Speaking PowerPoint

The **new language** of business

The business leader's guide
to boardroom-style slides

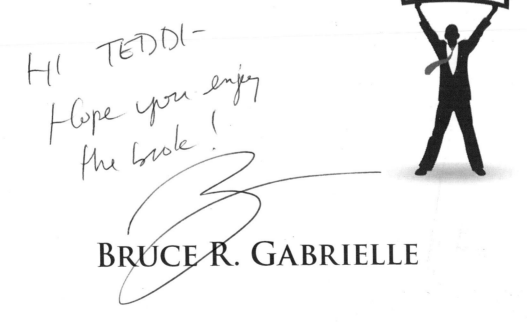

Hi TEDDI —
Hope you enjoy
the book !

BRUCE R. GABRIELLE

Insights Publishing
www.insightspublishing.com

ISBN: 978 0984 236046

Library of Congress Control Number: 2010911951
Bulk orders of this book for corporations, educational institutions or for premium giveaways are available by contacting Insights Publishing at www.insightspublishing.com

Cover design: Thomas Gorree, Jeanette Nguyen
Interior layout: 1106 Design
Interior images: Thomas Gorree, Bruce Gabrielle, Brent Dykes, www.VectorPortal.com

Microsoft Office PowerPoint, PowerPoint, Microsoft Office Excel and Excel are registered trademarks of Microsoft Corporation.

Bulk orders

Bulk orders of this book for corporations, educational institutions or for premium giveaways are available by contacting Insights Publishing at www.insightspublishing.com

Does your team want to learn how to *speak PowerPoint?*

Bring the research-based principles found in Speaking PowerPoint to your own company with a full-day onsite workshop. Help your staff use PowerPoint more effectively to influence and persuade in the boardroom.

After this full-day workshop, participants will be able to

1. Eliminate time wasters and complete PowerPoint decks 2-3 times faster.
2. Develop a presentation with a clear message, structure and slide order.
3. Develop a clear and persuasive slide using slide title, text, pictures and animation.
4. Enhance their credibility by creating professional-looking slides and charts using color, alignment and layout.

For details and pricing, please visit **www.speakingppt.com**

"Most PowerPoint trainings focus on product features. This may be the first I have seen on how to use PowerPoint to communicate *effectively.*"
- *Steve H, Microsoft*

"The ideas covered in this workshop can easily save someone days or even weeks the next time you build a presentation."
- *Sarah D, Prime 8 Consulting*

"Great material and easy to understand. This has definitely improved my PowerPoint skillset."
- *Pinak P, The Home Depot*

"The session makes you think 'Why aren't we doing presentations this way?'"
- *Steven B, Microsoft*

For my daughters Haley and Selena.
Always remember, girls, to follow your dreams. Dreams are like the stars
in the sky. You may not actually touch them. But follow them anyway and
they will lead you to beautiful lands you never could have dreamed of.

And for my wife Neena.
The night sky is full of stars, and it's my joy in life that we
always seem to be looking at the same ones together.

Acknowledgements

THIS BOOK HAS BEEN A JOURNEY, much of it spent alone in front of a computer screen studying research reports, writing and rewriting chapters, and experimenting with PowerPoint techniques. But the journey has been enriched by the people who joined me, even for short strolls, along the way.

Thank you to Professor David K. Farkas, Professor in the Department of Technical Communication at the University of Washington, for kindly reviewing several chapters. Dr. Farkas is one of the most thoughtful scholarly writers on PowerPoint as a new communication medium and it was refreshing to discover his writing and to see many of my own thoughts reflected there. His precise and expert feedback was invaluable in helping to shape some of the foundation thinking for this book, and especially his pointer to the STOP format was particularly influential to the book's final shape.

Thank you also to Nancy Duarte, author of *Slide:ology,* for her feedback and positive encouragement. Despite her busy schedule launching her second book *Resonate,* Nancy reviewed several of the chapters on design principles and her insights significantly altered and shaped my thinking in chapter 13.

Thank you to several PowerPoint-loving colleagues and authors, who provided me helpful advice when I was struggling with some thorny decisions, including Professor Michael Alley, Dave Paradi and Magdalena Maslowska for pointing me to useful resources.

Thank you to the many attendees at my workshops and business school lectures who provided positive feedback that let me know the principles worked, as well as constructive criticism so that I could revisit some of my thinking or find more compelling ways to explain it.

Thank you also to several friends and colleagues for reviewing early drafts of the book and providing useful feedback on the front cover, including Zubair Murtaza, Zimran Ahmed, Gaddy Radom, Tonya Fuhs Wallace, Stanley Keller, Rowland Savage, Stephen Schultz, Marcelo Prieto, Steven Silverman, Gerardo Dada, Tracey Pavlishin, Aaron Abraham, Brian Dominguez, Sarah Dziuk and Maria Potenza. A special thank you to my wife, Neena, for her courage to suggest making some final changes just before the book went to press, and for being a patient listener for two years. I'm sure talking about PowerPoint was a less than thrilling topic for you.

And thank you, dear reader, for selecting this book out of the thousands of other things you could be reading or doing right now. It's my sincere wish that all our hard work pays off for you.

Foreword

By Christopher Witt

YOU MIGHT THINK I WOULD BE THE LAST PERSON TO WRITE THE PREFACE FOR A BOOK TITLED *Speaking PowerPoint: The New Language of Business*. After all, I am the author of *Real Leaders Don't Do PowerPoint* (Crown, 2009). And I'm a long-time critic of the software and how it is used. When Bruce first asked me to review his book, I agreed mostly out of courtesy. I planned on giving it a quick once-over and sending him a note saying "nice job" or something equally non-committal.

To my surprise and to my growing admiration, I found myself reading—actually reading and thinking about—more and more of the book.

Let me tell you the reasons why I'm generally opposed to PowerPoint and how it's used, and why *Speaking PowerPoint* has changed (most of) my thinking about it.

I start with the assumption that PowerPoint is a tool, nothing more. It's a sophisticated tool, mind you, and one that has been almost universally accepted in business circles. But it's just a tool. Too many people, given the task of creating a presentation, produce a series of slides, and, by doing so, think that they've completed their task. They mistake the tool, PowerPoint, for the end product: a clear and compelling message, supported by evidence and visual aids, that meets the needs both of the presenter and the audience. PowerPoint is no substitute for a good strategy, a clear message, and a powerful delivery.

There are three questions you can—and should—ask about any tool. Is it a good tool? Is it a well-used tool? And is it the right tool?

First, is PowerPoint a good tool? I think it is good enough. PowerPoint 2010 is a clear improvement over previous versions. It's easier to use and more reliable, and it offers more advanced media-editing tools. But I don't think it's a great tool. The designs, color schemes, templates, and graphics that come standard issue on it are unremarkable. (If, for example, you use the pie charts that come with the program, you'll end up with an acceptable, not striking, pie chart.) While you can create visually stunning presentations, you really have to know what you're doing. It's neither intuitive nor easy to use.

Speaking PowerPoint shows you how to use a good-enough tool to produce excellent graphics and attractive slides. It leads you through pages and pages of both theory and practical advice for creating clear, appealing, and persuasive images. Just looking at the graphics in the book itself, all of which were created in PowerPoint, made me willing to reconsider my reservations about the graphic capabilities of PowerPoint.

Second, is PowerPoint a well-used tool? The short answer is, "No, at least, not most of the time." Many, if not most, PowerPoint presentations leave audiences confused and bored. There's a reason why the phrase *death by PowerPoint* has been coined. If you create clear slides with great graphics (using the book's guidance), you'll be a step ahead of most presenters. But your overall presentation may still be a disjointed mess, lacking an identifiable goal and a structured message to achieve it. But PowerPoint is not to blame for that. It's a tool, remember, and a tool can produce something good, beautiful, and worthwhile only if it is used with both skill and a plan.

Speaking PowerPoint shows you how to create a plan that will help you and your audience achieve a mutually satisfying goal. The first section of the book, in four thoughtful chapters, leads you through the questions you have to ask and answer before you even begin creating your slides. I especially like Bruce's advice about answering your audience's question first and creating a plan on paper.

Finally, is PowerPoint the right tool? The shovel you have at hand may be a perfectly good shovel, but that doesn't mean you'd want to use it to drive in a nail. This is why I believe leaders shouldn't use PowerPoint, at least not most of the time. Leaders speak—or should speak—to influence and inspire their audiences, not primarily to communicate information. They should tell stories, use evocative language, appeal to people's imaginations and emotions, and stand center-stage demanding people's attention. Leaders should so identify and be identified with the message they deliver that no one else can speak in quite the same way or say exactly the same thing without sounding like a cheap imitation. Would the speeches of King, Churchill, or Reagan move anyone if they had been given using PowerPoint?

And yet PowerPoint, used well, is the right tool for business. The first two chapters of *Speaking PowerPoint* ("The New Language of 21st Century Business" and "Boardroom-style PowerPoint") are worth the price of the book alone. They address the realities of the workplace and make a convincing case for how to use PowerPoint to enable collaboration and clear communication. (They also show why a lot of advice you've probably heard about how to use PowerPoint is simply wrong.)

I still believe, and Bruce agrees, that the most critical presentations require leaders to speak authentically and without PowerPoint slides. But it's equally true that PowerPoint is one of the most important tools for business managers to communicate and collaborate internally. That trend will only increase.

Over the past decade the use PowerPoint in business has produced, at best, mixed results. That's why smart businesses and smart business schools are already making a priority of training their people in a more effective use of PowerPoint. They would be wise, in my opinion, to adopt *Speaking PowerPoint* as their foundational text. It addresses the strategies, techniques, and skills that can turn a weak and ineffective presentation into one that drives a business's success.

Christopher Witt
Speech consultant and executive coach
Author, *Real Leaders Don't Do PowerPoint*
www.wittcom.com

Table of Contents

CHAPTER I

The New Language of 21st Century Business

IN 2000, A HIGH SCHOOL QUARTERBACK named Andrew applied to Arizona State University for a football scholarship. ASU students on the scholarship committee were divided into three groups and each was given the hopeful Andrew's high school football statistics.

The first group rated Andrew's application 4.5 out of 7; the second group rated it 5 and the third group rated it 6. All of the groups were made up of similar students, and each student evaluated the exact same statistics. But something was different about the application the third group saw and rated so highly.

What was it about the application that made group three more likely to approve it? And is it something you can use the next time you propose a new business idea? Or when you're coaching your team on how to convince another department to support your project? Or when you're selling a consulting engagement to a new client?

All three groups saw the same statistics, but each group saw them in a different format. The first group saw the data as a table in a text document. The second group saw it as a chart in a text document. The third group saw the data as an animated chart in a PowerPoint slide.

This study was conducted by three ASU researchers, including Professor Robert Cialdini, author of the book *Influence*. After seeing the results, he repeated the study with three groups of sports fans used to reading a player's statistics and found the same results. What he learned so impressed him, he resolved to use PowerPoint more in his own consulting work.

You hold in your hands a book that will change the way you think about driving business decisions in the 21st century. Using the old rules is like selling ideas to groups 1 and 2. But when you learn how to use the new tools effectively, it will be like selling ideas to group 3.

Fast forward six years. In 2006, I was a senior marketing manager at Microsoft leading a global brand advertising campaign for Windows Mobile smartphones. If I had known of this study, and other studies you'll read about in this book, I would have sold my ideas differently.

At the time, our ad campaign was focused on business professionals who needed to check email on their phones when they were travelling. I uncovered a segment of email users we were not focused on, a group much larger than the mobile professionals, and told my manager about this surprising market.

At the meeting, I showed her my findings in a table, just like the one seen by group 1 of the ASU study. And like that group's lukewarm reaction, my manager did not agree with my recommendation to divert some of our multi-million dollar campaign to this new segment. She couldn't see this audience as potential email users.

Later that summer, a young MBA intern independently discovered the same audience. He also recommended directing some of our massive advertising budget, but rather than show his idea as a table, he made a colorful and slick-looking bubble chart in PowerPoint, illustrating with the size of the bubbles this untapped audience was larger than the mobile professional audience. Soon, Microsoft meeting rooms were buzzing with this discovery. The elegant bubble chart helped people see things his way.

A few months later, RIM released the Blackberry Pearl, a stylish email device aimed at young, trendy hipsters. RIM had seen the same audience we had seen, but they were able to move faster.

Winning in the idea marketplace

Businesses are idea marketplaces where business managers compete for attention, budget and headcount by selling their ideas. Successful business managers, those rewarded with promotions, teams and bigger budgets, are the people who know how to sell their ideas effectively.

PowerPoint is no longer just a visual aid for presenters. In fact, more and more companies are shifting to PowerPoint and away from text for day-to-day business documents. PowerPoint has become one of the business leader's most important tools for winning in the idea marketplace.

How important? Increasingly, strategic discussions begin as PowerPoint decks, are circulated among stakeholders for input and come to represent the consensus view. Since major strategic decisions usually involve a presentation to executives, it makes sense for these strategies to begin life as PowerPoint decks.

In March 2010, Sarah Kaplan of the University of Toronto released a paper entitled *PowerPoint and Strategy*. She observed how one technology company used PowerPoint to drive strategy and concluded that PowerPoint had become not only the document that chronicles business decisions, but the *battleground* where new ideas advance, warring ideas duel, and champions prevail. Those who knew how to use PowerPoint effectively wielded an advantage over their peers.

PowerPoint has three central roles for driving strategic decisions, says Kaplan:

1. PowerPoint facilitates collaboration. The slides externalize assumptions, often through diagrams, where they can be debated and discussed leading to consensus. PowerPoint is modular, so one department can insert a few slides and so contribute to an ongoing discussion.

2. PowerPoint makes ideas "real". Ideas rattling around in someone's mind, or even composed in a text document, have not gone through the collaborative process of discussion and debate. More than that, as the ASU study shows, PowerPoint just makes ideas seem more credible. PowerPoint formalizes and legitimizes ideas.

3. If you control the deck, you control strategy. Important strategic recommendations always culminate in a presentation to senior management and represent the stakeholders' consensus

view. If your slide is not included in the final presentation, it is not considered by management and does not influence strategy.

In her report, Kaplan told of one manager, newly promoted to team leader, who rushed to prepare a PowerPoint deck for an important meeting. But the meeting stalled and a decision could not be reached because of his ad-hoc PowerPoint style. That manager lamented later that his lack of PowerPoint skills damaged his reputation as a leader.

PowerPoint, used well, can be your secret weapon to winning in the idea marketplace. First of all, as I'll demonstrate throughout this book, visual communication is a superior way to drive strategic decisions. Whether convincing others with a standup presentation, or standalone reading, visual communication is more effective than text alone.

Second, visuals lead to more productive decision making meetings because they externalize assumptions where they can be evaluated, debated and modified. And visuals help to depersonalize conflict because attention becomes focused on a shared visual rather than directed at other speakers.

Researchers at the University of Lugano, Switzerland found that visuals lead to more productive meetings. Conflict in those meetings is more likely to be amicable, focused on strategic issues and based on finding a common ground. In contrast, when visuals were not used assumptions remained hidden and conflicts were more likely to be resolved through argument and personality clashes. PowerPoint, used well, focuses discussions outward and leads to more productive meetings.

Third, visuals help executives understand complex problems and make better decisions. There is more data available than ever before, and more tools available on business managers' computers for analyzing that data. Displaying that data is done most effectively through charts and diagrams. Executives live in a world of complexity and information overload, and time is a scarce resource. Clearly showing complex information to executives makes best use of that scarce resource.

The shift to PowerPoint from text documents makes sense, given the complex environments of many businesses. And, in theory, it should lead to the best ideas winning in the idea marketplace.

But in practice, PowerPoint is not used effectively often enough. Too often it seems that good ideas are passed over while obviously flawed ideas find sponsors, only because this flawed idea is easier to understand, more persuasive and rolls off the tongue more easily.

Business leaders who want the best ideas to survive in the idea marketplace want their people to know how to use PowerPoint effectively. Executives who sponsor weak strategies will be at a disadvantage when they face tougher competitors powered by strong strategies. Executives who want the best ideas to be recognized and supported will want their managers to know how to compete in the idea marketplace. Those who develop the 21st century skills to use these new tools effectively will have an advantage in the idea marketplace as well as the broader global marketplace.

This all points to an important conclusion: PowerPoint is not just software for presentations, but the new language of business and a critical business skill. Said Clarke L. Caywood, associate professor of integrated marketing at Northwestern University in a January 2003 Chicago Tribune article, "No one in business today could pretend to be facile in business communications without PowerPoint. It's like being able to read."

This is a book about competing in the idea marketplace by explaining ideas clearly, persuasively and simply enough that they can spread. In the 20th century, we've used a certain set of tools, the same tools used to sell ideas to groups 1 and 2 of the ASU experiment. But the new 21st century tools, the tools used to convince group 3, can increase your odds of spreading ideas and winning in the idea marketplace.

Business communication has changed forever. In the 20th century, typical business communication happened through text documents, fax machines, phone calls and standup presentations with a few expensive visual aids. That era is fading away along with eight-track cassettes, drive-in movie theaters and Cabbage Patch Dolls.

Increasingly, effective business communication is visual. Those who master visual communication will be more effective driving business strategy in the idea marketplace. This is not a fad, but a fundamental shift that businesses and business schools are learning they need to embrace.

The secret to selling ideas in the boardroom

While the technology has changed, one thing hasn't changed: the way people think. In the end, all success depends on changing human behavior: buy my product, invest in my business, approve my proposal. Winning in the idea marketplace means understanding how the human brain works; what makes ideas more understandable, more persuasive and more memorable.

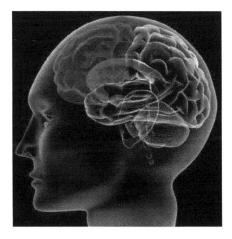

To start, let's take a look at an elementary classroom where two groups of third grade students are reading the same storybook. When they have finished reading, they take a test to see how many facts they can remember and what they think will happen next in the story. Group 1 does well remembering facts and guessing what will happen next. But group 2 remembers twice as many facts and is twice as good predicting what happens next.

What makes group 2 understand the story so much better than group 1? Is it a technique you could use to help make your ideas more clear?

Or let's look over the shoulders of university students at the University of Minnesota, listening to a speaker trying to encourage them to attend a workshop on time management. One group of students leaves the room *less* likely to attend the workshop than when they came into the room. Another group leaves the room *more* likely to attend the workshop. What did the second group see that the first group didn't?

Or let's go back to 1984, when students at a major U.S. Midwestern university were asked to view Yellow Page advertisements for several common industries: plumbing, automotive repair, construction and so on. They were then asked to recall all the companies that fit into each category. They were not told in advance they would need to remember. One group remembered nearly twice as many companies as the other group.

Two times better recall? What technique can make twice as many people remember your idea?

The difference in all of the studies mentioned above was the use of visual imagery. Among the elementary students, group 2 was asked to visualize what was happening in the story while group 1 was just asked to remember it. Among the University of Minnesota students, they became more interested in the workshop when the speaker's presentation included visuals. And it was the Yellow Page ads with words and pictures together, rather than words alone, that students found twice as easy to remember.

This is called the *picture-superiority effect* and has been well-known for at least 40 years. Advertisers know pictures make you more likely to notice, read and recall their advertisements. Instructional designers also know students learn better when pictures are part of the class materials.

Why do pictures make ideas easier to understand, easier to agree with and easier to remember later? The answer, according to some, is that most people, if not all people, think in pictures. Think of anything—the White House, Mariah Carey, the San Diego Chargers—and an image pops into your head.

For instance, neuroscientists using brain scanners report that when we read a novel we are actively converting sentences into pictures. You may be familiar with this phenomenon, reading a story of a pair of convicts being chased by dogs through the woods at night you can probably conjure up images of their panicked expressions and the thick branches tearing at their orange jumpsuits while they race away from the rising sounds of yelping hounds in the distance. You can see all this in your head.

A 1989 U.S. study had fifth grade students read poems aloud. Researchers stopped them along the way to ask if they had an image in their minds, and 60% of the time the students did.

Why does an image pop into your head? Can you understand and reason without the picture in your head?

Aristotle, one of the great thinkers of all time, said images were necessary for thought. He wrote in *On The Soul,* "To the thinking soul images serve as if they were contents of perception…that is why the soul never thinks without an image."

Rudolf Arnheim expounded on this theme in the book *Visual Thinking,* saying without pictures there is nothing for the mind to work with. He said further that seeing and thinking are the same function. "There is no basic difference…between what happens when a person looks at the world directly and when he sits with his eyes closed and thinks."

This is a remarkable statement! Our brain uses the same process to *see* the world as it uses to *think about* it? What does the brain science have to say about this?

Scientists were amazed to find that the area of the brain responsible for processing visual information—the visual cortex—is also active when we are thinking. This means that there is more than one way to project an image in our mind: pictures can come from outside through our eyes, but pictures can also come from inside the brain, using our imagination. Our brain does use the visual system to think.

Think about the metaphors you use to describe understanding. Do you *see* what I mean? *Look* at it this way? I don't think we see *eye to eye* on this. I can't quite *picture* it. What's your *view*? What's your *perspective*? What's your *outlook*? What's your *vision*? Isn't it amazing to realize we use words that describe seeing when we mean thinking and understanding?

Brain science is difficult because one cannot see what is happening in the brain. Thinking is an invisible process, so it's difficult to prove this theory conclusively.

But here is an experiment I use in my workshops to test the theory. Make a list of five things you want for your birthday. But if the thing you are writing down pops into your mind as an image, you must strike it from your list. You can only write down things that you cannot see in your mind. Go ahead, give it a try. Put down this book, get a pen and write out five things you want for your birthday.

Were you able to write out five things? How often did you have to cross items off your list because they popped into your head as images?

When I run this workshop exercise, people sit stock still in their seats, battling the impulse to imagine. They end up writing and striking out items constantly.

When they are done, I ask if they were able to complete the exercise. Many cannot; they aren't able to suppress images from coming to mind. Others are able to list five things. But when I ask, "Is this a good list? Is this what you really, really want?" they concede it's not a great list; it was a Herculean mental effort just to suppress the images.

Professor Richard Mayer, author of *Multi-Media Learning*, has conducted dozens of empirical studies showing university student remember more and understand better when they learn from words and images rather than words alone. Mayer postulates that words are processed in one part of the brain, images in another, and they are integrated together at the end to create meaning. When one or the other is missing, the brain has difficulty with the integration step and some of the meaning is not retained.

But this theory is controversial because some people report they do not see images in their head. Instead, they see words. Or they report seeing nothing at all.

Data on the number of picture thinkers versus word thinkers is slim. Research in the Netherlands by Linda Kreger Silverman finds 30% of the Dutch population thinks primarily in pictures, 25% thinks primarily in words and 45% thinks in both. Only a minority of the word-thinkers think exclusively in words, suggesting a vast majority think in pictures at least some of the time. Albert Einstein, for one, insisted he only thought in pictures and not in words.

If it's true that most of your audience thinks in pictures, you can encourage them to *see things your way* if you give them the picture.

A lack of skills and training

At this point you may be convinced you would be more effective at winning in the idea marketplace if you could use visuals. But PowerPoint? There are so few examples of good PowerPoint and many arguments against it: *I've seen what people can do with PowerPoint. And most of it is awful.*

And you may be correct that most PowerPoint is awful. But does it have to be? Couldn't it be better with better visual communication skills?

Despite its important role in strategy-making, most business managers do not know how to communicate clearly through PowerPoint. They struggle to create coherent slides, often turning to ornamentation to dress up otherwise unimpressive slides. If PowerPoint is so important in business, then where is the training?

It is not offered in business schools. Corporations offer training on the mechanics of PowerPoint but not on how to communicate complex information effectively. There are books on how to use PowerPoint for stand-up presentations but not for collaborating with colleagues to shape strategy and for boardroom presentations to drive complex business decisions.

There is no doubt we need better PowerPoint skills for driving smarter strategic decisions. PowerPoint's critics have been plentiful and vocal.

One of PowerPoint's most-quoted critics is Edward Tufte, a Yale professor and author of several pioneering books on information display. Tufte's *The Cognitive Style of PowerPoint* knocked the software because it "reduces the analytic quality of serious presentations." He continued the criticism in a Wired Magazine article entitled "PowerPoint is Evil" where he compared PowerPoint to a drug that is supposed to make you beautiful but instead makes you stupid.

Like Tufte, military leaders also argue that serious decisions are made with crudely constructed slides consisting of clip art and sound effects that over-simplify complex issues.

In July 2009 a senior officer in Israel's defense ministry, Brigadier General Erez Weiner, blasted the use of PowerPoint, saying "I believe the use of presentations has made the level of discussion, and the depth of study, more superficial." And in the U.S., Retired Marine Colonel T.X. Hammes continued the attack, saying PowerPoint "is actively hostile to thoughtful decision making" because of its over-reliance on half-formed bullet point thoughts. Former U.S. Marine Sgt. David Goldich didn't pull any punches when he said, "PowerPoint has largely become affirmative action for the inarticulate."

Educators also debate PowerPoint's merits. José A. Bowen, a dean at Southern Methodist University, attracted national attention in 2009 when he advised his faculty to *teach naked*. What he meant was *without PowerPoint*, saying professors are using it "as a crutch rather than using it as a creative tool."

In business, PowerPoint is derided through editorial cartoons in business magazines, mocking YouTube videos, online satires showing the Gettysburg address as a PowerPoint deck, and by self-proclaimed presentation experts. It's hard to find the PowerPoint supporters.

Most of the criticism is aimed at the *thoughtless* use of PowerPoint, and especially following the defaults that encourage bullet points and artless use of color and clip art. The criticism tends to fall into four categories:

1. Unclear messages, especially an over-reliance on half-formed thoughts delivered as bullet points, or unclear slide organization without a central message.

2. Incoherent slides jammed with information that overwhelms the reader.

3. Amateurish slides that elevate form over content, often caused by over-enthusiastic use of clip art, colors, effects and animations that buries the message in ornamentation.

4. Inappropriate use of slides during presentations, such as reading bulleted lists to the audience.

The most common defense is that the user, not the software, is to blame. *The poor carpenter always blames his tools.*

If people are using PowerPoint wrong, then what's the right way? Where are the classes? Where are the textbooks? Where are the answers to the critics' arguments?

They are in this book. Let's discuss all four concerns, and the skills that answer those concerns.

The Mindworks Presentation Method

This book attempts to close the skill gap, using language and examples to which business managers can relate. It is based on how the mind works to process complex information, and especially visual information.

I call this method the Mindworks Presentation Method. It is intended for business leaders who want to present their ideas clearly and persuasively, while creating visually pleasing slides in less time. My focus is PowerPoint because it's the standard for expressing business ideas, but the concepts are equally applicable if you are expressing ideas visually in a Word document, on a website or in email.

The principles of the Mindworks Presentation Method are not based on rule-of-thumb advice, but on 40 years of research in fields as diverse as neuroscience, cognitive science, instructional design, information design, graphic design and the legal profession. I use these principles in my own work as a market researcher who regularly presents strategic presentations to executives.

The principles are comprehensive and address all of the critics' concerns.

Criticism #1: Unclear message

The first criticism is lack of clarity. Section One of this book focuses on the brain science of crafting a message that is simple, clear and persuasive. For instance, did you know you can double the chance your message is understood by putting your conclusions before your supporting data?

Criticism #2: Incoherent slides

The second criticism is incoherent slides. In Section Two we discuss the brain science of learning and persuasion. For instance, you can make readers 15% more likely to understand your slide if you use a complete sentence as the title. How many slides do you see every day that could be clearer with that one simple change?

Criticism #3: Amateurish slides

The third criticism is overly-noisy slides where the message is buried in ornamentation. In Section Three we cover some easy-to-use rules of graphic design that will make your slides look more eye-catching and professional. For instance, using color makes the reader spend three times as much time on your slide as pure black and white, but too much color will make readers more likely to disagree with you. What's the right balance?

Images used in this book can be seen in color at www.speakingppt.com

Criticism #4 : Misuse of slides for presentations

The fourth criticism is presenters using PowerPoint as a crutch instead of an enhancement. Boardroom presentations are rarely one-way, but involve discussion and debate. Well-crafted PowerPoint slides facilitate that discussion. We devote one chapter to discuss what brain science has to say about the role of slides for presentations. For instance, did you know when you read the text on your slides your audience will learn less than if they read the slides themselves?

It's surprising how often you will catch yourself and others using PowerPoint in a way that collides with how the brain processes visual information. But it's also exciting to realize how much more effective communicators we can be once we know what we're doing incorrectly. We answer all of the critics' complaints in this book.

Even simple slides that are already easy to understand can be improved. For instance, here is a slide with a simple message. This is not a terrible slide. In fact, it is simple and uncluttered.

But what is the message? Go ahead and look the slide over. Does it take you three seconds to understand? Ten seconds? Thirty seconds?

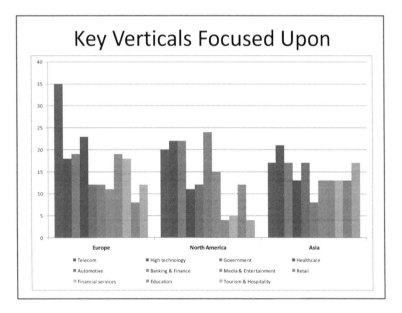

You can communicate the same information more effectively and even make your slide more professional looking. It is the same content, but organized to save time and get to the message faster. This slide uses the principles of the Mindworks Method.

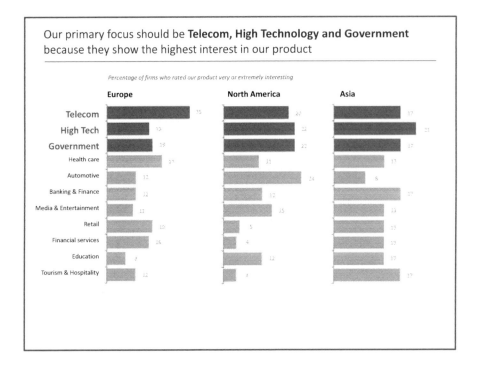

Do you see how much more quickly the reader can understand the slide's message? How much cleaner the slide looks? How much easier it is for an executive to *see what you mean*?

There are four main ways the Mindworks Method will make you a more effective communicator:

1. You will know how to create more clear and understandable presentations

2. You will know how to create more persuasive presentations

3. You will know how to create more visually pleasing and professional-looking presentations

4. You will create presentations two to three times faster

Ultimately, you will learn a skill for selling strategic ideas in the boardroom; a skill that most other business managers still lack.

The rest of this book is broken into three sections, covering the three critical elements of the Mindworks Method.

The Mindworks Presentation Method

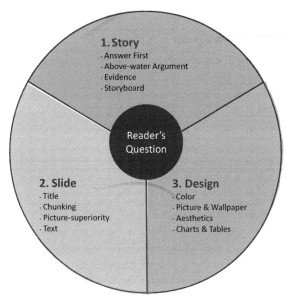

Section One: Story

Before you can develop a PowerPoint deck, you must decide what information the reader needs, in what order your slides will be shown and what evidence you will use to support your argument. This should be done before you even open the program. Using a storyboard to plan your document in advance can cut in half the time you spend creating slides.

In particular, we cover some of the brain science of organizing information so your message is clear and the supporting evidence is convincing. We also discuss the brain science of persuading through logic and emotion.

Section Two: Slide

After you have developed a storyboard, you will see that each slide has a single message that supports your overall argument. We talk about the role of slide titles, how to place text and visuals on the slide so they are easily understood, and how to explain complex ideas over multiple slides.

In this section, we cover some of the emerging research around effective slide design, as well as the brain science around working memory, our brain's whiteboard for understanding information. We also introduce a library of visuals that business managers can use on their slides to facilitate effective decision making meetings.

Section Three: Design

While creating your slide, you need to decide what you want to highlight. If everything is important, then nothing is important, and the reader has to spend extra time trying to prioritize the information on your slide. You can make it easy for the reader to see things your way by directing their attention.

We cover the brain science behind attention, and especially the impact of color and decorative elements. We especially spend time on charts, one of the most common visuals used in business. We'll learn why the default settings in programs like Microsoft Office Excel may actually hurt your ability to compete in the idea marketplace, and suggest a process for taking control of your business graphs.

The Mindworks Method does not depend on artistic skills. I'm writing this book assuming you will never be a good graphic designer and don't aspire to be one. I have a lot of admiration for those who can whip up gorgeous slides with lovely color and perfect placement. But that's not me. I assume most people in business, and most people reading this book, are like me—smart but not very artistic. This book was written for you.

Summary

1. PowerPoint is a critical business skill. PowerPoint has moved beyond being just presentation software and is now a critical tool for driving strategy in large companies. Businesses are idea marketplaces and selling ideas requires knowing how to communicate effectively with PowerPoint.

2. PowerPoint uses the power of visual thinking to make ideas clearer and more persuasive. This has been proven over the past 40 years and is called the picture-superiority effect. But business managers have not been trained how to communicate visually.

3. PowerPoint has not made it into the training curriculum of business schools or most corporate training rooms. What training exists is for simple slides that will be presented to a large audience, not for displaying complex data in a boardroom. The critics note four problems with our skills today: unclear message, incoherent slides, amateurish design and using slides poorly during presentations.

4. The Mindworks Method attempts to close the skill gap for business managers and address the critics' concerns. Based on cognitive science, it describes the most proven and effective strategies for communicating clearly and persuasively in business. There are three stages: craft a clear story, create coherent slides and use graphic design to organize information and improve aesthetics.

CHAPTER 2

Boardroom-style PowerPoint

THE TYPICAL ADVICE YOU HEAR is often not appropriate for boardroom presentations:

10 slides, 20 minutes, minimum 30-point font
7 bullets per slide, 7 words per bullet
Don't use bullets
Use a storytelling approach
Use a stock photograph that bleeds off the edges of the slide

If you're presenting to sleepy conference attendees, this advice is correct; you need simple but eye-catching slides to keep them awake and interested. But you can't present your marketing plan to senior management with advice like this.

Show this slide to a vice president of marketing and they will want more details. How large is the market? How profitable? How well does our product stack up against competitors in this segment? This slide is fine to introduce a recommendation but eventually you need to support your recommendation with data. The typical PowerPoint advice doesn't address the business reader's needs for complex information presented simply and concisely.

The rules for boardroom-style slides are different than the rules for large-audience presentations. So let's separate what works for sleepy conference attendees and what works for motivated business managers working together to shape strategy.

Boardroom- vs ballroom-style PowerPoint

Typically, PowerPoint slides are used to provide visual support for a speaker's presentation, usually in front of a large audience. Professor Andrew Abela, author of *Advanced Presentations by Design*, calls these *ballroom-style presentations* because they are often delivered in a conference ballroom.

Conference attendees are not always the most motivated or attentive audience. They are interested in what the speaker has to say, but they will tune out if the speaker is not engaging. They have many distractions. They may be checking email on their Blackberry or wondering if they should go get another coffee or checking out the people at the next table. The presentation is not necessarily critical to them and so the speaker needs to work a little harder to catch and keep their audience's attention.

But for a business meeting, the attendees are usually motivated. They may be looking for certain information in your presentation so they can make a decision. They may need to provide input into your plans or even provide the final approval. Because these meetings often take place in a meeting room or boardroom we call them *boardroom-style PowerPoint*. Boardroom-style decks include strategic plans, marketing plans, research reports, product planning decks, execution plans, program proposals and other business planning presentations.

For ballroom-style PowerPoint, the audience is far away from the slides and cannot read the text easily. In fact, as we'll learn later, asking an audience to read slide text while you're speaking is one of the least effective ways to persuade them. Ballroom-style PowerPoint slides are simple and meant to be seen from a distance.

On the other hand, boardroom-style presentations are studied up close. They are often provided as printed handouts in addition to, or instead of, projecting the slides onto a screen. The reader requires more details, including text and statistical data, so the slides have complex detail that can be studied close up.

Ballroom-style PowerPoint has a single use: to provide visual support for a speaker. It contains little text and so doesn't work well as standalone reading. Without the speaker, the slides make little sense.

Boardroom-style PowerPoint may have several uses. It may be read standalone at a computer screen—a *reading deck*—or printed and discussed in a team meeting—a *discussion deck*—or presented to a roomful of decision-makers—a *briefing deck*. Sometimes a single deck has to work in all three situations. The audience wants to read your slides before the meeting, or after the meeting, or instead of attending the meeting. They want to forward your deck to others in the company. Boardroom-style slides need to work as both presentations and standalone documents.

In ballroom-style presentations the speaker speaks and the audience listens. There may be opportunity for questions and answers at some point, but the speaker is not looking for feedback or lengthy discussion. The speaker controls the pace of the presentation.

Boardroom-style PowerPoint involves decision makers of different levels in the company. When you present to a vice president, they do not meekly listen; they have questions, they will challenge assumptions, they will tell you what they want to see modified. When you collaborate with colleagues, they have opinions and want to shape the deck. So boardroom-style PowerPoint is interactive.

Because boardroom-style slides are intended for a different kind of audience and different kinds of uses, the typical PowerPoint advice does not apply. In fact, the typical advice is often the wrong thing to do.

	Boardroom-style	**Ballroom-style**
Audience	Motivated	Easily distracted
Able to study the slides	Yes	No
Uses	Reading, discussion, presentation	Presentation only
Communication	Interactive	Lecture

Noted PowerPoint blogger Brent Dykes (www.powerpointninja.com) makes a similar distinction, using the analogy of ice cream. Strategic decks are like "soft" ice cream and are meant to motivate and inspire. But tactical decks are like "hard" ice cream and are meant to contain more details and tactical direction for the reader.

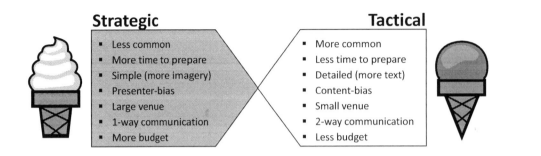

The biggest difference is how motivated the audience is to think deeply about the content on your slides. An unmotivated audience will not process lengthy details, and is too far from the slides in any case. But a motivated audience has more reason to think deeply about your content and is close enough to be able to study it.

If the goal of your presentation to sell your ideas, you need to know that research shows motivated audiences are persuaded differently than unmotivated audiences. Specifically, motivated readers are more sensitive to the merits of your argument and unmotivated readers are more sensitive to peripheral cues, like the speaker's credentials and the slide's aesthetics.

An experiment conducted in 1976 by Professors Richard Petty & John Cacioppo shows how the strength of your argument influences interested readers. University students were asked to evaluate a proposed 20% tuition fee increase. When the students thought the tuition increase was for the next year and would affect them personally, they agreed with strong arguments significantly more often than weak arguments.

But when students were told the tuition increase would take effect a few years later and so would not affect them personally, they agreed with weak arguments *almost as often as strong arguments*. Studies like this were repeated by several different researchers, with similar results.

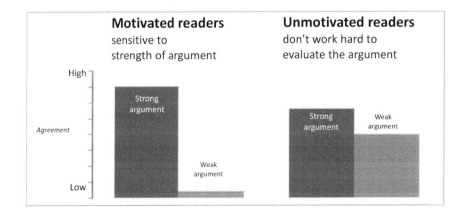

While the unmotivated reader was not sensitive to the strength of the argument, they were highly influenced by peripheral cues, such as the source's credibility or the number of arguments used. They were less motivated to think hard about the message and instead evaluated arguments based on other cues. For instance, in one study, students heard a strong argument or a weak argument for a new school policy. Some thought the argument came from a high school class (inexpert source) and some thought it came from a government task force (expert source). In this study, and multiple studies like it, the less motivated reader was heavily influenced by peripheral cues while the highly motivated reader was less influenced.

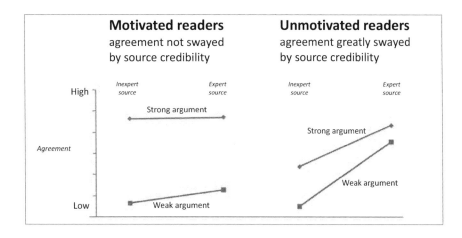

So graphically pleasing slides may be highly persuasive to an unmotivated audience in a ballroom-style presentation. But for a boardroom presentation, the audience is focused more on your facts than your slide's aesthetics. Structuring a strong argument is critical for boardroom-style slides and we cover it in Section One of this book.

This theory, that the approach to persuasion differs based on the audience's motivation, has been proven over dozens of studies and is called the Elaboration Likelihood Model (ELM).

Another important principle from the ELM is that adding distractions makes readers less likely to agree with your ideas. Strong arguments become weaker and weak arguments become stronger. That's because distractions interfere with thoughtful processing of the arguments and especially disrupts counter-arguments.

In the Petty & Cacioppo experiments, students were asked to approve the 20% tuition increase, but one group of students was distracted completing a computer activity while they read the proposal. The results were astounding. Those who were not distracted approved strong arguments significantly more than weak arguments, as before. But the distracted group approved weak and strong arguments about equally. Strong arguments got weaker and weak arguments got stronger. So distractions on slides can hurt you if you have a strong argument.

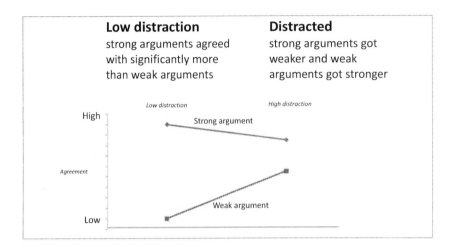

On the other hand, if your argument is weak, then adding distractions to your slides can make your argument stronger. But shrewd executives know that graphically beautiful slides are often a red flag that the underlying argument is weak. This book offers no advice on how to dress up weak arguments and focuses instead on how to highlight strong arguments by removing clutter from boardroom-style slides.

Distractions tend to annoy motivated readers because they interfere with them completing a specific task, like making a decision or locating information. Research found that people planning a vacation preferred brochures with specific details about the destination and were unhappy with brochures that used more persuasive than informative language. Learning a destination had "fun activities for the whole family" was less satisfying than specific details about those activities, including prices and schedules. When people have to make decisions, they are unhappy with distractions that keep them from getting the information they need.

In sum, boardroom-style PowerPoint requires a different approach than ballroom-style PowerPoint based on the reader's motivation and ability to study your argument closely. In fact, boardroom-style PowerPoint has more in common with a typical business document than a presentation.

Fortunately, there is a business document that, like PowerPoint, is both modular and highly visual. It was introduced over 40 years ago, and although it is not widely known today, it gave one company a competitive advantage in the marketplace. And we can apply those principles to boardroom-style PowerPoint.

The STOP format

In the early 1960's, as the Cuban Missile Crisis was heating up and the Vietnam War was escalating, the U.S. was increasing its war spending. Aircraft manufacturers were scrambling to keep up with the blizzard of RFP's for expensive fighter jets and other aircraft.

The Hughes-Fullerton division of Hughes Aircraft Company found it challenging to produce coherent and persuasive proposals, which could run to over a hundred pages. The proposal was written in sections by different engineering teams, and the writing was often poorly organized, rambling and difficult to integrate into a single coherent document without significant editing and rewriting. Hughes-Fullerton faced strict deadlines imposed by demanding officials at the U.S. Department of Defense and regularly had to scramble at the last minute just to send out relatively jumbled proposals.

The publications team, lead by Jim Tracey, began looking for a way to simplify proposal writing. They studied other Hughes business documents and proposals and noted a surprising consistency for a writer to use about 500 words to cover a topic before changing the subject and moving onto another topic. Sometimes they used 1,000 words, but these were often rambling and verbose passages that went off-topic. Some topics were covered in as little as 200 words, but these were often under-developed sections that could have been incorporated into another topic.

Based on this insight that a topic can be covered effectively in about 500 words, they developed a new approach to proposal writing called the STOP format (*Sequential Thematic Organization of Publications*).

Essentially, the STOP format imposed boundaries on proposal writers: each writer was to use a two-page spread to cover their assigned topic, they needed to explicitly state the topic they were discussing as well as a thesis statement—a short paragraph stating a conclusion they were now going to prove was true. They need to concisely support the thesis with about 500 words of text with no more than one level of sub-heads, and use a diagram on the right-hand page to help illustrate the topic.

TOPIC: _____

THESIS SENTENCE: _____

The secret was to treat each two-page spread as a *thought module* with a strict format. Text and images were laser-focused on supporting a single thesis statement. Turning the page meant the reader was starting a new topic with a new thesis. An entire document could be assembled by planning the thought modules out in advance, assigning them to different teams and then assembling them into a proposal as they arrived. Thought modules could be re-organized. If a thought module was too complex for two pages, it might be broken into two or more thought modules.

This method became a competitive advantage for Hughes-Fullerton. Walt Starkey, one of the coordinators on Jim Tracey's team, reports years later that their proposal success rate mushroomed and they had the highest win rate of all the major aeronautics firms in their time. The STOP format helped them win lucrative contracts to build air traffic control systems and satellite communications systems. The STOP format was so successful it was copied by other companies. A new form of business document was born.

Readers of these proposals raved that Hughes-Fullerton produced the most clear, and even distinctive, proposals of all the aeronautics firms. The proposal made clear assertions that were backed up briefly but completely, unlike the competitors' rambling text proposals where assertions were buried deep in the prose and often not stated explicitly at all. In the STOP format, readers found it easier to look up the information they needed to make a decision.

Engineers found the STOP format easy to work with. Once they finalized the module's thesis sentence, they knew exactly what they needed to write about. The clear format gave them explicit guidance on how much to write and where to place the image.

What's especially interesting about the STOP format is that it sounds a lot like a PowerPoint slide. Here are the rules followed by the engineers at Hughes-Fullerton that turned their proposals into the most clear and persuasive documents of their time:

- thought module that covers a discrete topic. Turning the page starts a new topic

- strict two-page format with thesis sentence, supporting text and image

- include an image in each module

- build an entire document by arranging these thought modules

We aren't required to accept the STOP format as a model for PowerPoint documents. But as I'll show throughout this book, there is a wealth of research showing these principles are worth embracing and will give you a competitive advantage in the boardroom.

The advantage of PowerPoint's boundaries

If Hughes-Fullerton can turn this kind of a document into a competitive advantage, can't we use PowerPoint in the same way to our own competitive advantage?

Along with being a visual medium, PowerPoint is differentiated most of all by its strict boundaries. A text document is forgiving; you can cover a point in one paragraph or explain it in greater detail in four or five paragraphs. And if you run to the edge of the page, your writing can flow onto the next page. In contrast, you run out of room quickly when you're placing text and images in PowerPoint and must find a way to work within the slide's boundaries.

But just as Hughes-Fullerton discovered, boundaries can be a source of competitive advantage.

First, boundaries are good for writers because it forces them to simplify ideas. Winning in the idea marketplace means, first and foremost, simplifying ideas. Successful business managers know their elevator pitch and can get to the point quickly, a trait busy executives value. A text document does not force writers to focus their ideas, and instead allows long rambling documents that work against you in the idea marketplace.

Second, boundaries are good for readers because it produces shorter documents that can be skimmed and read more quickly. This is important for everyone working in a fast-paced, too-much-email-too-little-time business environment. Readers can quickly understand the main point and support points and find information they need to make decisions. The STOP format requires more succinct writing than does a rambling, disorganized and poorly written text document.

Boundaries are not unique. Most writers work within boundaries. If you write email, you know that most readers can only tolerate 3–4 paragraphs before they tire of your message. Website designers know visitors do not like to scroll and so they develop the main ideas "above the fold". Executive summaries force writers to surface the main points for the busy reader. Advertisements, brochures, flip charts, postcards, business cards and even book covers impose boundaries that writers must work within.

But boundaries still present a challenge to writers. It's harder to write a brief, focused document than a long, rambling document. And it's harder to organize your thoughts in a PowerPoint slide than a text document, where you can write as much as you want until you clarify your own thinking. It would be naïve to say boundaries are all positive. Boundaries do force writers to make tradeoffs, leave things unstated and generally leads to "content cutting"—editing fully-articulated thoughts, or even deleting important details, to fit the slide. We will talk more about the unique challenge of working with text in chapter 10.

Boundaries, though, are not really the problem. Boundaries are simply of set of conditions writers must learn to communicate within. The real problem is a lack of guidance on how to work within those boundaries.

Here's an example of another group, which didn't know how to work effectively within PowerPoint's boundaries.

In January 2003, a group of engineers produced a slide deck for NASA. Space shuttle Columbia's left wing had been struck by large chunks of spray-on foam insulation (SOFI) which came loose after liftoff, and now Columbia and its seven crew members were orbiting Earth with possible wing damage. Would Columbia survive re-entry into Earth's atmosphere or would the wing damage cause the spacecraft to be torn apart?

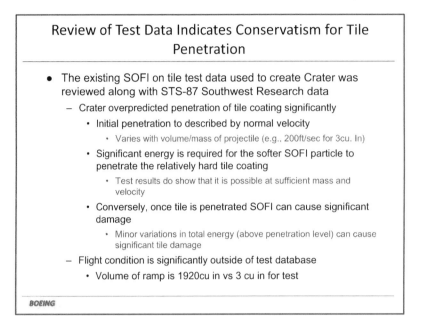

The working group of engineers produced a slide deck, including this slide using the default settings in PowerPoint: center-aligned title and bullet points.

Ambiguously written slides like this helped reassure NASA officials the damage was inconsequential and it was safe to attempt re-entry. On February 1, 2003 Columbia re-entered Earth's atmosphere at a blistering speed of 5 miles per *second*. Super-heated gases seeped into cracks in the damaged wing, eroding the wing's structure and, at 9:05 a.m., there was a loud boom and Columbia exploded over Texas. All crew members were lost. An independent review board concluded that incoherent slides like this were one of many contributing factors leading to NASA's fateful and flawed decision to attempt re-entry.

In 2006, Yale professor Edward Tufte released *The Cognitive Style of PowerPoint: Pitching Out Corrupts Within*. Tufte, an advisor to NASA during the Columbia investigation, seized on this slide to support his thesis that PowerPoint imposes a set of default settings and boundaries that constrains the author to a single slide, requiring them to "dumb down" serious ideas to fit PowerPoint's limited space. And for that reason, serious scientific documents should be written in a text document.

Perhaps Tufte is right, that in this specific instance with so much at stake, the readers would be sufficiently motivated to read a text document. But a text document is not necessarily any better or clearer than PowerPoint if the writer is unfocused and rambling. And Tufte's thesis that you cannot develop a scientific report in PowerPoint is not correct.

The problem with this slide is not that its boundaries force the slide creators to dumb it down, but that the slide creators didn't know the STOP-like principles to build it.

- treat each slide as a thought module with a clear thesis statement

- limit text to support that thesis statement

- use text and images to make your point

In fact, using these principles, you can create a slide that clearly and persuasively describes the threat to Columbia and the seven astronauts onboard.

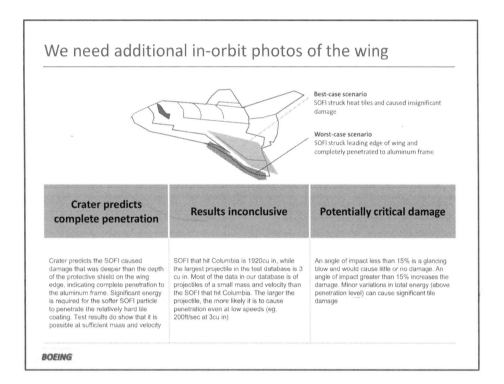

This doesn't look like a typical PowerPoint slide. In fact, there's not a single bullet point. But we can break out of the cognitive style of presentations and adopt whatever cognitive style suits our communication goal.

By following the STOP format for slide design, the slide creators must make a clear statement and then defend that statement briefly with text and images. Instead, the NASA slide does not fully state a position, and only lists a series of facts that need to be interpreted by the reader. This is not to say the engineers did not attempt to communicate this message in other ways, including verbally, but only an example of the impact of adopting STOP-like rules for clearer PowerPoint slide design.

PowerPoint vs text documents

Some critics argue that serious business reports should be produced as a text document. But as we saw from the experiences at Hughes-Fullerton, text documents have their own weaknesses. They can be written in a rambling style so that decision-makers cannot find the information they need, presented clearly so they can make a decision.

Is PowerPoint really better than a text document? There's no simple yes-or-no answer. A better question would be *when* is PowerPoint the best tool?

For presentations given in front of an audience, there are a lot of opinions and books written on how to use PowerPoint as a visual aid. I will cover this in more detail in a later chapter. For now, I'll say that a lot depends on the purpose of your talk. If you're sharing your experience backpacking across Asia, you'll probably want to present a lot of photographs. If you're giving a motivational speech, like introducing yourself as the leader of a new department or delivering a pep talk to the sales team, you may want to use fewer visual aids and focus on connecting with the audience personally.

But for standalone business documents like strategic plans, research reports, training documents, tactical execution plans and project updates, you will probably want to choose between a text document or a PowerPoint document. You can use visuals with both types of documents and both have their strengths and weaknesses.

The research comparing the effectiveness of a text document with a PowerPoint document is nearly non-existent. The Arizona State University study is one of the few, and it points to PowerPoint as the more persuasive tool, although it only considered a single page of information.

The main issue is readability. Most business documents are passed along through email, or printed and shared in team meetings. Reading a long text document on the computer is fatiguing in a way that reading a long PowerPoint document is not. And discussing a text document with a group of colleagues in a meeting room may be virtually impossible. Visuals give a team something to focus on and discuss while text may spread the same information over several paragraphs or even several pages.

PowerPoint forces the writer to simplify ideas. Many consulting firms produce final reports in PowerPoint because they know they are easier to read, and easier to pass onto others in the organization to read. Lengthy text documents are less likely to be read completely, rendering them less useful.

In practice, the reader could just print the long document. But human nature being what it is, readers are likely to just skim a long document rather than print it out, unless they are very motivated. But when you're trying to sell ideas, you don't want to depend on the reader's motivation or they may simply pass your idea by for another idea that takes less effort to understand.

Anecdotally, I know that if I get a 50-page Word document, I won't read it. I'll skim it or use it as a reference document. But if I get a 100-slide PowerPoint deck, I'll review each slide.

I've also prepared marketing plans and research reports in Word, and feedback from my readers was they did not read it. It seems reading time is at a premium in large companies, and people are discouraged by long text documents whereas they aren't discouraged by long PowerPoint decks.

The other issue is time required. Text documents can usually be prepared more quickly than PowerPoint documents because there is more reliance on words, which are familiar to us and don't require any artistic skills. We can begin writing without knowing what we are trying to say and crystallize our thoughts as we write. PowerPoint takes longer to prepare because it's often difficult to find the right visuals and it requires a more concise writing style that gets to the point.

There have been some efforts to encourage managers to stick with Word and wean them off PowerPoint, but I'm not aware of any successful efforts.

In fact, in 2005, Microsoft's CEO Steve Ballmer said at the annual conference to 15,000 assembled employees "Guys! You don't have to use PowerPoint for everything. It's okay to use Word." This was said to no avail. Microsoft managers continued to use PowerPoint for everything from project planning and operations reports to executive briefings and planning the company picnic.

Sun Microsystems in 2005 also informally banned PowerPoint. Again, to no avail. Employees continued to pump out business reports in landscape format instead of portrait.

Given this, your decision to use Word or PowerPoint might depend on several factors:

- Is this intended for a single reader, or for pass-along readership? If you're preparing a document giving instructions to a vendor, or a final report on a market research study for your client, then a text document may be sufficient briefing for a single motivated reader. But if you're trying to make an idea viral and get others to read it, a text document may not spread as well as a PowerPoint document.

- Is the reader motivated to read it? If you're an executive laying out the company strategy, then it's likely your readers are motivated to spend extra effort to print out your text document and read it. But if you are trying to persuade another department to see things your way, they may not be motivated to spend the extra time on your message.

- Is the goal to persuade? Or to inform? If you need to persuade the reader, the extra effort put into a PowerPoint deck may be worthwhile because of its superior ability to support visuals. But if your document is just to inform, such as an employee handbook, a text document may be sufficient.

- Is your topic heavily visual? Sales decks with screenshots of a new software application are probably best shown in landscape format to fill the screen, with text descriptions nearby. If your topic is not heavily visual, like the text for a survey questionnaire, a text document probably makes more sense.

Notice that I don't make a distinction between documents that require a lot of text. It's possible to add a lot of text to PowerPoint slides. An example is Nancy Duarte's book *Slide:ology,* which is not only one of the best books explaining how to prepare slides for presentations, but her book was also written in PowerPoint.

I also don't limit visual communication to PowerPoint. I frequently create diagrams in PowerPoint and then copy and paste them into a Word document if my goal is to inform rather than persuade. For instance, when I conduct a market research project in another city I might prepare a Word document for the client with a map showing the location of our hotel and the focus group facilities.

In summary, it may be that for short 1–3 page informational documents, or working documents intended for a small team, or longer documents for a single reader or where the reader is motivated to understand your message, a text document is superior because it can be produced quickly without losing potential readers.

But when the primary goal is persuasion and pass-along readership, it may be worth the effort to create a PowerPoint deck. This is especially true for market research reports, strategic plans and tactical plans where the reader needs to agree with your recommendations. The extra preparation time will pay off in increased readership, stronger agreement and more pass-along readership.

PowerPoint slides take longer to create than writing thoughts in a text document. It takes more skill to develop focused thesis statements and to express ideas briefly and visually. But when you need the persuasive power of visuals and the simplicity forced on a writer by PowerPoint's boundaries, PowerPoint gives you a competitive advantage selling ideas.

Summary

1. Most advice from experts is appropriate for ballroom-style presentations. But the trend in business is toward boardroom-style slides to sell ideas, and especially standalone decks or decks discussed in small groups, which demand a different set of rules: more focus on structuring your argument, more text and data, and fewer distracting slide elements.

2. Based on the proven success of the STOP format, boardroom-style slides should be thought modules which contain a clear thesis statement, use sub-heads and text to support that message and the module should include an image.

3. Working in PowerPoint's boundaries correctly can lead the writer to be clearer and allow the writer to use visuals to make the report more persuasive. Text documents may be more appropriate in situations where the reader has the time and motivation to read the text document, and the writer's objective is primarily to inform rather than persuade.

4. PowerPoint has higher readability because it is written more succinctly and uses visuals. Text documents are appropriate for reference materials that don't involve persuading an audience, or when the reader has the time and motivation to read your text extensively.

Recommended reading

Sequential Topical Organization of Publications by Jim Tracey is the ground-breaking internal report intended for Hughes Aircraft Company personnel that describes the STOP format. The 1965 document is even written using the STOP format. Search for the document title at http://www.scribd.com

The Cognitive Style of PowerPoint by Edward Tufte is a polarizing essay that damns PowerPoint's tendency to impose an overly-concise writing style on the slide creator and "dumb down" slides. While Tufte makes many fair points, this essay is very much an opinion piece which has found both supporters as well as heated critics.

A Heuristic for Reasoning about PowerPoint Deck Design is one of Professor David Farkas's many academic papers exploring PowerPoint as a unique communication medium. He cuts through the simple rule-of-thumb advice about PowerPoint design and offers a sharp and analytic look at a medium that is still developing its own identity.

http://faculty.washington.edu/farkas/TC510/Farkas-PowerPointHeuristic.pdf

STORY

Criticism #1: Unclear message

The first rule to persuading in the boardroom is to surface your arguments clearly. Some presentations and PowerPoint reports ramble and lack focus. There is no clear central message, which is the first reason ideas die in the idea marketplace.

Creating a clear message is the first step to selling ideas. But in a PowerPoint deck with 10, 20, 30 or more slides, how do you order your information? What slides come first? What slides come next? Do you break the deck into sections? What sections?

This challenge is similar to the one faced by the engineers at Hughes-Fullerton: how to break down a 100-page aeronautics proposal and create a document that was clear and convincing. They started by turning their proposals into a set of thought modules, each with a clear thesis statement. But how did they decide what each thought module would cover and their order?

They started with a storyboard. Engineers would gather in rooms and talk about the proposal at a high level: what categories they would cover, what main themes they would cover in each category. Then they taped paper templates to the wall and teams of engineers would start putting crude notes on the templates they were assigned: what major points they would cover, what major support points they would use, what images they would employ.

Hollywood directors face the same challenge: how to order hundreds of scenes in a movie to capture your interest, build conflict and ultimately deliver a satisfying climax. In Hollywood, the answer is also to use a storyboard: a hand-drawn image of each scene in the film, showing camera angles, camera movements, and actors' entrances and exits. A storyboard allows the director to visualize and think through the film's progression. Only after he's satisfied with the film's flow does he start the expensive process of filming.

You are the director of your deck. And before you start the expensive process of creating slides, you need to organize your thinking. If you are the manager of slide creators, you also don't want your people spending a lot of time crafting finely polished slides. You want them to work out their logic in advance, review it with you, and only when you're satisfied with the logic do you allow them to start the expensive and time-consuming work of creating slides.

This section covers:

Answer First: Write for the benefit of your audience. What do they want to know when they go through your deck?

Above-water Argument: Develop a strong argument with a few critical support points. This is what the reader will remember and what they will talk about with others.

Evidence: Logical arguments are only one way to win in the idea marketplace, and not always the most effective. When do you use emotional evidence, like customer quotes and video? How do you overcome resistance to an idea?

Storyboard: Planning your deck in PowerPoint is wildly inefficient. Mind mapping and storyboarding will save you time and help you be more creative as you plan the order of your slides.

CHAPTER 3

Answer First

Answer the reader's question first

Your boss Aubrey, the Vice President of Marketing, is a hulking figure, a former athlete from the UK, with a bumper sticker on his office door that says "I'd rather lose at rugby than win at baseball". He's sharp-witted and sharp-tongued, and reviewing others' plans is a sport for him.

He's ruthless at dismantling flawed thinking. At a meeting six weeks ago to review another team's plans, he grew impatient with the loose thinking and terminated the meeting early by loudly tearing in half the PowerPoint printouts and saying, "This isn't even halfway ready."

You are meeting with him next week to review your team's $2 million marketing plan.

It's 8 a.m. on Wednesday. You and Robert, one of your direct reports, are reviewing his part of the marketing plan. Robert has printed copies and you spend a few minutes flipping through the pages. The deck is a bit of a mess—slides densely packed with text and charts, and with obscure titles like "Segments vary based on criteria importance". You are having trouble following the logic of the plan.

You ask a number of clarifying questions as you go—*Which market are we targeting? Why that one and not the others? How will you measure progress?* You are having a hard time assessing this plan because of poor slide organization.

It's now 8:30 a.m. and you hardly know what Robert's plan is. This is not ready to go in front of Aubrey next week.

Take a moment and think about this problem. Robert is your direct report and needs your coaching. You have 30 minutes before your next meeting. What advice do you give Robert to pull this deck together?

Clarify the main message of the deck: Answer First

The first step to creating a great boardroom-style PowerPoint deck is this: Answer First. Answer First means understanding what the reader wants from your deck and providing that information quickly and clearly.

The main difference between a boardroom-style and ballroom-style deck is how motivated the reader is. Business readers are highly motivated to understand your message and supporting argument because they have to make a decision or provide input or plan their activities.

It's easier to sell an idea in the idea marketplace when it's an answer to the reader's question. People pay attention to things that are important them, not things that are important to you. So start by putting yourself in your reader's shoes and asking: *what is their question?*

Imagine your reader opening your deck on their computer. Whoever your reader—a client, your manager or your planning team—when they sit down to view a PowerPoint deck they do not have an empty mind—*hmmm...what's this?* They have a lot of other meetings to attend, email to read and PowerPoint decks of their own to work on. But they have taken time to look at your deck because they have an important question gnawing at them.

What is that question?

> *How do we win developers onto our technology platform?*
> *What features will I be able to sell in our next product release?*
> *Is business intelligence a promising area for us to explore?*
> *Is this new product ready to go to market?*

Barbara Minto, author of *The Pyramid Principle,* has been training McKinsey consultants, as well as other consultants across the world, on her method of organizing information for decades. And the first step she teaches is to get crystal clear on the reader's question you need to answer.

Based on *The Pyramid Principle*, McKinsey consultants are taught that if the client only has a little time, they can get the main point in the first minute. If they have more time, they can get the main supporting arguments in five minutes. And if they have an hour, they can dive into all the details.

Putting the Answer First ensures your deck has a clear message. The audience will be able to walk out of the room and know what you want them to do. You become crystal clear in your own mind what main point you want to stress. If you don't know what you're trying to say, it's a sure thing your reader won't know either.

Putting the Answer First also gives you increased confidence to know that, if you met your VP on the elevator and he said, "Hey, you know what, I'm really sorry but I'm going to have to bail on that meeting this afternoon. I've got five minutes now. Can you just give me the topline?" you'll be able to do that. Executives appreciate those who get to the point quickly, so training yourself to Answer First is a smart discipline for other types of executive communication.

Putting the Answer First helps you plan the rest of your deck. It helps you answer questions for yourself like: what supporting arguments do I need to present and in what order; what evidence do I have to support those arguments; what do I *not* need to show in this deck. Without this important anchor, you will find yourself adding slides that have no real purpose as you flounder in data without a coherent argument. By putting your Answer First:

1. You communicate your ideas clearly and quickly, the hallmark of a good business communicator. The reader knows what you are asking them to do and why it's important.

2. You provide context for all the information that will follow next, which makes it easier to understand your argument.

3. You give yourself a way to easily structure the rest of your deck, what evidence to use, what supporting data to use, and in what order to present it.

We cover the first point in this chapter, and points 2 and 3 in the following two chapters.

There are some instances where you will want to take a more indirect route and reveal the answer after you've provided more extensive background, such as when you need to deliver bad news or bring up a controversial idea. We'll talk about that in the next chapter. But even if you plan to *show* the answer last, if you know the Answer First it will guide you in structuring the rest of your deck.

First, find the question

The best way to know what is the reader's question is to ask them. When I'm preparing a market research report, I ask the client explicitly "to help me guide my analysis and the final report, what's the main question you need to answer?" There is rarely one question. But there is a central theme that will allow me to brainstorm a number of questions.

But even if you haven't asked explicitly, most business reports fall into one of three types of documents: a *Why* document, a *What* document and a *How* document.

In a *Why* document, the reader wants to make a decision and needs information that tells them why one option is better than another.

Sample Why documents	Reader's question
Research report	What do we need to do, and why?
Strategic plan	What do we need to do, and why?
Project recommendation	Should we do this, and why?
Business proposal	Should we hire this firm, and why?

In a *What* document, the reader wants to know what someone else is working on and wants the details explained to them. These are often reference documents others will use when they build their own plans.

Sample What documents	Reader's question
Product plan	What new product features are coming and when?
Project plan	What is your plan?
Update	What's the status? What needs my attention?
Executive briefing	What do I need to know?

In a *How* document, the reader wants to know how to do something and needs instructions and detailed steps.

Sample How documents	Reader's question
Training document	How do we do this?
Execution plan	How do we execute this plan?

This is a good starting point, but your reader will have a very specific question in mind. For a research report, their general question may be "What do we need to do?" but their specific question may be "What do we need to do to improve customer satisfaction?" or "What do we need to do to expand into China?"

An approach I use is to take a big red marker and write the question on my whiteboard. In fact, the customer's question is central to planning the rest of the deck, so I will brainstorm several different ways to ask the question. This sharpens my focus even further by asking myself, "Is this the real question they wanted answered?"

After establishing the reader's question and writing it on my whiteboard in red letters, I next write the answer to that question in black marker. This Answer becomes the idea I am selling and building my deck to support.

Answer First in Email

Putting the Answer First can improve all kinds of communications, including email. Consider this typical rambling email:

> Hey Bob,
>
> I was in a meeting with Ray Krebs today and we're planning for next fiscal's BTS promotion. Ray mentioned your team had done some focus groups with students in the past and he suggested I contact you to find out about your focus group results.
>
> Can you send me a link to your student focus group results?
>
> Thanks,
>
> Phil

Here, Phil has written in a chronological order, arranging information in the order he remembers it. His request is the last sentence. This makes the task easy for Phil because he just writes in the order things happened, without regard for what order the reader needs.

But poor Bob! He has to read this email, not really sure what is being asked of him until the end. The opening makes him wonder *Who is Ray Krebs? What does this have to do with me?* By the time Bob gets to the request, he may have to re-read the opening paragraph again to understand its relevance.

Consider how much easier it is for Bob when Phil writes in the order the reader needs information, and puts his request first:

> Hey Bob,
>
> Can you send me a link to your student focus group results?
>
> I was in a meeting with Ray Krebs today and we're planning for next fiscal's BTS promotion. Ray mentioned your team had done some focus groups with students in the past and he suggested I contact you to find out about your focus group results.
>
> Thanks,
>
> Phil

The only change was to move the request to the top of the email. You can see how much clearer this is. You can improve your own emails, as well as PowerPoint reports and other types of reports, when you put your main message first and the supporting information after.

Forcing yourself to write out the question and the answer makes you turn your abstract thinking into concrete words. You might have thought you had an idea, but if you can't summarize it in writing then you may realize you really didn't have a clear message. All you had was a lot of data. Forcing yourself to write out the answer imposes a discipline on you to walk into any presentation with a clear purpose and a clear message.

Writing out the answer also ensures the idea is short and easy to understand. Long answers can be studied and tightened into a simple big idea that you want to reinforce in the reader's mind. Long complex ideas will be too complex to sell to others. Writing out the answer forces you to articulate a simple message that will make you a more effective communicator.

Don't be surprised if this is difficult at first. Many business managers are used to pouring all their data and half-formed thoughts into PowerPoint with only a vague idea of what they're trying to say or what the reader wanted to hear. If you find it difficult to formulate concrete answers, keep at it. This is a muscle you can build to improve your focus and increase your ability to sell ideas.

Create interest with the Inciting Incident

The opening slides set the context for the reader. They answer questions like: what is this report about, why is this report important, what information will it provide?

If the reader is already familiar with the context, the opening slides do not tell them anything they don't already know. They simply show that you and the reader see the situation similarly. There should be nothing controversial in the opening slides.

But for readers who are not familiar with the topic, you will want to use the opening slides to tell them why the report is important. You want people to be hungry for your information. You want them to feel pain that only your report can satisfy. How do you make people care that much? By introducing a problem that needs to be solved.

I remember at Microsoft my group would often get requests from different country managers to fund local marketing campaigns or pilots. The country manager would send their deck explaining the project, but did not explain why this project was worth $20,000 from my budget. They failed to get me excited about their idea because I didn't know what problem this would solve.

If your goal is to sell ideas, you want people to feel some pain that you are going to solve. What is at stake if you don't solve the problem?

Consider this sentence: The woman sold her car.

This is a fine sentence. It's grammatically correct and easy to understand. But it doesn't make you wonder why she sold her car or what happens next. It's just a fact that you have no reason to care about or spend additional time on.

But consider this new sentence: The woman sold her car to feed her children.

Ah! Drama! Conflict! A solution to a difficult problem! Now the reader is hooked and wants to know the rest of the story. Did she feed her children? For how long? What will she do without a car? How did she get into this mess?

In storytelling, this is known as the *Inciting Incident.* Life is good for the hero, then suddenly something bad happens that puts life out of balance and now we have a story.

Research shows that starting a report with an Inciting Incident can also make it easier to understand the rest of the report, because it flags for the reader to what details to pay attention. In 2008, Luuk Lagerwerf, an associate professor at VU University in Amsterdam, conducted a study with business professionals to test what happens when you take a typical report and rewrite the opening of each chapter so it starts with a problem statement. The study found that readers were significantly more likely to understand the chapters that started with problem statements than chapters that started with the solution.

However the study also found that repeated use of the problem statement made people dislike the report and the report writer more, possibly because of the negative emotions caused by reminding the reader something was broken. Readers were also likely to remember the problem better, but there was no change in how well they remembered other key points from the report. For these reasons, over-use of the problem-solution approach may work against you if the negative words lead to less support for your ideas. But starting with the problem does prime the reader to know what to pay attention to.

When developing your deck, highlight what is the Inciting Incident that makes your idea important enough to care about. What was happening that made it necessary to work on your project? What's at stake if the problem isn't solved? There are at least three benefits to showing the Inciting Incident before introducing the answer.

1. If the reader is already interested, the Inciting Incident simply tells the reader what they already know, and reassures them that you see the situation similarly.

2. The Inciting Incident explains to others why your work is important. It explains to others in your organization what problem you are working on, justifies large investments in your project and is your chance to position yourself as working on significant initiatives.

3. The Inciting Incident makes disinterested readers more interested. If you are trying to sell ideas to others who aren't as familiar with the problem as you are, the Inciting Incident makes them more attentive to your idea.

Without the Inciting Incident, there's little urgency for the reader to act. If you feel the report lacks urgency, focus on strengthening the Inciting Incident. The bigger the conflict, the hungrier the reader is to hear your recommendation.

In *Moving Mountains,* author Henry Boettinger suggests several ways to frame the Inciting Incident. The following list is inspired by that book's list. Experiment with several of these approaches to find one that feels right for you and will resonate best with the many stakeholders you need to persuade.

Nostalgia. Tell a story about the past and appeal to the audience's pride for a glorious future.

"Seven years ago, the Jones brothers opened their first mobile phone manufacturing plant in Little Rock, Arkansas. Since then we've been selling mobile phones and have succeeded because of superior handset design. Now it's time to write the next chapter of our company's history."

Gathering Storm. Recite a list of bad news items and bring them together, like gathering storm clouds, to create a sense of anxiety and impending doom.

"Sales are flat or declining in all regions, competitors are coming out with new handsets every month, our margins are being flattened by powerful channel partners. We need to do something different."

Unpleasant Future. Talk with certainty about an unpleasant future if nothing is done.

"One thing is certain: we will continue to see steady and accelerating market share losses for the next five years unless we invest in breaking open new markets."

Crossroads. Argue that you have reached a fork in the road and you *must* make a decision. This works best if you can refer to a real transition that is happening.

"Handset sales are flat or declining in all markets. We just acquired Cosmic Mobile and our newly merged company must decide how to make the most of our combined strengths. We have two choices…"

Failure. Refer to decisions in the past that haven't worked out. Avoid blaming anyone in the room because people have a way of rejecting ideas that threaten their egos.

"We invested in a new line of handsets last year but sales have not taken off the way we expected. We need to learn from our mistakes and try something new."

New Development. Talk about how something in the environment has changed which creates an opportunity that wasn't possible in the past.

"Most phones have 3G wireless access, which wasn't available even three years ago! We've always been a handset company. But why can't our handsets come with access to online software downloads like games, ring tones and business applications?"

Evolution. Talk about how the world is changing and you must keep up.

"Five years ago we had three competitors. Today, we have nine. Five years ago email on the phone was a novelty. Today's it's a commodity. The industry has changed and so we must also change to stay ahead."

Dare. Appeal to people's pride by challenging them to meet a difficult-to-attain goal. It could include a competitor's taunt or a comparison to a company's past achievements.

"Our competitors say we're behind the times. Are we going to just let them steal our share? Or are we going to fight?"

Pay Your Dues. Show how some rule has been broken and now you are obligated to make amends.

"Handset sales are flat or declining in all regions and our shareholders are rightly upset. Their expectation is steady growth. We need to present them with a new plan that will achieve what we promised them."

Adventure. Create a desire to take on a risky new strategy by talking about the potential treasures, and also the dangers, versus the status quo.

"The mobile handset market is mature. We can settle in for steady three percent growth per year. Or, we can break out of the pack and invest in handsets with a completely new form factor. It's tough to predict what form factors will catch on so we'll have to be willing to experiment and have more failures than successes, but if get it right, it will mean strong and steady growth and pulling ahead of the competition."

The Great Dream. Paint a picture of a utopian future that is bold and visionary and builds a strong desire to get there by any means possible! This works best when expressed by a high-ranking officer and appeals to basic human emotions.

"I imagine a future where our handsets stand for pride of workmanship and rewards for a job well done. I imagine college graduates, filled with hopes and dreams and ambition, picking our phone because it says *I've arrived. I've worked hard, I've overcome every challenge, and I've arrived.*"

New Information. You tell people that what they thought was true is not true, or you just learned some new information that changes everything.

"We've believed that a good price, good form factor and widespread distribution are all that's needed to be successful. Well, we were wrong. Every mobile handset maker has that. We need something more."

This is not an exhaustive list, but a useful starting point as you think about how to approach your Inciting Incident. There are many ways to introduce an Inciting Incident and you should pay attention to other speakers to learn their methods for introducing a problem that makes the audience starved for the answer.

Sometimes the Inciting Incident is obvious and significant. But sometimes, the Inciting Incident isn't that obvious or is too mundane to really generate interest. In that case, I offer the following tips to help you strengthen it:

- Expand the scope: Look beyond the current problem to side effects and others who will be hurt if the problem isn't solved. For instance, losing market share to a competitor for one product may lead to losses for other products as well.

- Narrow the scope: Focus in on certain situations which are troubling. For instance, rather than talking about losing 5% market share overall last year, focus more narrowly on losing 30% market share among midsize customers last year.

- Make it concrete: Use pictures instead of words. For instance, rather than just name competitors or competitive products, show photographs and quotes from real customers who have stopped using your product.

If you cannot think of a strong Inciting Incident, it may be that you don't fully understand the importance of what you're working on. Or, you may be stuck working on non-strategic issues. At a minimum, you may want to clarify with your own manager how important they think the issue is, and why.

The Inciting Incident helps sell ideas by making people more interested readers and more hungry to resolve a problem. If your goal is to compete in the idea marketplace the number one thing you can do to heighten interest in your ideas is to craft a strong Inciting Incident.

Fine points of the opening slides

There are no hard and fast rules for the opening slides, but the following format works for me and may be a useful starting point for finding your own style.

The first slide should summarize the situation with three bullet points. This should be stated in a non-controversial way. You don't want the reader to disagree with you on slide one. You are just saying what the reader already knows.

- The current situation. What was happening before the Inciting Incident when life was good?

- The Inciting Incident. What new force is upsetting the current situation and what's at stake if it's not addressed?

- The reader's question that you will answer in your report.

Summary

- Our company needs to win 1,100 new customers onto our email platform
- Competitor is winning early adopters and becoming perceived as the market leader
- How can we regain the lead in customers' minds?

The second slide should lay out a more detailed answer to the question and suggest how the rest of the deck is organized. We'll discuss this more in the next chapter.

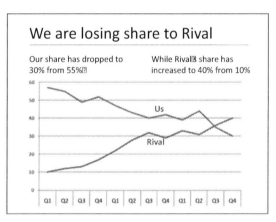

The third slide should summarize the Inciting Incident in more detail, such as showing sales trends falling or customer quotes saying why they're moving to the competition. The goal is to dramatize the problem.

It's best if you can summarize the Inciting Incident on one slide, for maximum impact. Spreading the threat over multiple slides is sometimes necessary to fully explain the threat, and if done right can even build more drama and tension, but it risks diffusing the impact by demanding the reader understand and remember too much. Both approaches can work.

The opening slides are intended to answer the reader's question quickly and generate interest with the Inciting Incident. In practice, you may need some administrative slides as well, such as the methodology for a research report or a recap of your marketing goals. All of this competes with answering the reader's question and generating urgency, so if at all possible, it's best to minimize these slides or move them to the appendix.

Back to Robert's deck

It's 8:30 a.m. and you need to give Robert some advice to get his deck on track. "Robert, let's imagine it's next week and Aubrey is sitting down to look at this deck. What's the main question he has in his mind?"

"I imagine he's going to want to know what plan we're proposing, how much it's going to cost and what it's going to accomplish. Probably our timelines too."

"I think you're right, Robert. But let's boil this down to the single most important question Aubrey will be thinking."

"Probably, what is the plan."

You write the question on the whiteboard. "So what is your recommendation?"

Robert begins scrabbling through his slides. "Here on slide 8 is the marketing mix. And slide 9 has the events and conferences recommendations. Slide 10 has the messaging, and the agency comped up a few potential ads…"

"Let's boil this down to the 2–3 things you think will get us 1,100 new customers. We can get into the details of how and budget later, but let's just get a topline on the whiteboard. What are your 2–3 recommendations?"

"Okay, well first, we should be doing call-downs to drive attendance to webinars and local seminars to hear directly from other customers. Second, we want to gather case studies and issue joint press releases with customers. And third, we want to invest in a heavy presence at trade shows to show our market dominance."

You write all that down on the board and circle the three recommendations in black marker with a dramatic flourish. "That's what the reader wants to see right away. Everything else in the deck just tells them why and how."

You tap the marker against your chin. "For anyone who doesn't understand why this is important, tell me why do we need to win 1,100 new customers? Why is this worth $2 million in marketing?"

"Because we're up against a pretty tough competitor and they are scooping up all the early adopters. That's bad. They are going to get market momentum and we'll be playing catch-up. So we need to press on the gas and get ahead of them."

This sounds like an Unpleasant Future approach, where you paint a picture of a gloomy future unless something is done. You rephrase it for Robert, "Let's make sure we really emphasize what the future will look like if we don't do the right things today; we will be playing catch-up with our competitor. To avoid that, we need to adopt your strategy."

You wonder if you should brainstorm a few more possibilities. You could use an Evolution approach, where you talk about how something in the environment is changing and you must keep up. Or a Gathering Storm approach, where you bring together a stack of bad news like angry storm clouds. You discuss some of these options with Robert, again expressing that it helps his recommendation get approved if the reader has a strong interest in seeing the problem resolved.

You both decide the Unpleasant Future approach will resonate with Aubrey, and later with the field, the best.

You get up and start writing on the whiteboard. "Let's call that our Inciting Incident. I want anyone who reads your report to know just how important your project is, and I want them to feel an urgency to read your recommendations."

Summary

1. Answer First is critical for selling ideas in the boardroom. Answering the reader's question helps ensure your deck has a clear main point, helps you organize the rest of your deck and gives the reader the information they need to make a decision.

2. Ask your reader what question they want answered, or else write out possible questions. Then write out the answer. The act of writing the question, along with the answer, helps you turn vague half-formed thoughts into a fully-articulated idea that becomes the foundation for the rest of your deck.

3. Introduce your deck with an Inciting Incident that explains why the information is important and increases the reader's interest in your recommendations. Experiment with a number of different approaches and choose one that will resonate with the audience. The number one way to increase interest in your report is to strengthen the Inciting Incident.

4. A suggested framework for the opening slide is: state the situation before the Inciting Incident, state the Inciting Incident, and frame the question you will answer. On slide two, summarize your answer and show how you will structure the rest of your deck (covered in the next chapter). On slide three, show the Inciting Incident.

Recommended reading

The Pyramid Principle by Barbara Minto is the resource used by consultants around the world on how to structure clear and persuasive business reports.

Moving Mountains by Henry Boettinger covers how to structure a persuasive business presentation. The book is practical and insightful and packed with useful advice and examples. *Moving Mountains* is one of the finest books ever written on business presentations and should be required reading for every business school student. It's not an exaggeration to say it's the modern-day equivalent of Aristotle's *Rhetoric*, the timeless classic on persuasive speech written 2,500 years ago.

Resonate, by Nancy Duarte, shows how to organize a deck using the proven principles of storytelling. In particular, Nancy shows how to create a sense of imbalance to increase interest (what we have called the "Inciting Incident") and keep an audience's attention throughout by constantly alternately between what is and what could be.

CHAPTER 4

Above-water Argument

Surface your 3–4 portable points

I T'S 8:40 A.M. You and Robert consider the text on the whiteboard. This is the main message for the field, and what you want Aubrey to approve.

At least, you think so. What is Robert's rationale? Why these three strategies and not others? Is this a plan you want to defend in front of Aubrey?

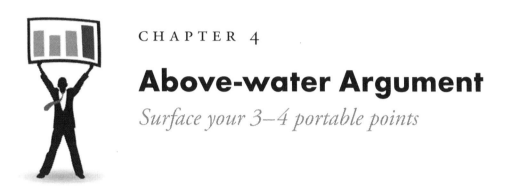

You watch Robert dutifully writing the whiteboard notes on a blank sheet of paper, the other 20 slides of his deck messily splayed on the table. Great, you've got a clear message. Is that the only change?

What's your advice to Robert to organize and structure the rest of the slides?

The long and winding road approach

Great ideas commonly die in the idea marketplace because they are too complicated to understand. You might have 10, 20, 30 slides or more in your deck. But the reader cannot remember everything. You must organize your slides so the reader can follow your logic easily.

Selling ideas requires simplicity. Colin Powell, former U.S. secretary of state, famously said,

> "Great leaders are almost always great simplifiers, who can cut through argument, debate and doubt, to offer a solution everybody can understand."

Robert Mayer, author of *How to Win Any Argument*, calls this brief summary of your argument your *portable points*. These need to be simple enough to recite quickly to others. The easier they are to repeat, the easier they are to remember and spread.

You have probably thought about your problem long and hard and the solution is complex. But if you want people to understand your argument, you need to simplify your important report down into a few portable points. The way you organize your slides will influence whether or not your argument is simple enough to follow.

The common way I've seen slides ordered is to present details first and then summarize those into conclusions and finally into recommendations. Steve Ballmer, Microsoft's CEO, calls this the *long and winding road* approach, where the slide maker takes you through their path of discovery and you arrive at a logical conclusion.

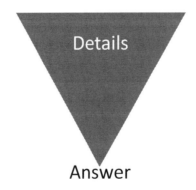

For instance, a marketing manager may build their deck showing:

Slide 1:   market sizes in 15 countries
Slide 2:   market share in each country
Slide 3:   competitive analysis showing our product's strengths and weaknesses
Slide 4:   channel analysis, showing sales by product by partner type in each country
Slide 5:   channel analysis, showing sales by customer segment by partner type in each country
            …and so on…
Slide 17:   recommendation is to focus on 5 countries with channel incentives

What the manager has done is re-enact their analysis. Theoretically, this makes sense. This is how the manager analyzed the situation and came to their conclusion, and they feel if they take the reader on the same journey, the reader will naturally and effortlessly arrive at the same conclusion.

There are at least three problems with this approach:

1. Forgetting. Readers do not have unlimited memory and so they will be selective about what they pay attention to and what they retain. For complex situations, it can be difficult to summarize multiple data points into a coherent conclusion. This type of report can feel like it has no focus—it becomes a cloud of data that the reader can't comprehend or form into a coherent argument.

2. Criticism. You may not even get to your recommendation if the reader disagrees with your data. Re-enacting your analysis means presenting a *deductive* argument. That means the reader must agree with each step in your logic to agree with your final analysis. For instance, you might argue A is true and B is true so C must be true. But if the reader disagrees that A is true they cannot agree with C. Because the reader must agree with each premise before moving on, it causes them to look for flaws. Presenting data invites questions like: *What was the sample size for this study? What is the statistical significance? Is there anything else that could explain the sales decline in Q4?* I have seen many meetings devolve into debates about survey design when a deductive argument is presented.

3. Disagreement. Taking the reader on a journey of your analysis may cause them to reach a different conclusion. Business persons like problem-solving and walking a reader through the data invites them to try to solve the problem you've already solved. They may have reached a decision by slide 8 that we need an awareness campaign in Europe. Now you are recommending sales incentives in Korea?

Disagreement is a serious risk because people tend to stick with decisions made early and be resistant to changing them later.

Research finds that when jurors are asked to make tentative decisions about a defendant's guilt or innocence—just *tentative decisions*—they are likely to stick with those decisions even after more carefully evaluating all the evidence and discussing different points of view with others. So you don't want to present information in any order that invites the reader to come to their own conclusions because it's difficult to reverse those biases later.

Steve Ballmer used to like the long and winding road approach. But not anymore. In a May 2009 *New York Times* article, Ballmer denounced the long and winding road:

> "That's kind of the way I used to like to do it, and the way Bill [Gates] used to kind of like to do it. And it seemed like the best way to do it, because if you went to the conclusion first, you'd get: *What about this? Have you thought about this?* So people naturally tried to tell you all the things that supported the decision, and then tell you the decision.
>
> I decided that's not what I want to do anymore. I don't think it's productive. I get impatient. So most meetings nowadays, you send me the materials and I read them in advance. And I can come in and say: *I've got the following four questions. Please don't present the deck.* That lets us go, whether they've organized it that way or not, to the recommendation. And if I have questions about the long and winding road and the data and the supporting evidence, I can ask them. But it gives us greater focus."

Does it make a difference if your conclusions come before, or after, your data? And how much more coherent does it make your argument?

Educators have studied this question extensively because teachers face a similar challenge: in what order to present information to students so they understand it, learn it and remember it later. The research suggests that putting your conclusion first makes it easier for the reader to understand and remember your main message, especially as the information becomes more complex.

In 1972, John D. Bransford and Marcia K. Johnson conducted a series of studies to determine how the placement of a paragraph summary impacted reading comprehension and recall. University students were asked to read a passage consisting of nine sentences. The passage discussed things that could go wrong with a particular situation, but didn't explain the situation in advance. The reader had to make some inferences based on the passage.

One group was shown a picture in advance illustrating the situation, the *context-before* group. Another group was shown the same picture after they had read the passage, the *context-after* group. A third group read the passage without seeing the picture, the *no-context* group.

What did the researchers find? Did it matter if the group saw the picture before or after reading the passage? And how much did it matter?

It turns out, seeing the picture in advance matters a great deal. Students in the context-before group understood the passage more than twice as well as the other groups and nearly three times better than the no-context group.

The study was repeated three times with different groups and found similar results: those who knew the passage's context in advance understood and recalled the passage better than the others groups.

This is an important brain rule. Telling people your conclusions before showing them the data primes the reader to know what information to pay attention to. This allows them to key on the most relevant information, understand its relevance and remember it longer. You see this principle at work when you read executive summaries, report titles, abstracts, section headers, lists of learning objectives and other *advance organizers* which signal what material will be covered in the upcoming section. The book you hold in your hands also signals upcoming material with section headers.

The more complex the argument, the more it requires a conclusion stated upfront. In the Bransford and Johnson studies, the passage was obscure, essentially a puzzle where the reader almost had to "solve" the context to understand it. Other researchers have found that simpler passages may be understood without a conclusion statement preceding or following the passage. But the more complex your argument and the more inferences readers need to make to connect the ideas in an argument, the more an upfront topic sentence will help the reader hold it all together.

Your above-water argument

When planning your main message and support points, think of your slide deck like an iceberg. Only 10% of an iceberg can be seen above the water. The other 90% is below the water.

Similarly, your slide deck may be 10, 20, 30 slides or more. But your reader doesn't need to see all of it. They just need to see the top 10%.

You want to surface your main argument before surfacing your details. Your main message includes the Answer along with 3–4 support points. The 3–4 support points are called your *above-water argument*.

The rest of your argument—your evidence and explanations—adds the necessary bulk to your argument but is kept under water until needed.

The more complex your argument, the more you need to surface your above-water argument before your evidence.

News reporters use this structure, called the inverted-pyramid, to write articles. They write the most important information in the first paragraph, then reveal additional details in the following

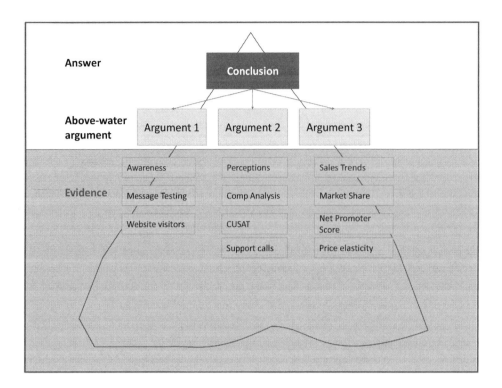

paragraphs with the most important information higher than the less important information. This allows editors, rushing to fit stories into a daily newspaper, to cut paragraphs from the bottom to fit the available space without cutting useful content.

The first paragraph is called *the lead*. When a reporter pushes important details into later paragraphs, they are said to be *burying the lead*. The lead is the most important part of the story; it's what the reader wants to know and experienced news reporters are good at sniffing out the lead and pushing it high in the article.

Compare these two approaches and decide for yourself which is more effective:

Approach 1: Details then conclusions (long and winding road)

The question we are here to answer is: should we expand our mobile phone sales into Canada?

There are 35 million Canadians, with 27 million who report using a mobile phone. Primary market segments are: urban professionals (33%), teens and students (24%), mothers (19%), small business and construction (12%).

The mobile carrier channel in Canada is highly concentrated among three primary wireless carriers. These partners serve 49%, 27% and 15% of the market respectively.

Mobile phone sales in Canada have increased at a rate of 3.5% YoY for the past three years, roughly the same growth rate as Canada's population overall. Canadians replace their phone every 17 months.

The market is there. And it's growing. We can get 90% market coverage through three channel partners. Therefore, our recommendation is to expand into Canada on a pilot basis.

Approach 2: Conclusions then details (above-water argument)

The question we are here to answer is: should we expand our mobile phone sales into Canada?

Our recommendation is to expand into Canada on a pilot basis.

The market is there. And it's growing. We can get 90% market coverage through three channel partners.

The market is there. There are 35 million Canadians, with 27 million who report using a mobile phone. Primary market segments are: urban professionals (33%), teens and students (24%), mothers (19%), small business and construction (12%).

The market is growing. Mobile phone sales in Canada have increased at a rate of 3.5% YoY for the past three years, roughly the same growth rate as Canada's population overall. Canadians replace their phone every 17 months.

We can get 90% market coverage through three channel partners. The mobile carrier channel in Canada is highly concentrated among three primary wireless carriers. These partners serve 49%, 27% and 15% of the market respectively.

Do you see how the writer buried the lead in Approach 1? Do you see how surfacing the lead to the top made the argument easier to understand in Approach 2?

Whether you agree with the recommendation and analysis or not, you understand the recommendation and the main supporting points. You don't need to store the details in memory and recall them later. You can evaluate the data as you read it.

The other reason this approach works is because as you share each conclusion, the reader's natural reaction is to ask questions. *Why a pilot? Why do you say there is low price competition?* Now that the reader wants the answer, it's the perfect opportunity to present it.

> "The fatal pedagogical error is to throw answers, like stones,
> at the heads of those who have not yet asked the questions."
> —PAUL TILICH, 20TH CENTURY PROTESTANT THEOLOGIAN

In *The Pyramid Principle*, Barbara Minto also recommends allowing the question to occur to the reader before you answer it. By delivering information in this just-in-time fashion, the reader can use your information as soon as they see it, rather than seeing information they had no need for, and having to hold it in memory and recall it later.

Compare the questions that may occur to a reader as they go through these two slide orders.

Details then conclusions (long and winding road)

Slide says	Reader thinks
There are 35 million Canadians, with 27 million who report using a mobile phone.…	*Okay, large market. Are they happy with their current cellphones? Would they buy ours?*
20 million are located in the three largest metropolitan areas in Canada: Vancouver, Toronto and Montreal…	*Okay…does that matter? Where is Montreal?*
Primary market segments in these cities is: urban professionals (33%), teens and students (24%)…	*There's our market segment— urban professionals. Is this a "go" recommendation or a "no go"?*
This competitive analysis shows our phones stack up well on form function and email – two things our customers value…	*Okay, great! How do we get into market?*
The mobile carrier channel in Canada is highly concentrated among three primary wireless carriers…	*Are they happy with their current cellphone providers? Will they be easy to work with?*
These partners serve 49%, 27% and 15% of the market respectively…	*Should I interrupt and ask questions as we go? How big was the market again?*

Conclusions then details (above-water argument)

Slide says	Reader thinks
Our recommendation is to expand into Canada on a pilot basis…	*Why a pilot basis?*
There is an addressable market of about 7 million who would want our phone, but it may be difficult to get distribution…	*Hmmm…large market you say? Would they want our phone?*
In terms of market opportunity, there are 7 million urban professionals who use a mobile phone in Canada's three largest cities…	*7 million users in three major cities! We should be able to do some targeted campaigns then.*
They value attractive handsets and reliable mobile email, and our handsets stack up well against what competitors offer…	*Great! How do we get into the market?*
But there are just three channel partners who control 90% of the market. They aren't highly competitive so it might be hard to interest them in carrying a new handset…	*What if we offered incentives? Or co-marketing funds? Or just marketed through direct mail?*
In our pilots, we would be experimenting with different approaches to interest the mobile operators, such as incentives or co-marketing funds…	*<notice how most of my questions have been answered?>*

Turning your slide deck order upside puts your conclusions first and supporting details last. It makes it easier for the reader to follow your logic because you prime the reader to look for your above-water argument and you don't introduce information until the reader needs it.

The direct approach of answer-argument-supporting data works when the audience is receptive to the message. But if you expect disagreement, you may want to take a more indirect approach of supporting data-argument-answer.

For instance, I developed a research report for a global technology firm to help them understand a market segment where they were having trouble growing. They believed the main challenge was high software piracy. This had become a sort of mantra so that in meetings people automatically assumed that the major challenge was piracy. Entire strategies were being built around this mantra.

But the data didn't support this. Or rather, most data didn't support this and some data was being misread. But as I shared my view in one-on-one meetings I found high levels of disbelief. People didn't want to entertain this contrary view.

So my final report revealed this data with a slide titled "Piracy: what does the data say?" which then went through the different data sources, and later revealed the data that was always misrepresented. This indirect route was necessary because there was a mental block against the recommendation that would have shut down further evaluation.

Developing your above-water argument

You now know why you want to present your 3–4 support points before your data. The 3–4 support points is called the above-water argument. It simplifies your argument, primes the reader to understand your line of reasoning and summarizes how the deck is structured.

The above-water argument is what the reader will remember when they finish reading the deck. They don't need to remember every piece of data you show them, but they should be able to walk out of your meeting and understand your most important points.

You should have no more than 3–4 portable points in your above-water argument and they should be complete thoughts.

Why 3–4 support points? We will cover this more in later chapters, but for now understand that most people cannot hold an unlimited amount of information in mind at the same time. The most they can hold is 3–4 ideas. This is called the Rule of Four in Stephen Kosslyn's book *Clear and to the Point*, and we will revisit this theme several times throughout the rest of this book.

For example, look at how much clearer your message becomes when you reduce an above-water argument of five points down to an above-water argument of three points. Imagine you are recommending a trial expansion into Canada. Your reasons, or above-water argument, are:

1.   20 million consumers (75% total population) in three markets

2.   7 million (33%) are urban professionals

3.   17 month replacement cycle

4.   Three resellers control 91% of the market

5.   Little price competition among competitors

These five points are difficult to understand and turn your smart analysis into an unclear data soup. But by combining them into no more than 3–4 points, the above-water argument becomes simple enough to understand.

1.   7 million urban professionals (33% of market) in three markets

2.   17 month replacement cycle

3.   Three resellers control 91% of the market with little price competition

Why complete thoughts? Because this ensures you articulate your above-water argument and not just the structure of your deck. Articulating your argument helps you to organize the evidence slides you need in order to get your reader to also agree with your above-water argument.

Complete thoughts might start as paragraphs. But challenge yourself to condense your thoughts down into single sentences. Remember, these are supposed to be *portable* points. If you can't simplify it for the reader then they won't be very portable.

Break your deck into sections and ask "what about" each section?

How do you decide which 3–4 supporting points will be your above-water argument?

One of the secrets of the STOP format, discussed in chapter 2, is how the report was organized. The engineers started by organizing the report into logical categories, like *Fuselage*, *Engines* and *Landing Gear*. Then they forced themselves to make a clear statement about each category. What about the fuselage? What about the engines?

Category	STOP format
Fuselage	The fuselage will meet the capacity and stability requirements
Engines	Engines will be high-performance and low-maintenance
Landing Gear	Landing gear can be fully engaged in 3.7 seconds

You can also use this successful approach to organizing your boardroom-style PowerPoint reports. Start by organizing your deck into some logical categories. For instance, you might organize the Canadian mobile phone pilot plan into the following categories:

1. Background

2. Market Segments

3. Channel Analysis

4. Competitive Analysis

This is a typical way to organize information in a business report. It doesn't require too much effort of the author. But this organization doesn't help the reader much. The category names don't communicate much of a message. This organization also doesn't help the slide creator surface their above-water argument or know what they are trying to prove.

To turn these categories into an above-water argument, make a statement about each of these categories. Say something that you plan to prove is true in that section.

You do that by asking "So what about...". So what about the Background? So what about the Market Segments? Turn each category into a clear message that supports your deck's Answer.

1. Background: Domestic sales are flat or declining. We need to open new markets...fast

2. Market Segments: 33% of the Canadian market is urban professionals

3. Channel Analysis: 90% of the market is served by three mobile operators, giving us broad reach if we can break into the channel

4. Competitive Analysis: We can compete based on secure email and a distinctive design

You can also see that organizing your deck around key ideas, rather than categories, makes your complete argument visible and easier to understand and critique. More importantly, as a seller of ideas, it makes your idea easier to understand, agree with and discuss with others.

However, you can also see that now each section requires additional thought modules to fully explain and support it. You can now begin to think about what evidence will be required to help the reader agree with your above-water argument.

1. Domestic sales are flat or declining. We need to open new markets…fast
   a. Sales have flattened for the industry overall, and our sales are beginning to decline
   b. Domestically, price wars are deflating profit margins
   c. Globally, several markets are growing fast including Canada and Australia

2. 33% of the Canadian market is urban professionals
   a. 20 million Canadians use a mobile phone
   b. In three largest markets, 33% are urban professionals
   c. Canadians replace their phone every 17 months

3. 90% of the market is served by three mobile operators, giving us broad reach if we can break into the channel
   a. Three carriers control 90% of mobile phone sales
   b. Little price competition. Channel competes primarily on location of retail stores

4. We can compete based on secure email and a distinctive design
   a. Mobile professionals are unhappy with the lack of secure email offered by the top three mobile operators
   b. Mobile professionals also feel they don't have enough design choices, especially executive-style flip phones

There are various ways you could break up a deck into sections and no one way is clearly the right way. You may want to experiment with different approaches to find the one that generates the most compelling above-water argument.

We are now developing a PowerPoint deck using thought modules, with a clear thesis statement that all adds up to support an above-water argument and overall deck message. The above-water argument is the important bridge between the deck's main message and all the evidence you will assemble to complete the deck.

We have not talked yet about the order to present your above-water argument. What argument comes first? Second? Last? We talk about the order of your above-water argument and your evidence in the next chapter.

Back to Robert's deck

It's 8:40 a.m. and you and Robert are looking at the whiteboard where you've written the recommendations you'll present to Aubrey.

"Let's think about how we structure this deck so Aubrey understands your reasoning. If you were writing this as a text report, how would you break your report up into sections?"

"Maybe…based on the three parts of the plan—telesales, case studies and trade shows?"

You scribble this on the board. "Okay, let's start with this. We might change it later, but let's see what it gets us." You tap the board where you've written *telesales*. "What's the main point you want to make about telesales?"

"Okay, well the most important thing is that our product isn't that much better than the competitor's. It's weaker in many areas, actually, but mostly it's the same so I don't think we can win on product features. We need to be first to talk to the customer. That's why we need telesales to get people to attend webinars and local events. We can't wait for people to find us; we need to find them."

You paraphrase this on the whiteboard. "What about case studies?"

"Lots of customers like our competitor better, especially end-users. Their product is simpler to use and they just have a better image. Customers don't believe what we say about our product, but they do believe what other customers say. So if we can do case studies and press releases, and let our customers talk about how satisfied they are, that will overcome any negative perceptions the market has of us."

You write this on the board. "And trade shows?"

"Well, trade shows have proven to be a good way to demo our product and gather leads. We can feed these back into the telesales lists. Also, showing up at trade shows gives us visibility as the market leader. Our competitor doesn't attend too many trade shows, so we have an opportunity to be perceived as the market leader."

You write all this down on the whiteboard and inspect it a moment.

1. Product isn't differentiated so we need telesales so we can reach the customer first

2. Competitor has a better brand image so we need customer case studies

3. Trade shows generate leads for call-downs and positions us as the market leader

Robert's argument is becoming clearer. You aren't sure if this is the correct order to present it, or if there's a better structure. But it is 8:50 a.m. and you have another meeting starting in ten minutes. Robert follows your glance then starts frantically writing the whiteboard contents onto his paper.

Above-water argument

1. The brain science of comprehension says that if you prime the reader in advance to your conclusion, they will be able to understand your argument better. Don't take the long and winding road. This is more likely to lead to forgetting, criticism and disagreement.

2. Develop an above-water argument to make your message clear and simple: present your answer first, above-water argument second and supporting data last. Answer questions as they come into the reader's mind, rather than requiring them to remember a lot of detail and recall it later.

3. Use 3–4 support points in your above-water argument and make them complete but brief thoughts. If you have more than four support points, combine similar support points.

4. Based on the success of the STOP format, create an above-water argument by organizing your deck into logical categories and then making a statement about each category you will now show to be true.

Recommended reading

The Pyramid Principle by Barbara Minto goes into greater detail on how to order your above-water argument and the rest of your business report. She especially suggests how to order problem-solution sets; should the problem come first or the solution? Should all the problems be listed first followed by all the solutions, or just introduce each problem followed by its solution? Barbara's principles apply to standalone business reports so can be applied to a reading deck or briefing deck.

Advanced Presentations by Design by Andrew Abela suggests ordering slides using the S.C.o.R.E. Method. Basically, each section of the deck is made up of a Situation, Complication, Resolution and an Example. This approach assumes the reader has a certain objection to your initial comment and you proactively address it. You proceed through your deck in this way, anticipating objections and proactively introducing and answering each one. This relies on the principle of storytelling that a story is developed by moving through a series of conflicts.

The Seven-Slide Solution by Paul Kelly covers another approach to organizing your deck. His method uses seven slides to set up the problem, build tension and ultimately introduce the solution. The presenter would extemporaneously cover the details that defend the solution so this is appropriate for a briefing deck but doesn't accommodate the additional slides needed to explain and defend a recommendation.

CHAPTER 5

Evidence

Choose and order your evidence slides

IT'S 8:50 A.M. AND YOU FEEL like the deck is starting to make sense. But you're going to need to defend this proposal to Aubrey.

"Let's focus on the first argument, Robert, that we need to reach the customer first. What data do you have to support that?"

Robert begins sifting through his slides then pulls out slide 6—a competitive analysis. "Here's a side by side comparison of our product with our competitor's. We're strong on integration and support, but our competitor is stronger on features and brand. They have a lot of features that we're way behind on. But overall, we both offer the main features all customers want."

Robert rummages again and pulls out slide 12, a SWOT analysis. He produces a few more slides, showing higher awareness and more positive perceptions for the competitor. Sales are also trending up faster for the competitor.

Does Robert have the right data? More importantly, how do you sequence these slides so Aubrey will agree with Robert's analysis? What's your advice to Robert?

Ordering your evidence

You've developed your above-water argument, which supports the main message of your deck, which answers the reader's question. Now you need to show the data that supports that above-water argument—your evidence.

Evidence is a broad term that includes many things. It can include data that "proves" your argument, like charts and tables. It can also include data that defines, explains or illustrates your argument, like conceptual diagrams, customer quotes, images, text descriptions and so on. It is basically everything you need to show to illustrate your above-water argument.

You will prove each leg of your above-water argument in turn, showing evidence until the reader is satisfied and agrees with your first above-water argument before moving onto the next leg and displaying data to prove that leg.

The challenge, for PowerPoint or any kind of writing, is finding the right order to present your argument. A PowerPoint deck, or any written or spoken report, is linear. Ideas are presented one at a time in some order to produce a coherent argument.

But thinking is not always linear. Ideas are scattered in our minds like stars in the sky and are connected in a chaotic web of associations. As we ponder a problem, its various parts are scattered in different areas of our brains and fade in and out of consciousness. We often arrive at solutions in a flash of insight, especially when the problem is unstructured and doesn't bend easily to simple analysis.

In a way, choosing an order for our slides is like untangling a ball of string in our minds and straightening it out so the reader can follow our logic in a linear order, which may not have been linear in the first place. How do we do this?

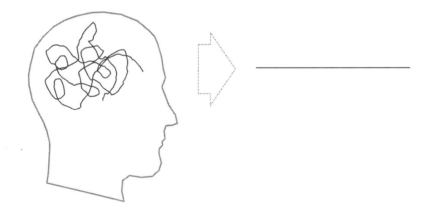

We will talk in the next chapter about a method for assembling your evidence. For now, imagine you have assembled all your evidence in front of you in a pile. How will you sequence this evidence for the reader? What is the "right" order that will make your logical argument clear?

There is no simple way to generalize this because your thinking was never purely linear. Instead, you will impose some arbitrary order on your evidence to start, and then modify your order later using your judgment.

Here are five possible ways to arbitrarily order your evidence:

1. Cause-Effect

The most natural place to start is to arrange your evidence so you can see the cause-effect relationships. For instance, if your above-water argument is "we should expand into the college market" you may have several pieces of evidence supporting this:

- analysis of your product versus competitor's product

- quotes from focus groups with college students

- market research showing high demand among college students

- data showing trends in usage for the product category is increasing

Is there a cause-effect order you can impose on this evidence? How about:

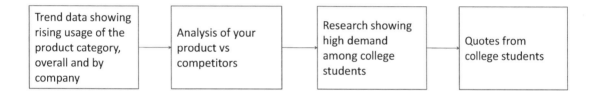

This is an acceptable order for the evidence so it forms a coherent argument for the reader. This order has a couple of advantages:

1. It has a story-telling approach. You could present these four slides with a narrative like: *College students are using the product more, and you can especially see how our competitors' sales are growing. But an analysis shows we are better on features X, Y and Z. College students also see value in these features and this data demonstrates what percent of the market would be interested in purchasing our product. Finally, here are some specific quotes we heard during that research.*

2. You can find holes in the evidence. By ordering the evidence in a cause-effect chain, you can determine what evidence is missing to support the narrative. For instance, in this order, I wonder why the competitor's sales are increasing so fast despite having an inferior product.

One problem with the cause-effect chain is it starts to look like the long and winding road approach, where you re-enact your analysis. This is what is called a *deductive argument*. The reader has to agree with each premise before they are willing to move onto the next premise. If they disagree at any point, they are less willing to agree with later parts of your argument.

So the cause-effect chain is most appropriate for short narratives that can be explained in 2–3 slides or that are non-controversial. Otherwise, you run into the problems of the reader forgetting data you presented earlier, questioning your methodology and disagreeing with your analysis.

2. Effect-Cause

An alternate arrangement is to start with the effect and work back to the cause. This is a root-cause analysis and just reverses the cause-effect chain.

For instance, in the earlier example, if we reverse the order we get:

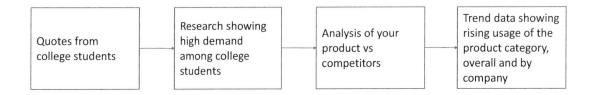

Now our narrative becomes: *We spoke to college students and they are very interested in our product. In fact, in a quantitative study we found 70% of college students would purchase our product. Compared to our competitor, we have many advantages that appeal to college students. Sales in the college market are rising fast, and especially for our competitor, so now is the time to increase our investments.*

There are two advantages to this approach over the cause-effect chain:

1.   It negates many of the problems of the long and winding road approach. Rather than re-enact your analysis, which invites disagreement, you reveal your analysis in reverse order.

2.   It's a more comfortable reading experience. Information is only revealed as the reader asks for it. For instance, in this example, you say "70% of college students want our product" and the reader asks *why*. You answer "because we have many product features the competitor doesn't". This reverse order appears to anticipate reader questions and simulates a conversation rather than an analysis.

For complex or controversial arguments, the effect-cause chain should be preferred over the cause-effect chain.

3. Categorical

Another approach would be to break the evidence down into categories, similar to how you developed your above-water argument by breaking your deck into categories. This is especially useful if you are describing something that is complex and needs to be broken down into components.

For instance, if your above-water argument is *we should increase our demand-generation activities*, you might organize your evidence into three categories: online marketing, print marketing and broadcast marketing. Then each slide would show mock-ups of each advertisement and a rationale for that recommendation.

Whenever you are describing something complex made up of many parts, you have a decision to make. Do you show the entire system at once and try to explain its components over the next few slides? Or do you show each component first and then bring them together to show the entire system on the final slide?

You will want to describe each component first. Instructional designers find that people learn complex material best when it is broken into categories and taught one category at a time. Later, the categories can be brought together to form more complex ideas. This is like learning the alphabet before learning to spell words, then write sentences, then craft entire essays.

For instance, you might want to build a perceptual map showing seven customer segments and how they match with four competitive products, demonstrating a gap in the market. Rather than show the entire perceptual map on slide one, your communication will be clearer if you describe each of the seven segments on their own slides and then culminate in a slide that brings all seven segments together on the final slide.

4. Ranking

You can order your evidence from most to least important, largest to smallest, or some other ranking order.

Here's an example. Say your above-water argument is *our competitor is planning to enter the college market*. You have several pieces of evidence:

- competitor has sponsored bowling competitions on 17 college campuses

- competitor is planning to release a new low-price product with a trendy design

- competitor is having trouble making progress with business customers

This is an example of an *inductive argument*. By presenting these three pieces of evidence, the reader is invited to reach a certain conclusion, even if there is no cause-effect relationship linking them. In this case, any order is sufficient to follow your logic, but ordering the evidence from most to least compelling lets you lead with your strongest argument and follow that with supporting arguments.

5. Solution/Problem

It's very common in boardroom-style slides to begin by presenting a problem followed by the solution. In theory, this is a good approach but in practice this is another deductive argument that has many of the problems of the long and winding road approach: if the reader disagrees with your analysis they are biased against your recommendation.

A better approach is to present the solution followed by the problem. The solution is what the reader is interested in, causes them to ask *why do you recommend that*, which allows you to now present the problem you will solve.

The best advice is to keep the problem and solution short and connected. Don't explain five solutions and then the five problems you will solve. The reader will have a heavy burden going back and forth matching solution number one with problem number one, then again for number two and so on. Instead, present solution one followed immediately by problem one.

This is just five possible orders but they are good starting points. My practice is to start with a cause-effect arrangement, if possible, which helps me analyze the data and look for missing evidence. I typically plan to reverse the order and present it as an effect-cause chain if the argument is deductive. This helps me develop a narrative approach which helps the evidence hang together for the reader. Then, I modify the order further based on how well the evidence flows.

This order also applies to your above-water argument. If there is a cause-effect relationship between the 3–4 pillars of your above-water argument, order your sections in that order. Or, if one pillar is clearly stronger than the others, lead with that one.

Which approach is the "right" one? In terms of presenting a logical and coherent argument, any of these orders will do because they all allow the reader to follow your logic. But your final choice should also consider which order is the most persuasive. We now talk about the important role of emotion for any argument and how that affects how you order your evidence slides.

The important role of emotion

Ordering your evidence helps to make it coherent, especially because it ladders up to support a clear above-water argument.

But being clear is only part of selling your ideas. Business leaders, sales professionals, military leaders, politicians, lawyers and others whose success depends upon persuasion agree: you cannot persuade with logic alone. The great sales guru Dale Carnegie said "When dealing with people, remember you are not dealing with creatures of logic, but creatures of emotion."

In fact, over 2,300 years ago in ancient Greece, Aristotle taught there are three basic approaches to persuasion:

- *logos*—logical appeals
- *pathos*—emotional appeals
- *ethos*—using authority figures

In his *Rhetoric,* Aristotle argued that all three are important to be an effective persuader, but emotion is critical for the acceptance of a logical argument.

"The orator must not only try to make the argument of his speech demonstrative and worthy of belief; he must also…put his hearers, who are to decide, into the right frame of mind… When people are feeling friendly and placable, they think one sort of thing; when they are feeling angry or hostile, they think…something totally different."
(*Rhet.* II.1, 1378a)

And in *Moving Mountains*, Henry Boettinger said of the important role of emotion and reason:

"Scissors cut cloth by combining two sharp tools. No one can say which blade of a scissors does the cutting. The most you can say is that *both* do. Passion and reason likewise cut through the fabric woven of doubt, inertia and fear…Neither can cut it alone."

Logic is necessary to compose your argument, but we are learning more and more that decision making is not purely logical.

If I offer you $20, with no strings attached, would you take it? Most likely, you would. Why wouldn't you? But what if I had $100 and was told to share it with you. If you accept my offer, we both walk away with the cash—you get just $20 and I keep the other $80. If you reject my offer, neither of us gets anything. Now would you accept the $20?

This experiment, called the Ultimatum Game, shows how illogical our decision making can be. In most cases, when someone is offered less than $30, they will reject the offer. This isn't logical; $20 for you is still better than nothing. Even $1 should be accepted if your decision was purely logical. But the human brain is often ruled (or overruled) by emotion.

Political and business leaders are masters of *pathos* and *ethos* to inspire confidence and rally support. Martin Luther King's *I Have a Dream* speech did not excite listeners with charts and graphs, or even statistics and appeals to logic, but with passion and picture words. Take a lesson from the great persuaders of history, and use *pathos* and *ethos* to sell your own ideas, even though you used *logos* to discover them.

Persuasion is a complex topic and it would take an entire book to cover it thoroughly. But through the rest of this chapter I will provide an overview of what brain science tells us about how people make decisions, and how you can order your evidence slides to be more persuasive.

The idea of cold Spock-like logical decision making in business, or anywhere else, is a fallacy. Fears, selfish desires and emotions cloud logic because the human brain is wired first and foremost for survival and last for logic. All decisions are colored by our instincts and emotions, which react more quickly than logic and are more responsible for driving human behavior.

There is more interest today in understanding how the brain affects decisions. Books like *Nudge*, *Predictably Irrational*, *Blink*, *Tipping Point*, *Brain Rules*, *Sway*, *Think Better*, *The Emotional Brain* and *Iconoclast* reveal new information to business and marketing professionals that helps us understand why people often make illogical decisions, and why logic is not always effective at convincing others.

Decision making happens in the brain, which is composed of different systems. Some of those systems are responsible for thinking, some for feeling, and some for survival. When you are selling ideas, you must understand how each of these systems becomes involved and affects decision making.

The brain is not one thing. There are actually three parts of the brain involved in decision making: the reptilian brain, the limbic system and the neocortex.

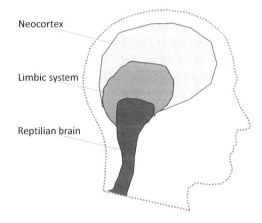

The *reptilian brain* is the small prehistoric stub of brain that starts where your spinal column ends. It's called the reptilian brain because it's the same brain found in alligators, lizards and other reptiles. Its main role is survival, and especially these four survival instincts: fight, flee, feed and mate. It is also territorial and controls the instinct to take ground by force and defend it. The reptilian brain is the oldest of the three-part brain, originating hundreds of millions of years ago.

The reptilian brain is fast! It responds instantly, without conscious thought. When a careless driver swerves into your lane on the highway, it's the reptilian brain that instinctively jams on the brakes. And when a peer challenges your ideas in a meeting, it's the reptilian brain that makes you defensive or aggressive to defend your "territory".

The *limbic system* sits on top of, and evolved out, of the reptilian brain. The limbic system regulates the emotions and behaviors we need for living in communities. Specifically, the limbic system manages emotions like fear, love, empathy, respect, trust, guilt, shame and obligation.

Networking is the limbic system in action. If we meet and I give you some advice that's useful, you will feel grateful. You will be willing to do a favor for me in the future. This reciprocity effect has survival value; it rewards cooperation and is an evolutionary trait that ensures tribes can exist. The limbic system operates slower than the reptilian brain but faster than the neocortex.

The *neocortex* is the large brain mass sitting on top of the limbic system, making up 85% of the brain. It evolved out of the limbic system and is the youngest of the three brains. The neocortex is involved in complex reasoning and logic. When you solve a math problem or learn another language you are using your neocortex.

The neocortex is large, but it's slow—five times slower than the limbic system. And as much as we like to think logic rules our decisions, you may be surprised to learn the neocortex can *receive* ten times as many signals from the limbic system as it can *send*.

The neocortex is composed of two parts: the left brain and the right brain. The left brain thinks in words and the right brain thinks in pictures. Importantly, the left brain cannot talk directly to the limbic system, which thinks in pictures, not words. Only the visual right brain can communicate directly with the limbic system and the reptilian brain. The left brain, which thinks in words, must pass messages through the right brain converted into pictures.

The order of these three brains is important. The reptilian brain reacts first, because we are hardwired most of all for survival. Our limbic system reacts second and our neocortex—the logical brain—reacts last.

Here's an example of how the limbic system can override logic. Consider how you would react if someone asked you for some spare change on a busy sidewalk. Some people will stop and dig out a few coins, but most avert their gaze and keep walking. Now, how would you react if someone instead handed you a flower first and then asked for some spare change? Now your limbic system is triggered—a feeling of obligation—and you are more likely to donate even though you don't want to. You may even throw the flower away as soon as you're out of sight. Robert Cialdini documented this persuasion technique in his book *Influence*, showing the subconscious, and even unwelcome, power of the limbic system to override logic.

The reptilian brain constantly compels us to establish and defend territory. This explains seemingly illogical workplace behavior like aspiring for a larger office or squabbles about which department is authorized to make an important decision. Respect for authority, resistance to change and social pecking orders are all rooted in the reptilian brain. These aren't logical behaviors but make perfect sense when you understand that survival instincts are biologically wired to trump logic.

So what does all this brain science tell us about how people make decisions? Most decisions, including business decisions, are not purely logical but are heavily influenced by emotions and territorial impulses. The decision maker may even be unaware of these biases, which happen instantaneously and largely subconsciously.

It would be a mistake, though, to conclude we are ruled entirely by the reptilian brain and limbic system and incapable of logical decision making. We regularly rally logic when we are making important choices in life. But emotion always reacts before reason and pure left-brain logic is always filtered through the visual right brain, even if we are not consciously aware of how emotion colors our thinking.

For boardroom-style slides, the reader will be looking at the strength of your argument. But take the advice of the great persuaders of history: logic is not the only way to convince readers, and you should not ignore the importance role emotions play in decision making.

Choose a persuasive order for your evidence

Your evidence slides will surface your analysis and logic. But a purely logical argument is not enough. You must consider the dual importance of *logos* and *pathos*.

Your evidence slides must, as Aristotle says, put the reader in the *right frame of mind*. How do we do that? Some options are:

1. Aesthetics. Using color and design principles artfully will help you design a visually pleasing slide that puts the reader in a positive frame of mind. We cover aesthetics throughout Section Three of this book.

2. Pictures. Another way is to add pictures to augment your logical evidence. Pictures have a unique ability that words do not to move us emotionally. We cover pictures in chapter 9.

3. Text. Another way is with word choice. Some words have more emotional impact than others. Especially, picture-words are more likely to affect us emotionally. Picture-words are words that describe a noun (person, place or thing) or an action (run, jump, fight). Some words have emotional power, like threat or danger, because they appeal to our survival instincts.

4. Use emotional evidence. Some evidence has higher emotional impact because it appeals to different decision areas of the brain. Certain types of evidence like quotes, anecdotes and metaphors have higher emotional impact than facts and statistics.

5. Slide order. Placing slides in a certain order, so evidence with high emotional impact is presented first, can put readers in a certain frame of mind that makes them more responsive to your logic.

6. Avoid any order that starts with controversial evidence or evidence that will put your reader in a negative frame of mind. It will affect how they view all the rest of your slides.

A business example is in order. Imagine you propose the company create a new product line for college students. A logical approach is to show market research demonstrating college students need this product and are willing to pay for it. You have assembled the following evidence and arranged it in a cause-effect chain.

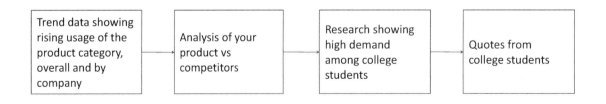

Images used in this book can be seen in color at www.speakingppt.com

This is a strong logical argument. But how strong is the emotional argument? We can try to score each slide for its emotional value. Here I've indicated my own score by changing the size of the box: large boxes for high emotional impact and small boxes for low emotional impact.

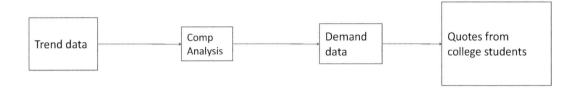

I believe the trend data, showing rising student usage, will be startling but since it's just a graph it is weak at appealing to the reader's emotions. The competitive analysis and demand data is also dry and factual. But the quotes from students saying things like "I'd buy one and tell all my friends" is emotionally powerful.

In this case, I'd reverse the order and lead with my evidence with the highest emotional value. This will help put the reader in the right frame of mind for the rest of my data.

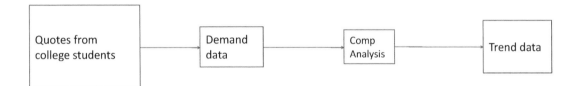

This is better, but I need to be concerned about the persuasiveness of this argument overall. It has high logical value but low emotional value. There are ways to enhance my evidence, by adding images or quotes to the logical evidence slides to make them more emotional.

For instance, imagine this is the demand data I want to show. How persuaded are you by this slide? Likely, this data is interesting but you still have many questions. I have not affected you emotionally.

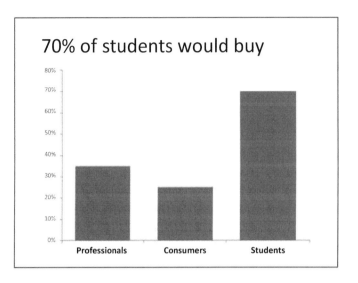

To increase the emotional value of this evidence and put the reader in the right frame of mind, I could add a quote to this slide to illustrate the point. Adding a quote increases the emotional value of this evidence and makes it more persuasive.

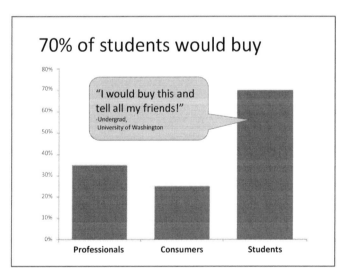

You can also increase the emotional value of this evidence with word choice. For instance, rather than saying "70% of students would buy" we can use picture words: nouns and verbs. In this example, I've used the verb *said* to indicate action. I've also used the phrase *college students* instead of *students* because a *college* is a physical place that conjures an image. Finally, I've written the slide title as a sentence that describes a physical scene.

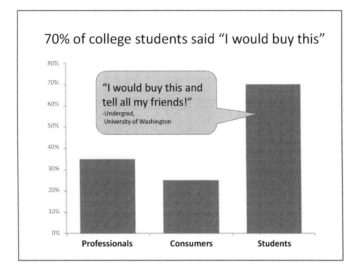

Making slides with emotional evidence does not mean they should be low-content, intended only to put the reader in the right frame of mind. Readers of boardroom-style slides have a task they need to complete, and they are looking for information to help them complete that task or to make a decision. Because of this, slides that are low in content, such as slides used exclusively to affect emotions, are easily recognized and, more importantly, make the reader more resistant.

Research conducted by IBM Netherlands with technology decision makers found that readers preferred a business proposal that used neutral and informative language *three times more than* a similar proposal that added a few persuasive words to enhance the vendor's reputation and the product's promised ease-of-use. Similar research found that people planning a vacation preferred brochures with specific details about the destination and were unhappy with brochures that used more persuasive than informative language.

For instance, this slide saying "the next growth opportunity is students" has an image with little content value. Some readers will tolerate it, but motivated readers may question why you spent time creating a slide with so little content.

This low-content slide would be unwelcome as part of your evidence. One option is to make this slide an above-water argument slide that introduces a section of your deck. Above-water argument slides may include a summary statement with an attractive image just to break the deck into sections. You can also use images like this on the title page.

The important point is that boardroom-style slides assume an interested reader looking for information to help them complete a task or make a decision. Low-content or no-content slides make the reader dissatisfied and even suspicious. So ensure your emotional evidence slides augment your logic, rather than replace it.

If your goal is simply to inform, you may not need to worry about using emotional evidence. A simple factual description of what you are doing or what the reader needs to do may be sufficient. But make that decision deliberately and don't assume your logical argument is sufficient to convince the reader.

> "If the world were a logical place, men would ride sidesaddle."
> —Rita Mae Brown

You have an obligation to present well-reasoned arguments. But the great persuaders of history understand the dual role of emotion and logic to sell ideas. A logical argument can be made more persuasive by consciously choosing to order your slides to surface emotional evidence early and put the reader in the right frame of mind.

Inserting audio in PowerPoint 2007

Including audio in your slides can be powerful. In market research reports, I will embed sound so readers can hear first-hand not only what customers are saying, but the emotion in their voices. This can be an impactful way to make your evidence more emotional.

To insert audio (.wav files only)

1. Click Insert > Sounds > Sound from File. Browse to your .wav file and select it.
2. This produces a small speaker icon on your slide. You can move this icon to anywhere on your slide. If you delete it, you also delete the sound.
3. If your audio file is larger than 100 kb, you will need to change the defaults. Click on the speaker icon once and select Sound Tools > Options. In the field "Max Sound File Size" increase it up to the maximum 50,000 kb (50 MB).

Only .wav files can be embedded. Other audio file types like mp3 can be linked, not embedded, which means you'll need to send the audio file along with the PowerPoint file, which may not be practical. There are tools online that will convert audio files into .wav. I use Wavepad Sound Editor.

Overcoming resistance

Putting readers in the right frame of mind means making initial emotions more positive. Sometimes those initial emotions are indifference. Sometimes they are outright resistance. The bad news is there are no sure-fire ways to overcome resistance. On the other hand, this is also good news. Would you want to work in an office where people could convince you to approve their ideas as easily as operating a joystick?

The best you can hope for is to reduce the reader's subconscious barriers to listening to your argument with an open mind. This section will talk about some ways to do that.

Persuasion is the art of overcoming objections or turning inertia into action. To gather and order a persuasive set of evidence, decide how much resistance to expect and consider the following options to overcome it.

Resistance

Low (Indifference)   High (Bias)

←———————————————————————————————————————→

Storytelling   Humor   Anticipate Objections   New Info   Loss Aversion

First, there's storytelling. Brain scientists think we listen to stories because it has survival value. When our ancestors survived an attack by a wild beast or enemy tribe, telling that story to other tribe members made them more informed and more likely to survive a similar attack. This theory has some merit. In *The Leader's Guide to Storytelling*, author Stephen Denning tells of Xerox copier repairmen who swapped stories of copier problems they solved in creative ways. Passing knowledge along as stories is an effective way to prepare other repair technicians to succeed when they run across a similar technical problem.

Stories also tend to use picture words—the hero, the setting, the villain—and generate images in our minds. Because we think in pictures we understand and remember stories better than other types of information. Whatever the reason, we know that messages shared as stories are more interesting and memorable, and are evaluated less critically than other message structures.

I learned the power of stories when I taught leadership workshops at the University of Chicago. When I coached individual students on how they could improve their leadership skills, people listened defensively. But when I modified my approach and told stories, especially stories about how I had run into similar challenges as a leader, people relaxed, became more interested and even appreciated the advice more. There is something about stories that causes people to drop their guard and listen openly.

Storytelling can include using examples, quotes and anecdotes. When I conduct focus groups, customers tell great stories about good and bad experiences they've had with products. My clients love to read these quotes and hear these stories because it puts a human face on the research data. And listeners accept these stories uncritically because they really happened; there's nothing to disagree with.

I have also used storytelling to structure my entire deck. For instance, I produced one research report explaining how customers form long-term relationships with the client's brand. In this context it made sense to introduce a fictional character and tell a story of how he first learns about a brand, how he continues to use that brand and tells others about the brand. The story provided a context for all the details of the research findings and made readers more enthusiastically interested and accepting of the findings.

Second, there's humor. While people often evaluate facts critically, humor can slip in undetected. Advertisers use humor frequently because they know you are more likely to just accept the message and less likely to evaluate it critically.

A very good example of this is the Mac vs PC commercials, where a hip young guy (Mac) constantly one-ups the stuffy businessman (PC). The message—Macs are cooler than PC's. But how likely would you accept this message if it was direct and logical: "Macs are just cooler than PC's. We've won over thirty design awards." Now your mind stops the message at the door while you decide if you believe this claim. But when the same message is conveyed humorously, it gets a free backstage pass to your limbic system.

Smart use of analogies and metaphors is one way to slip humor into boardroom-style slides. I once attended a small group meeting where the speaker was telling us about three different software licensing programs. But instead of the typical detail-packed table to describe each program, he used pictures of 7-11 Slurpee cups: small, medium and the Big Gulp. This unexpected imagery got people smiling and, more importantly, they accepted that one licensing program was the more desirable one.

Other uses of humor include adding cartoons, humorous videos and funny quotes. This tends to work on disinterested readers more than resistant readers, but if you find your reader isn't responding to your message you may want to try humor.

Third, there's anticipating objections. This is effective when the reader has mild objections to your ideas but is willing to be won over. In this case, you look at the evidence you're presenting and try to imagine what objections the reader will raise. Then, you build a slide that proactively raises and addresses that objection.

For instance, let's say want to sell your organization on entering the college market and you've prepared some emotional and logical slides to present your argument. However, you expect the reader will be concerned *we've never sold into the college market before.*

To overcome this objection, you may add a slide titled "What will it take to enter the college market for the first time?" and then provide a detailed plan.

There's an important addition here: some people are automatically unnerved by new ideas. There's a scientific explanation for this. There is a part of the limbic system, called the *amygdala*, which is like a fire alarm in the brain. The amygdala, shaped like miniature berries and hanging in the middle of the brain, is constantly on the alert for danger. When it feels there's a threat, it triggers a chain reaction in your body to prepare for fight or flight, causing a rise in anxiety.

The amygdala is activated by anything that is perceived as a threat, and in many people that includes anything that is unfamiliar or reminds them of something that was unpleasant in the past. This is another survival instinct that is hardwired into the brain, a trait that kept our ancestors alive by making them alert and cautious in strange places or when around something that hurt them in the past.

That's why it's important when introducing new ideas to keep the amygdale calm—don't let it pull the fire alarm! One way to do that is to make the new idea seem like a familiar idea.

For instance, in the example of entering the college market, you can remind the reader that this will be similar to when the company entered the small business market for the first time and how sales are now $45 million for the market. The goal is to appear familiar and safe so the amygdala doesn't pull the fire alarm.

These three strategies work best with indifferent or skeptical readers. But what if the reader has real concerns and sees your proposal as risky? The amygdala is already fingering the fire alarm. Here are two more strategies to consider.

The first is by revealing new information. The theory goes that people are resistant to logical arguments and opposing views when they feel the argument is a win-lose proposition. If they have an opposing position and you are trying to prove them wrong, it's difficult for them to agree with you because they lose face. Their reptilian brain is responsible for self-preservation and won't let them back down.

One way to help them agree with you without losing face is to introduce *new* information—a recent development or something the company didn't know before and had no way of knowing. For instance, to convince your reluctant VP to enter the college market you might point out that you *just learned* the competitor is test marketing a new product in one college town. This is a *new development* and you make it easier for the vice president to reverse his previous position.

The second is the concept of loss aversion. Research shows that people are more sensitive to losses than to gains, and more willing to take risks to avoid a loss than to achieve a gain.

For instance, imagine you drop a $10 bill down a busy stairwell. You are likely to rush down two flights of stairs pushing past others to retrieve it. But if you spot a $10 bill lying at the bottom of a stairwell two floors down, you are less inclined to hurry down the stairs against oncoming traffic to retrieve it. Why the different reaction? Ten dollars is ten dollars, right? Not to the human mind. That's because losses cause us pain that we want to reverse, while gains offer rewards but do not ease any suffering.

In a business situation, you may be trying to persuade your executive to invest $10 million to enter the college market. Consider your persuasive approach. Which will be more effective? "We stand to gain $50 million over the next three years" or "Our competitor is moving to be the first entrant in a $50 million market." Fear of loss is more persuasive than promise of gain.

Be careful with this approach because it has the faint scent of manipulation. Master persuaders will recognize it easily. But it there truly is something at risk then it's a powerful form of evidence that will bulk up your logical argument.

Overcoming resistance is rarely simple. Once people form opinions they tend to filter information to fit their biases rather than look for evidence which might prove them wrong. But if you understand the brain rules that influence the reader's biases, as well as the types of information they are receptive to, you can arm yourself to reduce their subconscious barriers to hearing your argument.

Back to Robert's deck

It's 8:50 a.m. "Let's recap the evidence we have for the telesales strategy." Robert begins pulling slides out of his deck as he lists the evidence for his above-water argument *Product isn't differentiated so we need telesales so we can reach the customer first.*

1.   Competitive analysis showing mostly feature parity

2.   SWOT analysis showing field force and telesales is main advantage. Telesales can be copied by competitor

3.   Higher awareness for competitor

4.   Better perceptions for competitor

5.   Sales trends growing faster for competitor

"Let's arrange this in a cause-effect chain, just to see if we have the right information." You and Robert decide better perceptions of the competitor is causing more word of mouth, leading to higher awareness, which in turn is leading to faster sales growth for the competitor. The competitive analysis and SWOT don't fit into the cause-effect chain.

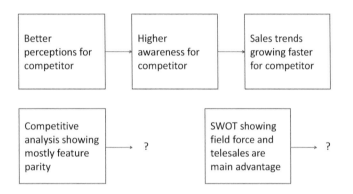

"Robert, if our product is better, then why does the competitor have more positive perceptions? What's causing that?"

Robert explains that the competitor's product is simpler to use and gets more word-of-mouth from end-users than our product. They are also positioning themselves as the underdog in the market, which fuels additional word of mouth. Another reason we need to invest in telesales.

"How do we know that? Do we have any evidence?"

"Well, the field tells us this," says Robert. "And our own customers tell us this. I remember one customer told me *they have all the air right now.* That's a pretty powerful statement."

"Yes, it is. Perhaps we should include a list of field and customer quotes in the deck. Maybe we adjust this flow a little bit, by explaining that we have mostly feature parity but the competitor is simpler to use and that is generating word of mouth. It's not completely true that we have feature parity; we are actually at a disadvantage." You quickly write on two sheets of paper and add them to the flow.

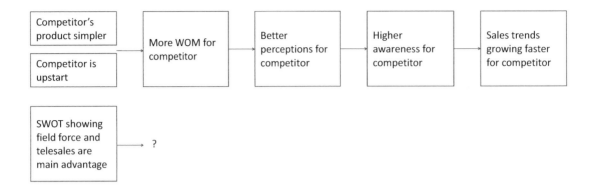

"Let's reverse the order of this flow. I don't want to start this section with something controversial, like saying our product is harder to use. I also don't want to re-enact the analysis for Aubrey. I just want him to be able to follow the logic. Let's also collapse the point about word of mouth on the perceptions slide and combine the point about having a simpler product and being an upstart on a single slide."

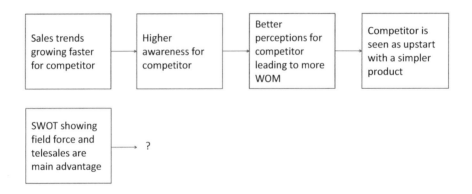

"Okay, I think I understand the narrative. We need to invest in telesales so we can get to the customer before our competitor does. The competitor is winning more customers today because of higher awareness and more positive perceptions. This is being driven by word of mouth because the competitor's product is simpler to use and because they are perceived as the underdog."

You ponder a bit. "This is starting to look like a problem-solution story. So let's fully explain your recommendation on the first slide, explain your rationale on the second slide and then bring in the effect-cause chain showing the problem."

Details of telesales plan	→	SWOT showing field force and telesales main advantage	→	Sales trends growing faster for competitor	→	Higher awareness for competitor	→	Better perceptions for competitor leading to more WOM	→	Competitor is seen as upstart with simpler product

"Do we have any examples of deals we won just because we called the customer first?"

"We have data on how we've been able to convert customers into trial customers if we get them on the phone. There is one customer I can think of who almost went with the competitor because the competitor's sales guy called them. But then their sales guy dropped the ball and stopped returning calls and emails. So the customer got frustrated and called us."

"Let's plan to highlight those examples on the first slide, where you introduce and explain the telesales plan, perhaps by adding the customer quote. I want Aubrey to know we have won deals in the past because of this strategy before we present our analysis."

Above-water argument

1. Place some linear order around your non-linear thinking. Choices are: cause-effect, effect-cause, category, ranking and solution/problem. You can order your above-water argument as well as your evidence slides in this way.

2. The great persuaders of history know that you must use emotion, in addition to logic, to sell ideas effectively. Brain science explains that decision making takes place in three parts of the brain: the reptilian brain (instincts), the limbic system (emotions) and the neocortex (logic). Although business slides depend heavily on logic, and your reader is motivated to understand your logic, do not overlook the importance of emotion when selling ideas.

3. Emotion is needed to put people in the right frame of mind and helps you sell ideas. Order your slides to put the reader in the right frame of mind by using emotional evidence early in the slide order. Do not use low-content slides to affect emotions; readers of boardroom-style slides are looking for content to help them make a decision and low-content slides will make them more negative. Don't begin with controversial evidence or your reader will be resistant to all of your other evidence.

4. Strategies to overcome resistance include: storytelling, humor, anticipating objections, new information and loss aversion.

Recommended reading

Predictably Irrational by Dan Ariely reveals numerous examples and studies where people made completely illogical decisions. This book will convince you that decision making is ruled, not with cold computer-like logic, but with a complex mix of logic, emotion, instinct and heuristics.

Influence by Robert Cialdini is the seminal business book exploring the curious process of human decision making, and how it is influenced by subtle things like appearance of authority, social pressure, a desire for internal consistency and other factors.

Think Better by Tim Hurson explores the three-part brain and how it influences decision making and problem solving.

Iconoclast by Gregory Burns is a highly readable and expert discussion of how the brain is quietly working for or against you.

Smart Choices by Hammond, Keeney and Raiffa discusses shortcuts your mind makes when making decisions and how much of decision making is illogical.

Nudge, by behavioral economist Richard Thaler, provides numerous examples of how so many of our decisions are made automatically and without effortful thought.

CHAPTER 6

Storyboard

Plan on paper before opening PowerPoint

IT'S 9 A.M. AND YOU HAVE TO DIAL in to lead a conference call with colleagues in Europe. Robert has jotted down the notes on the whiteboard. What next?

"Okay," says Robert, getting up to leave. "I'll work on the next rev of the deck and let's plan to review it in, say, two days?" Robert tucks the slide printouts under the arm holding his orange Styrofoam coffee cup and clutches his laptop with the other hand. He nods goodbye with a quick jerk of his chin and turns toward the door.

Today is Wednesday. You won't see the next version until Friday. Your meeting with Aubrey is next Friday.

You imagine Robert, hunched over his computer working late into the evening to get the next version ready. What do you say? Yes, I'll see you in two days? Or do you have some advice for him as he leaves your office?

Save time. Get away from the computer

People waste an extraordinary amount of time creating slides. There's no research measuring the amount of waste, but my own experience is that two-thirds of the time spent on slides is completely wasted. It may be higher.

The problem is we approach PowerPoint the same way we approach a text document. We typically refine our thoughts by writing them out. The act of writing actually helps turn hazy half-formed thoughts into concrete ideas that can be evaluated, critiqued and improved. Even though a text document allows for long rambling paragraphs, at least it allows the writer to clarify on paper what they are trying to say. Writing leads to good thesis statements.

People often work in PowerPoint the same way they work in a text document. They start by dumping thoughts and images onto the slide—a chart, some summary text, a brief slide title. They use PowerPoint as a workspace to assemble their thoughts, just as they use a text document to start assembling their thoughts.

But PowerPoint is not a good tool for writing and clarifying thoughts. This is partly because the default settings—bullet points—immediately encourage the writer to express ideas in 32-point font and the bullet encourages summarized thoughts. A writer may only get 40 or 50 words into the slide before they run out of room. Since they often need to pour charts, tables and images onto the slide as well, PowerPoint's boundaries stop a writer before they have had a chance to fully develop their thoughts. Hazy ideas remain hazy on the page.

That's why it's important to not plan your slides in PowerPoint, but to plan your slides on a whiteboard, paper or word processing software. You need to fully articulate your ideas before you start working in PowerPoint.

I'll illustrate the point with a personal example. In spring 2007 I completed 30 phone interviews with university technology directors to help me prepare a marketing plan. I found the information I needed. But it took me until June 2007 to complete the final research report—three months later! I had difficulty organizing all the information into a logical flow.

Fast forward to April 2009 when I was preparing a final report for a similar set of phone interviews with technology leaders discussing how they were preparing for new technology trends. At the client's request, I completed the final report in two days.

From three months down to two days? How was I able to cut my time by such a staggering amount?

The answer is: In the second example, I planned my deck before I opened PowerPoint.

It's wildly inefficient to create slides without a plan. The common approach is to simply open PowerPoint and begin typing. You start by dutifully filling in the title slide, then add an agenda slide, then ponder a bit before reminding the reader of the campaign goals on slide 3. What goes on slide 4? How about our target segments? Now, what about slide 5? Hmmm…

Creating a deck without knowing what is going to be on each slide is like building a house without architectural drawings. You'll find yourself with only a vague idea of what you're trying to say and you'll add slides hoping that the logic will fall together. Instead, you'll get to slide 10 and realize you don't have a coherent argument.

Even after you've worked out the slide order, you will still find yourself wasting time playing with different font sizes and colors, inserting clip art, moving shapes around on the slide. And half the time, you'll get disgusted with your slides and move them into the appendix because you can't bear to delete something you spent so much time producing.

This is a very inefficient use of time. The first draft of any deck usually needs lots of revision. So it doesn't make sense to spend a lot of time creating lovely slides if you're likely going to change them later.

Or as authors say: "There is no great writing; only great rewriting."

Garr Reynolds, author of *Presentation Zen*, believes planning on paper improves your creativity. "I could use the computer, but I find—as many do—that the act of holding a pen in my hand to sketch out ideas seems to have a greater, more natural connection to my right brain and allows for a spontaneous flow and rhythm for visualizing and recording ideas."

PowerPoint is great for *creating* the final slides. But there are other tools that are better for *planning* slides and will cut your design time in half—or more.

As a manager, you don't want your team wasting valuable hours playing with colors and fonts and searching for clip art. You want to be the team that delivers on time. So before reviewing any final slides, you will make your work much easier, and your direct report's work more creative, if you insist they create a first draft on paper.

Use mind maps to develop your above-water argument and evidence

Your above-water argument is the scaffolding you build your deck around. It summarizes the key ideas and organizes the evidence into sections.

Mind mapping is a good way to discover and organize your thoughts. In mind mapping, you write a central thought on a paper or whiteboard, then draw radiating lines from that central thought to associated thoughts, and then draw radiating lines from each of those thoughts to other associated thoughts.

It looks something like this:

Mind maps work because they reflect the way your mind works. The mind doesn't think linearly, but through associations. If I say "dog" your mind can instantly recall images like dogs running, dogs with tongues hanging out, angry dogs, a dog bowl, a dog collar and hot dogs with onions and relish. The mind organizes ideas in clusters of related ideas, so mind mapping helps you convert your internal chain of associated ideas into an external model you can work with.

There are several advantages to using mind maps to organize your above-water argument and evidence:

1. It helps you visualize all your information in one place. Meaningful clusters of information begin to form naturally. You can see what evidence you have and what evidence is still lacking.

2. It helps you organize and order your information. You can look for cause-effect relationships and simplify ideas by grouping related ideas together.

3. It helps you expand on your ideas. Each idea on the mind map is associated with a multitude of other concepts so a mind map naturally radiates out and suggests new ideas.

Mind mapping is especially useful for people who are intuitive and solve problems, not by following a linear trail through the data, but in a flash of insight. A mind map helps them put some order around their otherwise chaotic (but efficient) thinking process.

Here's the process I use when I create a mind map. I prefer to work on a whiteboard and use different colored markers. I'll start out by writing the reader's question on the whiteboard in red marker. The red is a reminder that the reader's question is the most important aspect of the deck. If the reader's question isn't answered, the deck has failed.

Next, I'll write the answer to the question in black marker. I've already done a lot of thinking and analysis so I'm just formalizing my thoughts in writing. I write the answer in the middle of the whiteboard and circle it. This is the moment of truth. If I can't produce a simple and understandable answer to the reader's question, I know I'm about to create an unfocused and rambling deck. I'll spend a bit of time here to get the answer down to a thought-sized chunk.

Now I want to organize my evidence to support my answer. I draw radiating lines from the center circle and create new circles that explain my answer in more details. These new circles tend to answer a question raised by the center circle—*what, why* or *how*—and I may end up with 5–10 new circles linked to the center circle.

Reader's Question: Should we expand into Canada?
A: Yes, on a trial basis

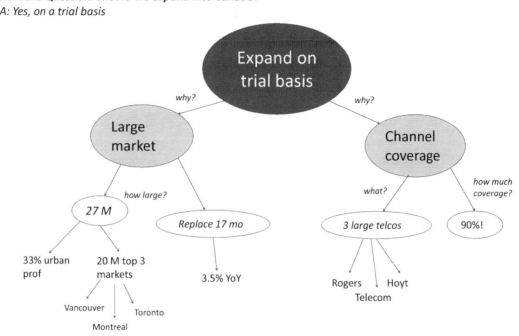

Now I continue connecting ideas together, adding more lines and more detailed pieces of evidence, like specific data points, examples and quotes. In the end, I can see all my evidence in one place. I look for groups of ideas that can be combined into even larger ideas so I end up with an above-water argument of 3–4 ideas with clusters of smaller ideas—my evidence—surrounding them.

Arranging information like this lets me review my above-water argument—does it make sense? Is it persuasive? What evidence am I missing? I can also start to think about what order I will present my evidence. Is there a cause-effect relationship in the evidence I can highlight? Do I need some more emotional evidence? In this mind map, I can see I haven't addressed some critical questions like who are our competitors, how is our product better and do Canadian urban professionals want a phone like ours.

I may have other evidence and analysis I've done. But if this evidence and analysis doesn't support the answer, it doesn't belong in the deck. I may add it to the appendix, but it will just muddy my clear message if I try to force it to fit into any the idea groups.

This entire book was developed using mind maps and each chapter was also developed using mind maps. Here's the mind map I used for this chapter.

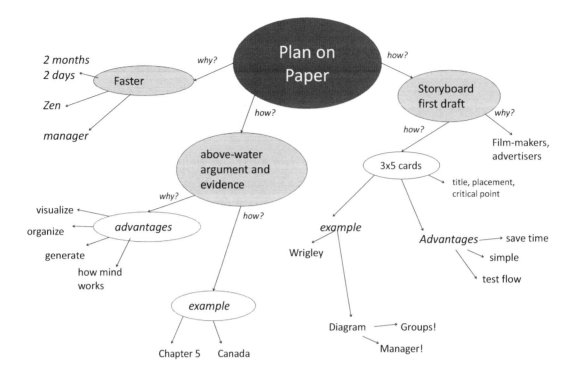

You could start your mind map with the categories you've decided to break your deck into. Or, you could start your mind map first and discover ways to break up your deck. Either way works, as long as you end up with 3–4 portable points that are complete thoughts. In practice, I find it helps to attack it from both directions and see which method generates the most powerful above-water argument.

Some people use Post-It notes rather than a whiteboard. This makes sense because you can move things around easily. On a whiteboard, when I combine ideas I need to erase and rewrite things. This requires some inefficient duplication of effort, but I prefer the freedom of writing ideas without constraining myself to the sticky note size and feel it lets me tap into the more free-wheeling creative side of my brain. It's all a matter of personal preference.

There are other tools for developing your above-water argument and evidence. I will sometimes do my thinking in a text document or Excel document, writing summary thoughts followed by the supporting evidence in bulleted lists or different spreadsheet cells. Then I can move things around to re-order evidence, join similar ideas into larger groups and so on. But like Garr Reynolds, I feel mind mapping on the whiteboard allows me to think in more expansive and creative ways, so I tend to use Word and Excel just to formalize my whiteboard thinking and refine my groupings further.

A mind map is a useful way to organize your above-water argument and evidence and generate new ideas to make your idea stronger. Once you're satisfied with your above-water argument and evidence, it's time to start creating a storyboard.

Use a storyboard to create a first draft of your deck

A storyboard is a rough draft of what the finished product will look like. In film-making, it could include crude drawings hung on a wall showing each scene, actors entering and exiting the scenes, and different camera angles to build the story's mood, pace and rhythm. This lets the director and others involved in the filming check the story's flow, re-arrange scenes and experiment with different camera angles before beginning the expensive process of filming.

One of the secrets to the success of the STOP format was the use of paper storyboards. Engineers would meet in a room with paper templates hung up around the walls and they would discuss what topics needed to be covered and what thesis statements they would write about. They'd also discuss the key support points in each thought module, and develop some ideas for images. This gave them a structured way to discuss the proposal with other engineers and make suggestions to improve other thought modules. At the end of the meeting, the engineers would take the paper storyboards off the wall and begin writing. It was one of the reasons the STOP format worked so well for Hughes-Fullerton.

Other professions that use storyboards include instructional designers, website designers, consulting firms and advertisers. Creating the final product is expensive and time-consuming and the final product is improved if they can review and edit it in some rough format first.

As a slide creator, you can also use storyboards before beginning the expensive process of designing slides.

I recommend using a 3 x 5 notepad. Notepads are inexpensive and each sheet is about the same dimension as a PowerPoint slide. You can quickly sketch out the slide title and the slide's basic outline. You will want to include:

- the slide title, summarizing the slide's main message

- the rough placement of elements like graphs, pictures and text

- anything that needs to be emphasized, like calling attention to certain data points on a graph

Planning on paper in advance has the following advantages over designing your deck in PowerPoint:

1. You save time. You can sketch out a 20–30 slide deck in about a half hour with crude hand-drawings. It would take you a half day or longer to sketch out a lengthy deck on the computer.

2. You simplify ideas. If it's simple enough to fit on a piece of notepaper, it will be simple enough to understand on a full-size PowerPoint slide. If it's too complicated for a piece of notepaper, it may be too much information for a single slide.

3. You can test your deck's flow. You can arrange your deck easily, test how well the deck flows, rewrite slides and throw away slides that aren't working. Since you didn't invest a lot of time in each slide, you don't feel compelled to keep slides that don't belong in your deck.

Re-arranging your slides is a critical step. I cannot tell you how many times I've put together my deck outline on paper and then realized that it didn't quite flow right. There was a piece of logic missing that called for another slide. Or one slide had too much crammed on it and really needed two slides. Or an idea that took three slides to explain really bogged down the presentation and needed to be summarized more crisply on one slide.

Once you are satisfied with your paper version you can open PowerPoint and start creating finished slides. There's a real sense of relief and purpose when you know exactly what you're putting on each slide and don't face that frustrating moment of looking at a blank slide. You get your work done very fast and your first draft is ready to present for feedback immediately.

Here's an example of how storyboards improved my own slide making. I was preparing for a workshop with the William J. Wrigley Company in Chicago. I was reworking part of my workshop based on feedback from other workshops and some new research I had found. I ended up adding 20 slides to my workshop deck. Even more amazing, I did it in four hours the evening before the Wrigley workshop.

I shared this story with the folks at the Wrigley workshop and they were impressed. One participant noted, "It would have taken me a week!"

It would have taken me a week too if I had designed those additional slides in PowerPoint. But I started by designing my slides as a storyboard and only when I was satisfied with my crude drawings did I open PowerPoint and quickly create all 20 slides.

Managers can use storyboards to review their team's deck before the team member puts too much effort into it. Using rough drafts rather than finished slide copies creates a better atmosphere for review and improvement because so little effort has been invested in each slide; it's easier to treat it all as a work in progress.

You can review the storyboard as a stack of notepapers. Or you can lay them out on a conference room table or tape them to a wall. A good format is to run the above-water argument across the top and the supporting evidence placed in order vertically below each above-water argument. This allows you to see your main argument across the top and discuss which evidence, and the order, is needed to support the above-water argument.

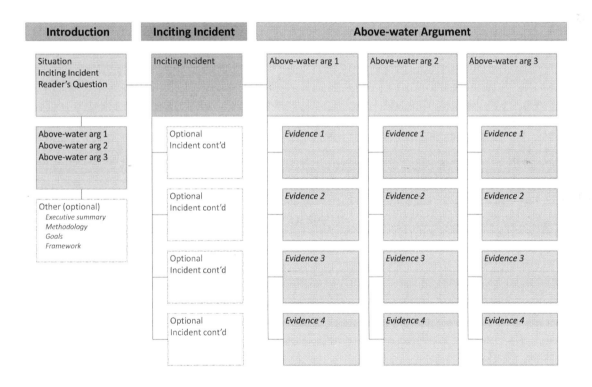

Storyboards are a good tool to help groups collaborate and develop a PowerPoint deck together. Rather than assigning each person a section of the deck and then letting one person try to merge it all together, you can meet in advance and discuss the contents of your storyboard. Taping rough slides on the wall lets people talk about the above-water argument and supporting evidence, move slides around, add new slides, add comments to slides and suggest slides to be removed. This collaborative approach builds consensus and fosters innovative thinking that can result in a more effective presentation.

In practice, you will not need to build a storyboard for every single deck. Mind mapping and storyboarding take time so they are most appropriate for longer decks meant to persuade the reader. Shorter decks may not need such extensive planning.

The Mindworks Method Planning Grid

One tool I use to help me get organized before working on my storyboard is a planning grid. I've included a copy on the next page for your personal use, or you can create your own planning grid in any spreadsheet program.

Start by writing out the reader's question and your answer. The answer is the main message in your deck.

Complete the Inciting Incident. This explains to the reader what is at stake and why your report is worth their attention.

Then break your deck into 3–4 categories. Don't worry at first about the exact above-water argument you'll compose; just find 3–4 natural ways to divide your report.

Now, write an above-water argument for each category. Ask yourself "What about…" this category? For instance, if you break the deck into Product, Place, Price and Promotion ask yourself what about the price? You may decide your main point here is "We need to establish a prestige price to position ourselves in the market." Great! That's one part of your above-water argument.

There will be more than one way to break your deck into 3–4 categories so you might try a couple of different approaches to determine which results in the strongest above-water argument.

Now list 3–4 pieces of key evidence you'll use to support each above-water argument. Think about both logical and emotional evidence. You may have more than 3–4 pieces of evidence but start out by identifying your key pieces of evidence. Don't worry about the order of the evidence at this point. You will likely want to experiment with different orders as you create your storyboard.

Now quickly sketch out each slide on a notepad, showing the opening slides, above-water argument slides and evidence slides. You can spend some time arranging the order of the evidence slides until you feel your argument has a clear and persuasive flow.

The Mindworks Method planning grid allows you to see your entire argument and evidence on one page and decide if you have the right argument and supporting evidence.

If you are the manager of a team, I urge you to require your reports to develop their storyboard using a planning grid or paper storyboard before asking them to spend a considerable amount of wasted time crafting slides. Their time is better used analyzing problems and executing strategies.

You've now planned your entire deck and are ready to begin creating slides, which we'll cover in Section Two.

Mindworks Presentation Method Planning Grid

Download this handout at www.speakingppt.com

Reader's Question	
Answer	
Inciting Incident	

Category	Above-water Argument	Evidence
1.		a
		b
		c
		d
2.		a
		b
		c
		d
3.		a
		b
		c
		d
4.		a
		b
		c
		d

Back to Robert's deck

Before letting Robert leave to work on the next version of the deck, you ask him to develop a storyboard you can review together. This will eliminate many wasted hours creating slides.

"Tell you what, Robert. Why don't we meet later this afternoon?" You quickly review with him how to develop a storyboard using the Mindworks Method planning grid.

You and Robert meet at 3 p.m. and Robert has developed some hand-drawn slides and organized them on his desk. You and he spend time discussing the above-water argument and supporting evidence. Both of you write on the crudely-drawn slides, move them around on the table and add new slides. Although the slides don't contain much detail, the key information is there and Robert easily answers questions about his thinking. This becomes a way not only to critique Robert's slide order but to understand his analysis and coach him on how to present his recommendations.

At the end of the meeting, you feel better about the plan. You've been able to collaborate with Robert on the plan and coach Robert on the final presentation. You understand what will be presented to Aubrey next week and feel prepared to answer questions.

After you leave, Robert pulls the slides into a pile next to his computer. He feels good knowing exactly what slides he needs to build. So good, in fact, he leaves the office at 6 p.m. after finishing the first 10 slides in two hours. He'll finish the other 10 slides tomorrow morning, in time to review the next version of the deck with you at 3 p.m.

Above-water argument

1. Plan your deck on paper before opening PowerPoint. It will cut in half the time you spend creating slides and lead to more creative and effective communication.

2. Use mind mapping to develop your above-water argument and evidence because it lets you visualize your information, organize it into intelligent groups and generate new ideas for areas that need more evidence.

3. Create your first draft using a storyboard. You will be able to build your first draft more quickly, simplify ideas, and experiment with different slide orders. Creating a storyboard with a group is a good way to build consensus and improve ideas. Storyboards are also a good method for managers who want to coach their team members on good report design.

4. Use the Mindworks Method planning grid to quickly assemble your above-water argument and evidence slides. This allows you to see and critique your entire argument on one page and lets you build your paper storyboard more quickly.

Recommended reading

The Mind Map Book by Tony Buzan clearly explains how to develop mind maps and why they reflect your brain's natural thinking process.

SLIDE

Criticism #2: Incoherent slides

You've got an idea to sell. You've developed a storyboard. And now you see that each slide has a main message that supports an above-water argument which further supports your deck's main message. But you can't sell ideas with slides that readers can't understand. A major complaint about PowerPoint is slides are often incoherent, contain too much information and do a poor job of conveying any meaningful information.

What causes incoherent slides, so packed with text and images and half-formed sentences that the reader struggles to comprehend them? The misunderstanding that just because you put it on the slide, people can understand it. This isn't true. The brain processes information in a certain way and if you don't understand and respect the brain's limitations then the information you placed on the slide will not transfer to the reader. Your communication will fail.

The STOP format provides a good model to follow: treat each slide as a *thought module* that supports a single clear message, and use a combination of thesis statement, supporting text and images to develop that thought module.

This section covers the brain science of organizing information on a slide so it's easy to understand and easy to agree with. There are different parts of your slide including slide titles, body text and pictures.

> ***Slide title:*** The most important part of every slide is the slide title. An unclear slide title makes the rest of your slide unclear, to both the reader and the business communicator. This is a single easiest thing you can do to improve your slides.

Chunking: The reader can only understand 3–4 pieces of information on a slide before it starts to become a confused mess. This section talks about how to chunk information into 3–4 meaningful groups that the reader can easily understand.

Picture-superiority effect: People think in pictures. This section explains the brain science of picture-thinking and covers how to select the most effective images for your message.

Text: PowerPoint's boundaries mean slide creators must write in a summative style. Is it okay to use bullet points? Are the rules different if you're presenting the slides to an audience?

CHAPTER 7

Slide Title

Write out a full sentence title

O NE OF YOUR DIRECT REPORTS, Alex, has a habit of cramming a lot of detail into a slide. He's a smart guy, and can explain his ideas with perfect logic, but his slides are packed so densely they are a chore to read and virtually impossible to present.

At a recent meeting with another department, Alex gave a briefing on the product roadmap. Everyone had a printout of Alex's deck. But faces looked dazed as they swept over the densely-packed slides.

When they got to this slide, Alex paused and asked "any questions?" The room was silent as a library.

Mission & Vision

Vision
By RTM:
Copenhagen v3 will be the Social Hub on the web and the single destination for consumer end user services

Business Goals
• Build loyal customer base
• Increase relevance of online services offering

Copenhagen v3 will let people around the world:
• try and buy Copenhagen and other services via token/subscription
• locate and connect with long-lost friends.
• anywhere access with any OS (Windows, Mac, Linux)
• connect and share with others while having fun at the same time while using the web and online
• access games, entertainment and social activities
• maintain their single online social identity

Roadmap

2011 ⯑ v3.3 Begins
Q1 – ABCv: Canada launch
  – DEF: Russian, Polish, Korean, Chinese, Dutch, Italian, Portuguese
Q2 – ABCv: India and Mexico launch
  – DEF: Nordic Languages, Czech, Turkish, Greek
Q3 – DEF: Slavic languages
Q4 – v3 Begins, AgX Beta 1, More languages

2012 ⯑ v3 .4
Q1 ⯑ RTM again beta 2, AgX Beta 2

Q2/Q3 ⯑ RTM again Availability
• OXOG and BLLR merge into a single site
• BLLR services available in all 38 AgX languages (14 countries where a fee is charged)
• VPBX (Burt) Rollout in Botswana

2013 ⯑ RTM

• OGOX,RTM, BLLR and ABCv3 in a single site
• RTM online services available in all 38 RTM languages
• VPBX (Ballyr) Rollout in Madagascar

2011 Goals
• 700 gross adds
• 50% YOY unique visit increase
• 50% YOY page view increase
• 50% OxenRo Net Promoter score
• 5K web site designers, developers or elbows developers listed

2012 Goals
• Trillions of gross adds
• Continued progress in engaging developers for web sites and online fun and games
• Improved NPS + 45
• Increase in Unique Visits and Page Views

Longer-Term Goals
• 603M AgX/DEF registered users by FY12
• Substantial trial and cloud performance issues assured

You rock back in your chair, looking at the dazed faces and realize these people don't understand. What advice do you give Alex to make this slide easier to present and his communication more effective?

The most important slide element—the title

Incoherent slides is a major complaint among critics like Edward Tufte. It is as if the slide designer just dumped all their data onto the slide and said *YOU figure out what it means*. This failure almost guarantees the reader will have to spend five to ten times longer on each slide trying to decipher the meaning and may arrive at a different conclusion than you intended.

But it doesn't have to be that way. There's a very simple fix for incoherent slides that takes just a few minutes—write out your slide title as a full sentence.

There's very little research on slide titles, but some of the most important research was conducted at Penn State University by Professor Michael Alley. He wanted to know how slide design affected student learning, and especially what happened when you compared an instructor using the traditional bullet-heavy and briefly-titled slide against an instructor using slides with a full sentence title and more visuals on the slide.

Test scores showed the power of full sentence titles. One group of students saw slides with full sentence titles. Another group saw the same slides with that title demoted to a bullet point on the slide and the slide title replaced with a short phrase. When students learned from slides with phrases for titles, about 7 of 10 students answered test questions correctly. With full sentence titles, 8 of 10 students got the right answer—a 15% improvement in student test scores.

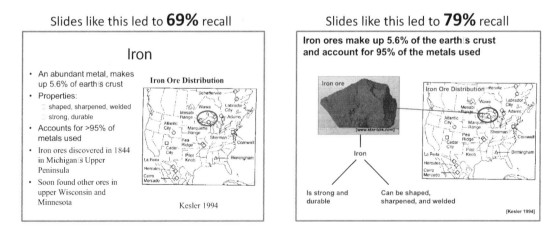

Is an increase to 79% from 69% significant? It's the equivalent of taking an entire classroom of 200 university students from a C+ average to B+. It's extremely significant. The additional effort in moving the main point into the slide title made the instructor a more effective communicator.

In business, you may be able to see an even greater improvement. Unlike your readers, students are motivated to study and remember details from the slides because it affects their final test scores. Business readers may be less motivated to understand every detail on your slide, so the slide title ensures your important message is highlighted. And in the case where there is no speaker, the reader is entirely dependent on your slides.

You don't need research to be convinced that using a full sentence in the title makes it clearer. A casual inspection makes the point. In fact, by adding a full sentence title to even the most incoherent slide, the reader can still understand the message.

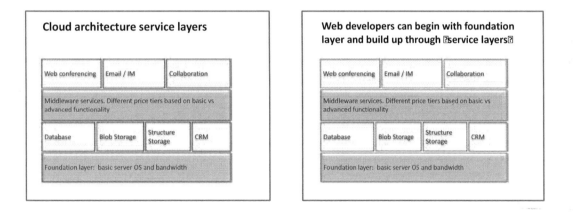

This is a simple principle but it's staggering to see how often business slides fail to use a full sentence title. In order to sell ideas, you need to present clear arguments by summarizing evidence into an above-water argument. If you don't clearly state that argument, then you leave it up to the reader to figure out what you were trying to say. The reader has to spend more time on each and every slide in your deck to understand the points you are trying to make. This wastes the reader's time. But more importantly, the reader may arrive at a different conclusion or miss your point completely.

It doesn't make sense to turn control of your message over to the reader. You have done the analysis, haven't you? You have come to some conclusions and have some well thought out recommendations, right? Why wouldn't you want to *ensure* that the reader can follow your logic? Lack of clarity is lack of leadership. You signal, by your lack of involvement in crafting the message, *I'm not sure what we need to do. You decide.*

Executives don't have time to waste trying to dig your meaning out of the slide. Instead of reading and appreciating your idea, they will skim it. In fact, everyone you work with is busy. If you make your slide messages instantly clear, you save time for everyone. If you fail to make your message clear on the slide, you disadvantage yourself in the idea marketplace.

Slide titles force discipline on the author

The second reason a full slide title is important, and perhaps the more critical reason, is it forces you to clarify for yourself what you're trying to say.

One of the reasons slides are unclear is because there is no message. The slide creator wasn't sure what they meant when they created the slide; they just needed a place to put all their data without thinking through the main point.

Creating a storyboard forces the slide creator to justify why each slide is in the deck. Rather than a place to hold data, it now contains an important message that ladders up to support an above-water argument which ladders up to support their big idea. The storyboard forces the slide creator to have a main message on each slide.

Often, you know what you want to say in your head. But you don't really know until you can express it in words. You may find that you *don't* actually know what you were trying to say, that you need *several slides* to fully articulate what you were trying to say, or that the data you have doesn't actually *support* what you want to say. These are all important discoveries because it forces you to think harder about the data you are using and the conclusions you have drawn.

Writing clear slide titles may even force you to re-think the conclusion of your entire deck. There have been times, in fact, when my recommendations changed because I forced myself to fully articulate the purpose of each slide, which forced me to concede that the data didn't actually support that conclusion. By whittling the sentence down to a fully supported conclusion, it forced me to re-look at other data and re-interpret existing data. These experiences significantly improve not only your PowerPoint report writing, but your critical thinking as well.

Don't be surprised to find that it's difficult to summarize your thoughts crisply on two lines of text, but I encourage you to pursue that as a discipline. It forces you to continue refining and focusing your thoughts, which will in turn help you to focus and simplify your slide design.

A clear slide title is the foundation for every other element you put on your slide, including your choice of visuals, how you'll use color and which graphs you'll use. Alley posits that the full sentence title also improved the selection of evidence on the slide "Once the headline assertion has been determined, the presenter is in a much better position to select persuasive evidence to support the assertion." A clear slide title is the first step to more effective communication.

Writing slide titles

As a manager who reviews slides, every slide can be improved by asking the slide creator *what is your main message?* Whatever their main message is, it should become the slide title. If they don't know what they were trying to say, it's guaranteed the reader won't know either. If they have more than one message, ask them which message is most important and make that the slide title. Practice simplifying ideas and sharpening your communication focus.

Every slide makeover starts by reviewing the slide title. An unclear slide title usually indicates a slide has no foundation and the reader will have to go hunting for meaning on their own. By forcing the slide creator to tighten their thinking and provide a main message for the slide, they will often find that the data and evidence they are using can be improved, which gives them direction on how to improve each slide in the deck, resulting in a clearer deck and an idea that is easier to sell.

In keeping with the STOP format's *thought module* approach, you will want to summarize the slide's main point in the title. There are four basic approaches to slide titles: the conclusion title, the thesis title, the category title and the question title.

In a *conclusion title*, you write out the slide's main message as the slide title using no more than two lines of text. When slide titles extend to three lines they become less inviting to read and suggest that the slide author is trying to cover too much on the slide. Having a discipline of two-line slide titles forces the slide creator to think harder about their main message. I will cheat and expand the size of the slide title box if absolutely necessary, rather than wrap around to a third line.

When writing a conclusion title, you may also want to add a short 2–4 word category label above the conclusion title. This tells the reader what is the topic of the slide before reading the conclusion. I have used this technique with good feedback from clients. You should experiment and find a style you and your readers like.

Another type of slide title is the *thesis title*. This is used when you simply can't fit your slide title on two lines because the message is more complex. In this case, you write a short category title to let the reader know the topic of the slide, and then write out in smaller font a full thesis of several sentences. This works especially well for reading decks, where the reader can comfortably read the text on the screen or on printed handouts. But this also works in a briefing deck where the audience can see the category title. If you use a light color like gray for the thesis sentence, it will be faint on the screen and discourage reading while you are speaking.

Mission & Vision
Our vision of a PC on every desktop is driving our 2011-2013 goals and roadmap. In order to achieve our three-year goal of 603 million registered users, we must build a product that appeals to their specific needs.

Vision
By RTM:
Copenhagen v3 will be the **Social Hub on the web** *and the* **single destination** *for consumer end user services*

Business Goals
- Build loyal customer base
- Increase relevance of online services offering

Copenhagen v3 will let people around the world:
- try and buy Copenhagen and other services via token/subscription
- locate and connect with long-lost friends.
- anywhere access with any OS (Windows, Mac, Linux)
- connect and share with others while having fun at the same time while using the web and online
- access games, entertainment and social activities
- maintain their single online social identity

Roadmap

2011 ▯ v3.3 Begins
Q1 – ABCv: Canada launch
 – DEF: Russian, Polish, Korean, Chinese, Dutch, Italian, Portuguese
Q2 – ABCv: India and Mexico launch
 – DEF: Nordic Languages, Czech, Turkish, Greek
Q3 – DEF: Slavic languages
Q4 – v3 Begins, AgX Beta 1, More languages

2012 ▯ v3 .4
Q1 ▯ RTM again beta 2, AgX Beta 2

Q2/Q3 ▯ RTM again Availability
- OXOG and BLLR merge into a single site
- BLLR services available in all 38 AgX languages (14 countries where a fee is charged)
- VPBX (Burt) Rollout in Botswana

2013 ▯ RTM

- OGOX,RTM, BLLR and ABCv3 in a single site
- RTM online services available in all 38 RTM languages
- VPBX (Ballyr) Rollout in Madagascar

2011 Goals
- 700 gross adds
- 50% YOY unique visit increase
- 50% YOY page view increase
- 50% OxenRo Net Promoter score
- 5K web site designers, developers or elbows developers listed

2012 Goals
- Trillions of gross adds
- Continued progress in engaging developers for web sites and online fun and games
- Improved NPS + 45
- Increase in Unique Visits and Page Views

Longer-Term Goals
- 603M AgX/DEF registered users by FY12
- Substantial trial and cloud performance issues assured

In most cases, you will want to use a conclusion or thesis title that clearly summarizes the main point of your slide. However, there are exceptions. There will be times when the slide has no summary message but is more of a reference slide. In these cases, there is no need to stretch to find the main message on the slide. There is no main message. You can use a *category title:*

- Agenda

- Research Methodology

- Definitions

- Team Members

- Interview Participants

Always challenge yourself. Category titles can often be turned into conclusion titles if you ask yourself *So what? Why does the reader need to know this?*

For instance, I developed a report in PowerPoint after completing eight focus groups with 60 university students. I dutifully added the Research Methodology slide. Then I asked myself *why does the reader need to know this?* Because they want to know who we talked to and how many people, to understand the robustness of the results. So I changed Research Methodology to "We spoke to 60 students at four major universities". A small change, but one that summarized the slide for the reader and helped them get the message instantly, rather than spending extra time gathering the meaning themselves. I used "Research Methodology" as the small category label above the title.

Titles do not need to be statements. They could also be *question titles*. This approach works well in market research reports, where your entire deck provides summary answers to a list of questions from a survey. In fact, one of the most interesting results from Michael Alley's research on slide titles is that of 15 slides used in the study, *the two slides students learned from the best had questions for slide titles.*

Questions are effective because they get the audience actively thinking and processing an issue and pique their interest. Educators use questions as a form of *advance organizer*, an instructional tool to prime students for learning. For instance, a teacher may ask students "Why do flowers smell so sweet?" before beginning a lecture on pollination and the role of scent to attract birds and insects. The question activates the student's thinking and desire to know. The instruction may be less effective if the teacher begins with a statement like "Now we're going to learn how flowers spread their pollen."

The few research studies on using questions as advance organizers are very positive. In addition to Alley's study, researchers in Iran tested questions and statements as advance organizers with 64 pre-university students. When the instructor used statements to introduce a topic, students scored 13 out of 20 on tests. But when the instructor used questions to introduce topics, students scored 15 out of 20; a statistically significant improvement in learning.

It appears, then, that questions can make your communication more effective because they activate a desire in the reader to learn the answer.

But you must ensure the question is answered clearly. Questions may work best in standup presentations where you can provide the answer verbally. Alley's practice is to show the question title first and then replace it with a full sentence title, to give students a chance to wrestle with the question before he provides the explicit answer. A modification of this for boardroom-style slides could be to write out a question title but add a thesis sentence below it, in smaller font, that answers the question posed.

This is a short chapter with a simple message. But don't let its length fool you. The slide title is the most important element to get right because it directs all decisions you'll make about the rest of the slide. When you are viewing a confusing slide the first question should always be *what are you trying to say on this slide?* Whatever that answer is should become the slide title.

In the following chapters, we will refer back to the title again and again. The title is the launching pad for determining slide content, layout and design so investing in clear slide titles will

Automatically create slides with slide titles

Want to create a deck with 20 slides? Rather than trudging through each slide to write in your title, use this shortcut to automatically create all the slides with titles.

1. Open a new slide and type the 20 slide titles in a bulleted list. Don't worry about the font size. Shrink the font down to 5 point if needed to get all the slide titles on one bulleted list
2. Make sure the "Home" tab on the Ribbon is active
3. Click the "Outline" tab of the Slides Pane visible to the left of your slide
4. Using your cursor, select all the bullets in Outline view
5. Press Shift + Tab
6. This will automatically turn each bulleted item into its own slide

make the rest of the slide design much faster, easier and clearer. Clear slide titles will make you a more effective communicator.

Back to Alex's slide

You meet with Alex to give him feedback on the channel deck. Turning to the Mission & Vision slide, you ask, "What's the main message on this slide?"

Alex isn't sure there's one message, "There are a couple of messages. We are adding new languages to our next three releases and new features. And we have some recruitment goals as well. And the goals and features are being driven by our overall strategy of putting a PC on every desktop."

"And which of those messages is most important?" you ask.

"Well, the overall goal is to put a PC on every desktop. The software languages is how we're going to reach more markets and the number of users is how we're going to measure it. But the main message is that it's our corporate vision driving everything for the next three years."

"Okay, that's a good message. Why don't we make that the title of this slide? It will be easier to get people excited if we make that message loud and clear."

Now you have a slide title that the reader can understand and ultimately get excited about.

Before: Category title   **After:** Using Mindworks Presentation Method

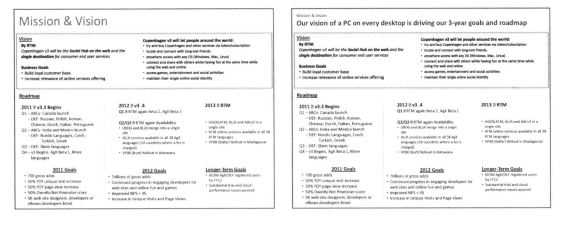

Above-water argument

1. The title is the most important part of your slide and can make even an incoherent slide understandable. Use a full sentence to increase comprehension 15% over a category title.

2. The slide title also forces the slide creator to clarify their message for themselves. It can cause them to re-think their conclusions and recommendations. The slide title will affect every other decision you make about the slide, including content, layout, visuals and color.

3. There are four types of slide titles: a conclusion title is a complete sentence that summarizes the slide message, a thesis title contains several sentences that more fully explain the slide content, a category title just labels a slide but doesn't summarize it, a question title poses a question that is then explicitly answered on the slide or verbally. Category titles can often be turned into a conclusion title by asking *why does the reader need to know this?*

4. As a slide reviewer ask *what is the main message on this slide?* That should be the slide title. If the slide creator doesn't know what the main message is, the slide reader won't either.

Recommended reading

The Craft of Scientific Presentations by Michael Alley focuses on communicating complex scientific and engineering data in oral presentations. Chapter 5 discusses slide titles in more detail.

The Visual Slide Revolution by Dave Paradi is a real gem packed with tips on how to clarify the meaning of each slide and especially the critical role of the slide title. The before and after slide examples show how much more impactful conclusion titles can be.

CHAPTER 8

Chunking

Only use 3—4 chunks of information on a slide

Alex's slide is clearer with a conclusion title. But this is a challenging slide to present. There is so much text! Is the audience supposed to read all this? How can Alex present this to an audience?

Mission & Vision

Our vision of a PC on every desktop is driving our 3-year goals and roadmap

Vision

By RTM:
*Copenhagen v3 will be the **Social Hub on the web** and the **single destination** for consumer end user services*

Business Goals
- Build loyal customer base
- Increase relevance of online services offering

Copenhagen v3 will let people around the world:
- try and buy Copenhagen and other services via token/subscription
- locate and connect with long-lost friends.
- anywhere access with any OS (Windows, Mac, Linux)
- connect and share with others while having fun at the same time while using the web and online
- access games, entertainment and social activities
- maintain their single online social identity

Roadmap

2011 ⬚ v3.3 Begins
Q1 – ABCv: Canada launch
— DEF: Russian, Polish, Korean, Chinese, Dutch, Italian, Portuguese
Q2 – ABCv: India and Mexico launch
— DEF: Nordic Languages, Czech, Turkish, Greek
Q3 – DEF: Slavic languages
Q4 – v3 Begins, AgX Beta 1, More languages

2012 ⬚ v3 .4
Q1 ⬚ RTM again beta 2, AgX Beta 2

Q2/Q3 ⬚ RTM again Availability
- OXOG and BLLR merge into a single site
- BLLR services available in all 38 AgX languages (14 countries where a fee is charged)
- VPBX (Burt) Rollout in Botswana

2013 ⬚ RTM

- OGOX,RTM, BLLR and ABCv3 in a single site
- RTM online services available in all 38 RTM languages
- VPBX (Ballyr) Rollout in Madagascar

2011 Goals
- 700 gross adds
- 50% YOY unique visit increase
- 50% YOY page view increase
- 50% OxenRo Net Promoter score
- 5K web site designers, developers or elbows developers listed

2012 Goals
- Trillions of gross adds
- Continued progress in engaging developers for web sites and online fun and games
- Improved NPS + 45
- Increase in Unique Visits and Page Views

Longer-Term Goals
- 603M AgX/DEF registered users by FY12
- Substantial trial and cloud performance issues assured

What advice do you give Alex about the right amount of information to include on a slide?

How much information is too much?

The question *how much information on a slide is too much* is one of the most frequent questions I hear at my workshops. And the answer is based on an important rule in brain science we have called the Rule of Four, which states that a person can only understand 3–4 ideas at one time.

There's a mistaken belief that if you put 100 ideas on your slide, the reader will understand all 100. And if you want to give them 200 ideas, well, the reader's mind is big and flexible and it can hold everything you throw at them. This is like believing the reader's head is a big empty elastic container that expands to whatever size you need and you can pour a giant pitcher of information into them.

And it you have twice as many ideas, you can just put them all on the slide and they will all be poured into the reader's mind without spilling a drop.

This view of unlimited attention and memory is incorrect. The mind has serious limitations on how much information it can hold at once. For instance, I can put ten numbers up on a slide. But can you hold all these numbers in mind at once? Do they mean anything to you?

What if we group these numbers differently, so we have five two-digit numbers? Can you hold it all in mind at the same time yet?

20   65   55   02   68

How easy is it to hold all five numbers in your mind? Can you see all five numbers at the same time? Most people cannot.

Holding ideas in your mind is like writing them on a whiteboard. This "whiteboard" is your working memory. And just like a whiteboard, the working memory is the place where you store ideas temporarily, inspect them, understand them and look for relationships and meaning.

But most people can only write about 3–4 ideas on their whiteboard. If they want to hold more, they need to erase one idea so they can write down a new idea.

So, you can probably hold this in mind and see everything at the same time

65   07   68

Or this

55   20   02

And maybe even this

20   65   02   68

That's because your "whiteboard" can comfortably hold four ideas; numbers in this case. But in order to add the fifth number, you need to erase one number and replace it with another.

That's why it's difficult to hold this in your mind. It exceeds your "whiteboard's" available space.

20   65   55   02   68

But what if we do this?

206   555   0268

What happened? It's the same ten digits, but they've been arranged into only three groups. And now we can actually hold this in working memory. In fact, now we can recognize it as a phone number. We have held everything together at once, we've interpreted meaning and we've understood.

The point of creating your slide was to pass information to the reader and help them understand your meaning. But realize they can only receive 3–4 chunks of information and still understand it in working memory. When you exceed 3–4 chunks of information on your slide, the reader simply cannot hold your slide information in their minds. Their whiteboards do not have room for it all.

The Rule of Four also says that each idea can further hold up to four other ideas inside it. In this way, by nesting four smaller ideas within four larger ideas, you can convey 16 ideas to the reader.

Here's the Rule of Four in action. Say you have a list of grocery items to purchase. They are listed here in alphabetical order:

apples	eggs
bananas	fish sticks
bread	hamburger
butter	milk
cheese	muffins
chicken drumsticks	oranges
cookies	pears
crackers	yogurt

How easy is it to keep all 16 items in memory at once? It becomes easier once you chunk them into smaller units, using the Rule of Four to nest them inside four categories: fruits, breads, meats and dairy products.

apples	chicken drumsticks
bananas	eggs
oranges	fish sticks
pears	hamburger
bread	butter
cookies	cheese
crackers	yogurt
muffins	milk

The Rule of Four will be your powerful ally as you create slides with a lot of detail. When you find you have more than four chunks of information for a slide, look for ways to summarize some of those chunks into larger ideas. The reader will be able to hold onto that larger idea and then "unpack" the four smaller ideas nested inside it more easily than treating each smaller idea as its own chunk of information.

The Rule of Four will dictate how much information you can put on a slide. There are two exceptions where the reader may be able to comprehend more than four ideas:

1. High IQ readers. Brain research finds that people who do well on standardized tests, like SAT's and IQ tests, are able to hold more items in working memory than others. That's what makes them great problem solvers—they can see more relationships and imagine more combinations by holding

Wait! I thought it was SEVEN items in memory!

You may have learned that you can hold seven items in short-term memory, plus or minus two. That's why our phone numbers are seven digits long. But short-term memory and working memory are different things. Short-term memory is where you can store information after repeating it and practicing it, like when you're walking out the door and your spouse shouts—*Honey! Can you go to the store and buy some milk, cheese, apples, bread, carrots, butter and chips!* All the way to the store, you will be mentally repeating to yourself *milk-cheese-apples-bread-carrots-butter-chips.* Or, if you're smart, you'll get out a pen and write it down.

Working memory is where you evaluate information to determine its meaning and how it connects to other ideas. It's where you do your understanding and problem solving.

The research that found the number seven comes from George A. Miller in a 1956 article entitled "The Magical Number Seven, Plus or Minus Two: Some Limits on Our Capacity for Processing Information". It involved university students viewing a random string of numbers. First one number, then a second was revealed, then a third and so on. Miller's study found students could, on average, remember up to seven digits before forgetting set in; some only five, some an astounding nine. They also found memorization was easier when all the items were similar in some way (eg. 1-5-7) versus different (eg. cow-7-universe).

Even seven digits is hard to hold in memory the first time you see it. Have you ever checked your cell phone voicemail where someone left you a number to call and you didn't have a pen to write it down? If you're like me, you may have said to your friend "I'll remember the first three numbers, you remember the last four." Even remembering seven digits takes some rehearsal.

more information on their whiteboard at the same time. *That's why you often see the worst slides created by the smartest people*—they understand it and don't realize that it's too complex for others.

Business executives tend to be able to process more information than others. That's one reason executives like slides packed densely with data—they are able to process it more comfortably than others. If you are one of these people, you need to be especially careful that you aren't overwhelming your reader with overly-complex slides.

2. Familiar mental models. The more familiar the reader is with the mental model, the more information they can comfortably hold. For instance, if I show you the seven days of the week you will have no problem holding this in your head because you already have a high familiarity with this model. Similarly, if your company has six market segments that everyone is familiar with, you can show all six segments on a slide because people have already learned that mental model and can conjure up the necessary connections to hold it all in working memory.

The Rule of Four is very powerful and will influence many things about slide design—how much information to put on a slide, how many slides needed to describe a concept, how to treat bullets, and so on.

You don't automatically transmit information to the reader just because it's on the slide. You need to reduce it to 3–4 chunks of information so it fits the reader's working memory. The question is: what is a *chunk* of information?

What is a *chunk* of information?

A chunk of information is anything that your vision can see as part of a group and separate from other groups. A slide will have many elements on it—boxes, arrows, text boxes, graphs, images. How does your vision organize all this into four separate groups, or *chunks*?

Gestalt Theory is a set of principles which explains how the brain organizes parts into whole units. According to Gestalt Theory, the brain chunks information based on things like proximity, alignment and similarity. Here are four ways the brain chunks information that are most relevant for slide design:

- Law of Proximity   00 00 00 00

- Law of Similarity   00**xx**00**xx**

- Law of Connectedness   0--0--0--0   0--0--0--0

- Law of Enclosure   [0000][0000]

The Law of Proximity states that objects that are *close together* are seen as part of the same thing and objects that are *separated by whitespace* are seen as part of something else.

The Law of Similarity says that objects that share a *common characteristic* like color or shape are seen as part of the same group.

The Law of Connectedness says that items that are *connected with lines* are seen as part of the same group.

The Law of Enclosure says objects that are *enclosed by a border* are seen as part of the same group.

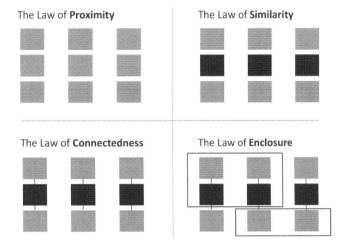

Some of these perceptual Laws are more powerful than others. Notice how the Law of Proximity, although effective, can be contradicted by the other Laws. When you introduce colors, the Law of Similarity causes you to see the same-colored shapes as part of a group, even though they are not in close proximity. You can introduce connecting lines and the Law of Connectedness will overcome the Law of Similarity. And the strongest of all is the Law of Enclosure, which overcomes proximity, similarity and connectedness.

There are other Gestalt principles, but these are the four you are most likely to encounter as you group shapes into chunks of information on a slide.

Whitespace, the blank space between objects, is an important tool for chunking and sometimes you can use it accidentally. Whitespace tends to push elements away from each other, making it difficult to chunk them together. Look at the blocks in the Law of Proximity diagram. You can see how whitespace helps to push the columns apart into separate chunks. You can use whitespace intentionally to push items apart.

But you can also use it unintentionally, introducing whitespace accidentally and making it harder to chunk information. Be aware of *trapped whitespace* on your slide, where two elements are supposed to be part of the same chunk of information but whitespace creeps in to push them apart. Notice the line graph on the left has the text labels tucked up close to the line. On the right, white space is "trapped" between the lines and the labels, pushing the elements apart and making it harder to chunk them.

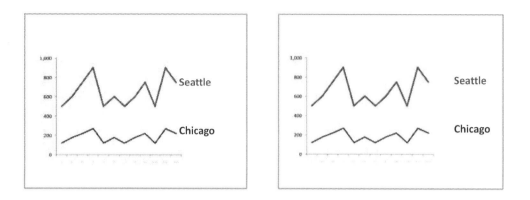

Let's look at an example. Imagine you're presenting a marketing plan to your VP and you are explaining you have eight market segments. This is too much to hold in working memory so your VP won't be able to comprehend this slide.

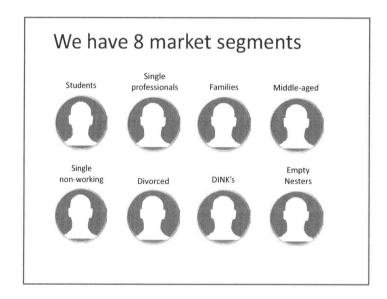

But if you chunk these into two groups of four using the Law of Enclosure, now the VP can hold these two chunks of information in working memory and see what you mean. Notice also how we used whitespace between the two chunks to push them apart, rather than press them up close to each other.

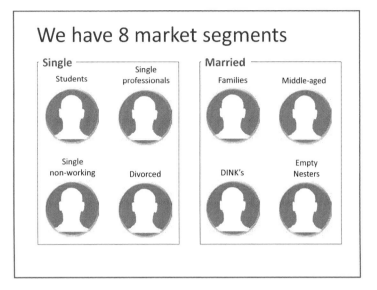

Labels are the handles on the briefcase

Chunking information is not enough. You also need to tell the reader what each chunk of information means. Remember, the reader needs to hold 3–4 ideas in mind so each chunk of information needs to be labeled as a concept or idea.

Labels are like the handles on a briefcase, with the ideas like the papers inside. The mind holds the idea by the handle then carries it over to working memory to unpack the contents. Short descriptive labels help you easily transmit the idea to the reader.

For instance, recall our grocery list example where we chunked the grocery items into four categories.

apples	chicken drumsticks
bananas	eggs
oranges	fish sticks
pears	hamburger
bread	butter
cookies	cheese
crackers	yogurt
muffins	milk

How much more quickly does the reader understand these four chunks of information if we just add labels?

fruits	**meat**
apples	chicken drumsticks
bananas	eggs
oranges	fish sticks
pears	hamburger

carbohydrates	**dairy**
bread	butter
cookies	cheese
crackers	yogurt
muffins	milk

Consider a slide like this, which shows seven steps in a customer journey. We can make it easier for the reader if we chunk this into three groups.

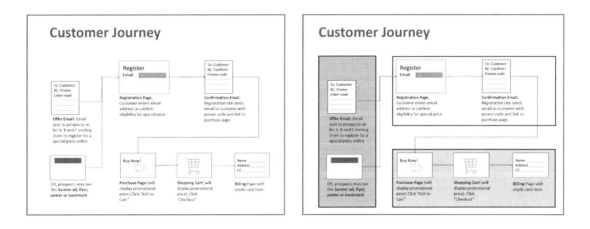

But what does each chunk mean? Chunking information helps but you still need to tell the reader what each chunk means. They still need a handle so they can pick it up and transfer it into working memory. We do that by adding a label to each chunk.

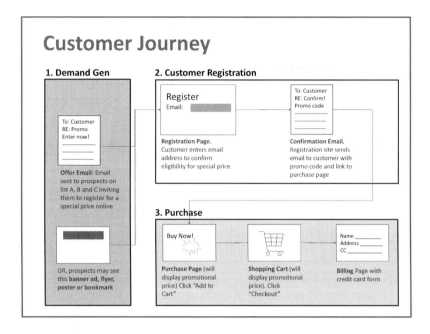

Each chunk of information on your slide should be clearly labeled. If you have a chunk of information on the slide that has no label, it will take longer to read through the contents of that chunk and identify its meaning. Your label is critical to transferring that knowledge to the reader.

Labels should also be located as close as possible to the information chunk. This will become especially important in our chapter on charts and tables. Consider the following slide with the labels placed on each pie slice. This chart is easy to read because the labels are integrated with the chart.

But look at how much harder the reader has to work to understand the slide on the right. The reader needs to keep flitting back and forth between the legend and the diagram, matching colors to understand each segment size. This is an unnecessary tax on working memory. Integrating the labels simplifies reading.

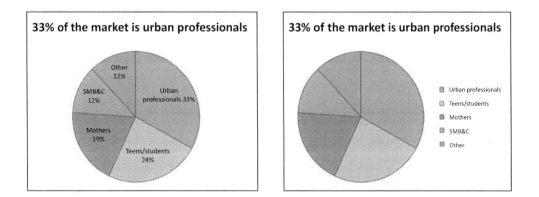

Research with university students by Professor Richard Mayer, author of *Multi-Media Learning*, found that integrating pictures and text close together lead to better test scores than moving the text farther away from the image. That's because it takes more cognitive resources to take a "snapshot" of the image, hold the image in working memory and then search for the matching text. But placing them close together does not use up valuable working memory space; everything is visible at the same time.

When you have too much content on a slide

You now know that anything more than four chunks of well-labeled information on a slide is too much. Sometimes, it will be easy to reduce your slide to four chunks of information. But what do you do when you have more than four chunks of information on a slide?

First, ask yourself if you really need all this information on the same slide. Sometimes we push too much information onto a slide because we are trying to conserve slides or because we had some extra white space on a slide and just added more information.

I call this the *spaghetti and meatball* problem. Spaghetti and meatballs taste better when they are together on the same plate. Similarly, there are times when you need the reader to see all the information together on one slide. The message is more difficult to understand if the information is on different slides.

One example is when you want to compare sales data in different cities next to website data, to show how website visits is a leading indicator of sales. You need this data on the same slide. You don't want the reader to have to flip between slides to see the correlation. This is an example of spaghetti and meatballs; it's better for them to be on the same plate.

But what if they don't need to be on the same slide? This is what I call the *spaghetti and cake* problem. There's a reason you keep spaghetti on one plate and cake on its own plate—they taste worse when they're on the same plate. In the same way, some slide creators jam too much information on a slide just because they have extra whitespace to fill. I've seen some market research reports where each slide is jammed with four unrelated graphs. There's no need for the reader to see all four graphs together at the same time, and the message from each graph would be clearer if it had its own slide.

So when you have more than four chunks on a slide look at your various chunks and ask: is this a *meatball*, or is this *cake*? Do these taste better on the same plate? If it's a meatball, and it needs to be on the same slide, then find a way to keep the ideas together. We'll discuss some ways to do that below.

But if it's cake, and doesn't need to be viewed together, then give it its own plate. Move it to a separate slide. You will make it easier for the reader to fit your message in working memory and be a more effective communicator.

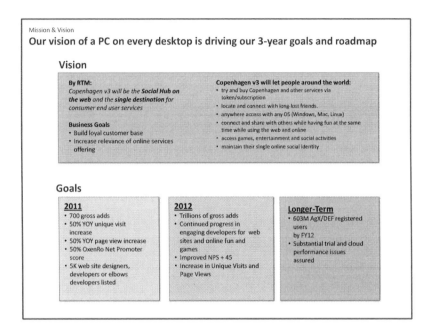

Moving cake to its own slide may solve the problem. But what if it's a meatball and you need to have all these ideas together on the same slide? Here are a few ways you can solve that problem:

1. Chunking it further. Maybe there's a way to combine two chunks of information into one, by setting them inside another larger idea. This allows the reader to understand the slide on first glance, and then understand the richer levels of detail as they slowly unpack it. The Customer Journey slide we saw earlier is an example of chunking units into smaller units.

2. Graying out text. There may be some parts of the slide you can gray out by using a lighter color. This sends a signal to the brain *you can ignore this for now.* The brain will not try to process that as a separate chunk of information but it will still be available on the slide as the reader spends more time with it.

3. Use lines to break the slide into smaller units. You may need to separate your slide into two or more distinct areas, each with its own conclusion. This is essentially two or more different slides compressed to fit together in one slide. Executive slides often follow this format so that a lot of information can be presented in a compact space. But using lines to separate each section tells the reader—you can ignore the other three sections and pay attention to each section by itself.

4. Sequencing. Some ideas are complex and can only be explained over several slides. For instance, you may want to describe a process that has seven steps in it. You could force it all onto one slide using 8-point font and every available pixel of whitespace. Or, you could break the slide into three different slides where you introduce steps 1–2 on one slide, steps 3–4 on another slide, and then steps 5–7 on the third slide.

1. Remove all the chunks except for one and give it its own slide

2. Introduce the next chunk of information. Gray out the first item so it isn't competing for attention

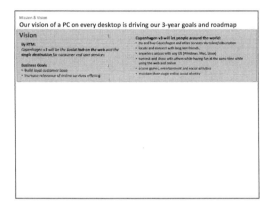
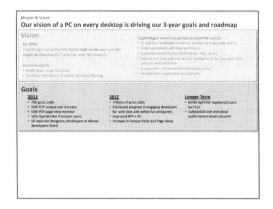

3. Introduce the last item. Gray out the items that have already been discussed

4. Finish with one slide that shows how they all fit together

The more detail you need to communicate to the reader, the more you will need to use sequencing to introduce the different elements and then the supporting details. As we discussed in the chapter on ordering your evidence, instructional designers find it's most effective for students to learn one chunk of information at a time and then bring it all together at the end. For instance, for Alex's slide, you may want to introduce each chunk of information on its own slide.

5. Animations and "builds". Instead of using sequenced slides, isn't it better to just use animations? In theory, building a slide using animations should make sense: you introduce some part of the slide you want people to pay attention to, then you click and another layer of information fades in that the reader can now pay attention to.

There has been some research done on the use of animations to build complex slides, but the findings are not very encouraging.

First, the research around animated text is bleak. There are several studies showing people learn *less* when you animate text. In 2002, Professors Donald Dansereau and Jason Blankenship conducted a study with four groups of university students. One group saw text slides, another saw animated text slides, a third group saw a process flow diagram and a fourth saw an animated process flow diagram. The group who saw the animated text slides remembered the least and did the poorest on tests.

A 2009 study found similar results. Professors Stephen Mahar, Ulku Yaylacicegi and Thomas Janicki tested two versions of a narrated PowerPoint lecture, one with animated slides and one with static slides. Students who viewed the animated slides scored 71% on an assessment, while those who saw the non-animated slides scored 82%. The animations included revealing text as the instructor spoke, and revealing screenshots as steps in a process. The results were published in the June 2009 *International Journal of Innovation and Learning* under the bleak title "The dark side of custom animations". The study was repeated and similar results were found.

What explains the difference? The researchers postulated that the static slides allowed the readers to view the information longer, leading to better recall. The animated slides required excessive processing that interfered with comprehension. In general, research suggests that students learn best when they control the pace of information being presented to them.

I also have a hypothesis why students learned less from the animated slides. When I reviewed the non-animated slides, I was actively engaged trying to match the speaker's voice to the bullets on the slide. In a sense, I was forced to process the instruction, understand it, and locate the accompanying text in order to follow along. I could not be a passive observer. In contrast, the animated slides had bullets that flew in, and text and images that were revealed as the speaker spoke. With the animated slides I found myself disengaging, waiting for the slides to "do something" that made it all make sense.

Watching a non-animated slide versus an animated slide is like the difference between reading a book and watching a television show. Reading a book requires you to use your imagination and make an effort to understand. Watching television is passive, requires no imagination and little effort to follow. The extra effort may explain the increased retention.

However, the research around animated images is more promising. When there is some meaning in the animation, such as "growth", animations appear to make the message more believable. As mentioned in the opening chapter, the Arizona State University students gave the highest rating to the scholarship application delivered as a PowerPoint slide where an animated graph was revealed as bars growing upward to illustrate the high school football star's statistics.

In the 2002 Dansereau and Blankenship study, students who watched the animated process flow map learned some parts of the lesson better than any other groups, primarily the steps in the process. However the students did not do better learning the details of each step. The researchers wonder if animation may have had a distracting effect, focusing learners more on the structure of the lesson and less on the details.

Even though the students learned the steps in the process better, the static process map used in the study was purposefully designed to be overly-complex so that animations were needed to guide the viewer through the steps. The authors note that a process flow map with better design could be as effective as using animations.

Clearly, more research is needed to understand when animation is helpful and when it's detrimental. But the evidence is clear that animated text tends to decrease understanding and animated images may be helpful when the animations reinforce a key message, or the static images are too complex to navigate easily.

There's a practical reasons animations may be an inferior way to sequence slides, or to control the reader's attention in general, in reading decks. First, the reader may not be viewing the slides in slide-show mode which is necessary to see the animations. If they print the slides, they lose the animation effect. Instead, they get the full cluttered slide.

I'm sure there are good examples of using animation to explain difficult concepts, and to be fair, I have seen them used. But my experience has been that animations are routinely misused to add novelty to a presentation rather than clarity. In the absence of research that says animations make communication more effective, and the existing preponderance of quantitative and empirical evidence that animations actually hinder audience learning, I recommend the use of sequencing over animations.

Back to Alex's slide

Later that day, you sit down with Alex. You explain that this slide has an overwhelming amount of information, and explain the limits of working memory and the concept of chunking.

You and Alex look it over to see how many chunks of information you are asking the reader to carry into working memory. Based on the Law of Enclosure, you agree the top box is one chunk of information. And based on the Laws of Proximity and Enclosure, there are appear to be six more chunks of information at the bottom, each broken into separate chunks by whitespace. So there appears to be seven chunks in total—too many.

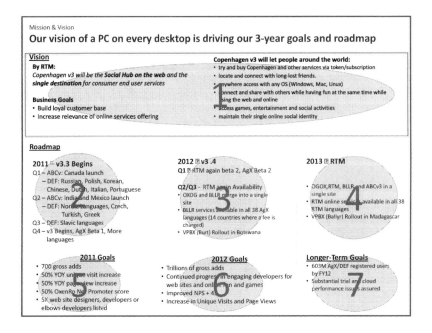

You and Alex decide you can group this into just three chunks of information, using the Law of Enclosure.

The information is now chunked, but the reader isn't clear what is in each chunk. The top two boxes have labels using a small text size with underlining so it's challenging to read quickly. You agree that adding prominent labels to each chunk makes it easier for the reader to understand.

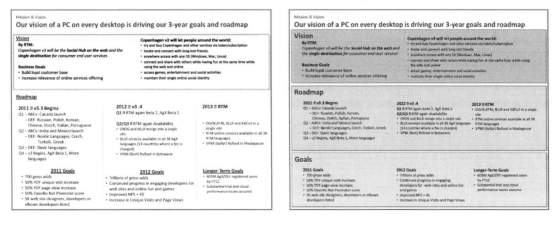

This slide isn't perfect, but at least it's coherent. You know what Alex is trying to say within a few seconds, rather than searching frantically for meaning and giving up.

Before: Information overload   **After:** Using Mindworks Presentation Method

Above-water argument

1. The brain can only hold 3–4 chunks of information in working memory so limit your slides to four chunks of information.

2. Chunk information through proximity, similarity, connectedness and enclosure.

3. Label each chunk, and make sure the label is seen next to the chunk of information, to assist in immediate understanding. The label is like a handle on a briefcase that allows the reader to pick up a chunk of information and carry it into working memory.

4. Use the spaghetti and meatball test to break complex slides down. Does all this information need to be on the same slide? Or can you move the cake to its own slide? If you need to keep items together, simplify them into four chunks by: chunking them further, graying out some of the text, dividing the slide into several sub-slides, or using sequencing.

Recommended reading

Clear and to the Point by Stephen Kosslyn discusses PowerPoint slide design from a brain scientist's perspective.

CHAPTER 9

Picture-Superiority Effect

Use the persuasive power of pictures

A LEX'S SLIDE IS EASIER TO UNDERSTAND by chunking the information and adding meaningful labels. But it still takes a long time to work through all the text! You remember the blank faces registered by your colleagues in the last meeting, and realize how difficult it is talk through a slide like this in a small group.

Mission & Vision

Our vision of a PC on every desktop is driving our 3-year goals and roadmap

Vision

By RTM:
Copenhagen v3 will be the Social Hub on the web and the single destination for consumer end user services

Business Goals
- Build loyal customer base
- Increase relevance of online services offering

Copenhagen v3 will let people around the world:
- try and buy Copenhagen and other services via token/subscription
- locate and connect with long-lost friends.
- anywhere access with any OS (Windows, Mac, Linux)
- connect and share with others while having fun at the same time while using the web and online
- access games, entertainment and social activities
- maintain their single online social identity

Roadmap

2011 ⊡ v3.3 Begins
Q1 – ABCv: Canada launch
  – DEF: Russian, Polish, Korean, Chinese, Dutch, Italian, Portuguese
Q2 – ABCv: India and Mexico launch
  – DEF: Nordic Languages, Czech, Turkish, Greek
Q3 – DEF: Slavic languages
Q4 – v3 Begins, AgX Beta 1, More languages

2012 ⊡ v3 .4
Q1 ⊡ RTM again beta 2, AgX Beta 2

Q2/Q3 ⊡ RTM again Availability
- OXOG and BLLR merge into a single site
- BLLR services available in all 38 AgX languages (14 countries where a fee is charged)
- VPBX (Burt) Rollout in Botswana

2013 ⊡ RTM

- OGOX,RTM, BLLR and ABCv3 in a single site
- RTM online services available in all 38 RTM languages
- VPBX (Ballyr) Rollout in Madagascar

Goals

2011 Goals
- 700 gross adds
- 50% YOY unique visit increase
- 50% YOY page view increase
- 50% OxenRo Net Promoter score
- 5K web site designers, developers or elbows developers listed

2012 Goals
- Trillions of gross adds
- Continued progress in engaging developers for web sites and online fun and games
- Improved NPS + 45
- Increase in Unique Visits and Page Views

Longer-Term Goals
- 603M AgX/DEF registered users by FY12
- Substantial trial and cloud performance issues assured

What advice can you give Alex to make this slide easier to share and discuss in a group meeting?

Pictures can be your secret weapon to selling ideas

Some slides are dense with bullet points and sentences, or what I call the *Great Wall of Text*. And just like the Great Wall of China, these slides are often impenetrable. Unfortunately, your great idea is held locked inside.

There is 40 years of research showing that adding pictures to a text document can make the message easier to understand, easier to agree with and easier to remember later. This is called the *picture-superiority effect* and it can become your competitive advantage when you sell ideas in the boardroom. That's why, whenever you create a slide, you should ask yourself, "How can I use the picture-superiority effect on this slide?"

Professional persuaders, like advertisers, politicians and lawyers, understand the picture-superiority effect. And numerous studies have shown people are more likely to *see things your way* when you give them a picture.

A sobering 1997 study with jurors found pictures more than doubled the chances of a guilty verdict. In this study, participants watched a mock trial; a widow was suing her insurance company for refusing to pay the life insurance benefit when her husband, a construction worker, fell to his death from an eight-story building. The insurance company contended the man did not fall, but jumped to his death. They produced evidence that the widow was pregnant with another man's baby, a motive for suicide, and that the husband's father had also committed suicide.

When jurors heard the argument that the man's body landed just 5–10 feet from the building, consistent with the slip-and-fall argument, they agreed with the widow 33% of the time. But when the widow's lawyer introduced a crude animation showing the trajectory of the fall using a simple stick-figure man, the jurors agreed with the widow a shocking 75% of the time.

A similar study in 2004 at the University of New South Wales had university students, playing jurors, read the transcripts of a hypothetical murder trial. Jurors found the accused guilty 9% of the time. But when they were shown neutral crime scene photographs, not of the victim, but of things like the room where the murder happened or rumpled clothing, conviction rates jumped to 38%. There are similar studies, as early as 1976, which corroborate that juries are more likely to side with a lawyer's argument when they introduce a picture.

It's only natural that lawyers today routinely use pictures and animation to convince jurors. Given the persuasive power of pictures, the judicial system is struggling with how much to allow pictures in the courtroom. In countries like the United States and Australia, courts have strict guidelines that prohibit pictures that may unfairly prejudice a jury.

The persuasive impact of pictures is not limited to courtrooms. In an amusing 2007 study, Colorado State University students were asked to read scientific articles. Some articles were bogus, like the one that said watching television improves your math skills. But students were more likely to agree when the article included a color picture of a brain than when the article contained a graph, or no picture at all.

The ASU study, which opened chapter 1, is another example of how a graph made a scholarship application more likely to be approved than an application with text only.

Educators have also studied the picture-superiority effect, to find ways to improve learning for students. One of the most extensive set of studies was conducted by Professor Richard Mayer as documented in his book *Multi-Media Learning*. Students were taught how lightning forms, how car brakes operate and how bicycle pumps work. In dozens of experiments Dr. Mayer shows that educating with both pictures and text roughly doubles understanding and recall over educating with text alone.

There are many studies which corroborate these findings. In a review of 150 research studies over three decades, Joel Levin found that students learn 50% to 140% more when relevant pictures accompany the text.

A similar research review by Levie and Lentz found pictures increase learning. In 45 of 46 studies reviewed, students learned an average 36% more when the image illustrates something explained in the text. Even when the image only partly illustrated the text, learning was improved an average 25% in 38 of 48 studies.

The important point for business managers is that, for most readers, pictures make your message easier to understand, easier to agree with and easier to remember. This makes images a stronger foundation for ideas than text alone and can be your competitive advantage when selling ideas in the idea marketplace.

That's why, whenever you create a slide, you should ask yourself, "How can I use the picture-superiority effect on this slide?". Do not be content with a Wall of Text. That wall can be a barrier to selling your ideas. Set your ideas free with pictures.

Use concrete images suggested in your slide title

When choosing your picture, look at the keywords in your slide title. Forty years of research has demonstrated the picture-superiority effect is most effective when the picture and text are addressing the same message. That message is contained in the slide title you have so carefully crafted.

Always strive to use concrete rather than abstract pictures. Concrete pictures include things that exist in the real world, like icebergs and college students and jurors. Abstract pictures like graphs and diagrams and icons summarize things that are too complex to represent with concrete pictures. For instance, in describing the college student market, it's more effective to use pictures that represent your customer segments rather than simply a pie chart. The reader will understand you more quickly, remember your message longer and feel more persuaded.

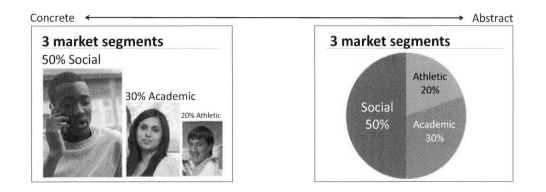

Why? The research on the picture-superiority effect finds that concrete images are more effective than abstract images at making ideas understandable, memorable and persuasive.

The picture-superiority effect works because most people think in pictures. In the early 1970's, Allan Paivio of the University of Ontario proposed the Dual Coding Theory, which argued that readers store words in one kind of memory and pictures in another. Not only are they stored separately, but words themselves have no value unless they are connected to a picture.

This makes intuitive sense. Words are just a man-made convention to stand for a real thing or activity. We learn the word *computer* to stand for that object. We learn the word *type* as a set of activities to create a document on a computer. We learn the word *office* to stand for that place where we type on our computers. Without words, we would still have pictures as the basis for thinking.

A helpful analogy is that words are like money. A hundred-dollar bill has no value by itself. You can trade it in for quarters or dollar bills, but it still has no value until you trade money for goods and services. Words are the same way; they are valuable only in their ability to conjure a picture. In your mind, you are always trading words for pictures in order to understand written or spoken words.

Educators have long-believed that pictures play a critical role in learning. They know, for instance, that pictures pop into students' minds automatically while they are reading. For example, read this passage:

> Little Red Riding Hood skipped happily through the forest to her grandmother's house. Little did she know that the Big Bad Wolf was close behind.

When you read this passage, does a picture pop into your mind? What do you see? When researchers interrupt student who are reading, 60% of students report seeing a mental image. Students who struggle with reading comprehension are also poor at visualizing. Brain scans confirm that the visual system is firing when people are reading. In studies where people are directed to *not* think in pictures, those studies fail because people are unable to suppress their mental images.

So always strive to use a concrete picture on your slide to activate the mental images your reader needs in order to understand. There are two types of concrete pictures to consider:

1. Illustrative images

If your goal is primarily to *explain*, use an image that literally overlaps with the text. For instance, in chapter 5 I described the three decision areas of the brain using a picture which illustrated exactly what was described in the text.

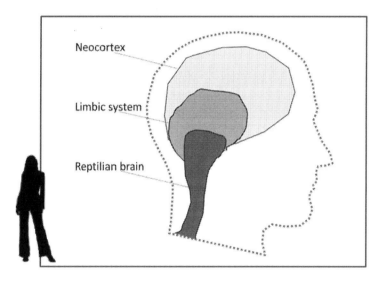

According to educational research, students learn the most from pictures that overlap with the text or provide additional detail that could not be covered well in the text. Carney and Levin summarized the results of 150 studies in the 1970's and 1980's and found that illustrative images increased learning by 25% to 75%. Learning is not improved when the picture does not overlap with the text or only provides visual interest.

Learning is improved because the picture tells the reader which mental images to activate. There is usually a lot of text to read and the mind will be struggling at first to understand what pictures it needs to mentally activate to understand the text. A picture tells the reader what is important and helps activate the relevant mental images.

In this regard, pictures act as a sort of "hook"—a *conceptual peg*—that we chunk new information around. Conceptual pegs give us something concrete to think about as we try to understand a new idea. In a boardroom presentation, the audience is trying to quickly understand your main message. A picture conjures up the relevant mental image instantly and helps them quickly assimilate the supporting text.

Look at your slide title. If your slide is talking about a specific person, place or thing, consider using an illustrative image. For instance, if your slide title says "Software developers in India are increasingly using free developer tools online" the keywords that are concrete nouns are: *software developers*, *India* and *free developer tools*. Do you have photographs of software developers in India? How about a map of India? How about a screenshot of free online developer tools? Or, you might combine pictures, showing a map of India with a screenshot of free developer tools inserted over the major cities.

Whenever they keywords in your slide title include people, including specific people or a class of people, try to find ways to use an image of that person in the slide. If the slide title is talking about teachers or travelling business professionals or Bill Gates, consider adding an illustrative image of that specific person or type of person.

Why? Pictures of people are especially powerful. There are some scientists who insist there are actually three unique processing centers in the brain—for text, for pictures and for faces. Eye-tracking studies show that when we look at a picture we spend the most time fixating on faces. In fact, our gaze is temporarily frozen exactly on the eyes of the people in the picture. Scientists suppose this is an inborn survival instinct; we can detect which people are threats, which are allies and which are potential mates by studying the faces, and especially the eyes, of those we meet.

One word of caution: eye-tracking studies also show we ignore stock photography, such as a picture of a nurse who is clearly a professional model. Avoid stock photos that are supposed to represent real people, and instead use an authentic picture or else silhouette images.

Illustrative images are especially important if the reader doesn't have a mental image to work with. For instance, if you are describing your competitor's new mobile phone, the reader may struggle to activate a mental image. Adding a picture gives them the needed mental image.

2. Metaphorical images

If your goal is to *persuade*, or *explain an abstract concept*, consider using an image that makes an abstract idea more concrete. Metaphorical images are of concrete things but not a literal illustration of the text. For instance, in chapter 4 I used a picture of an iceberg to explain how to structure a PowerPoint deck, to activate a familiar mental model that would help you organize and assimilate new information.

An interesting study by Luuk Lagerwerf found that people are more persuaded by pictures that are metaphorical than illustrative. In this study, he showed advertisements to people. Some of the ads stated their case explicitly, such as an ad that said "This car gets 21 miles per gallon". Another ad showed the same picture but the title read "This car sips gas". The metaphorical ad, which stated nothing explicit that could be agreed with or refuted, was more persuasive.

Pictures may be more persuasive because they activate our emotions. In jury research, jurors report higher levels of emotional arousal caused by seeing the crime scene photographs, to explain their guilty convictions.

Recall from chapter 5 that the limbic system, which modulates emotional responses, is pre-verbal. It reacts to images, not words. Verbal descriptions, in print or through voice, do not generate detailed enough mental images to trigger emotions as effectively as a picture. If I ask you to imagine a group of college students, you may be trading the words "college students" in for a generic image that represents an average or prototype of the many college students you've ever seen, rather than any specific flesh-and-blood college students.

But a picture contains more realistic details that can trigger an emotion. No matter how hard you try to imagine a group of college students sitting on the lawn, nothing you imagine can compare to the visceral experience of seeing real human beings and human expressions. Mental images lack the details and cannot match the emotional impact of a picture.

Students next growth opportunity

It's also possible that pictures are more persuasive because they are processed in a different part of the brain than text. There is a phenomenon, called the *illusion of truth effect*, where people are more likely to agree with statements they have heard before, regardless of whether they were true the first time they heard them. In a 1977 study by Hasher, Goldstein and Toppino, university students read 60 statements and rated how confident they were the statements were true or false. Then students returned two more times and again rated statements, 40 of them new and 20 repeated from previous sessions.

Researchers found students became more confident over time that statements were true if they were repeated from earlier sessions. Even when students were told originally the statements were false, when statements were familiar from previous sessions, students became more confident they were true.

This effect works best when the person does not think about it deeply. The more they think critically about the statement, the less likely they will be over-influenced by the familiarity.

Is it possible that there's a *picture illusion of truth effect*? Agreement is triggered by many cues, including cues we don't process consciously. People are more likely to agree to do something if they are instructed by a man wearing a business suit than they are by the exact same man dressed as a construction worker. Similarly, pictures are not processed in the verbal channel, but the non-verbal channel, so is it possible the lack of semantic processing makes them more susceptible to an *illusion of truth* effect? Like a business suit, does a picture increase the claim's authority? Is it possible that *seeing is believing*?

It's interesting to speculate that this could be true. It's certainly supported by studies like the ASU study and the brain science article study. But there are no studies which have investigated an *illusion of truth effect* for pictures. It remains an interesting speculation.

Finding concrete pictures

Perhaps the hardest part of communicating visually is not just finding the right concept, but finding professional-quality pictures for slides. This is a big problem and there are no easy solutions, but here's some advice for finding concrete pictures:

1. Take pictures with your own digital camera.
2. Perhaps your company has a library of images, or you can re-use images from others' PowerPoint slides. You should always confirm with them that they have the rights to use those images.
3. Flickr allows commercial use of some of its images. To find approved Flickr photos, click on Advanced Search and scroll to the Creative Commons section to search for images where the owner has given rights to use the image for commercial purposes. Or, even better, there's a new website that lets you search the Flickr collection for re-usable pictures (www.compfight. com) Typically, the photographer just wants you to attribute the photo to them, possibly in the notes section of the slide.
4. Hand draw images using PowerPoint's scribbling tool, especially if you have a tablet PC or a tablet mouse. Or hand-draw them on paper and scan them.
5. I like to find images online, copy them into a PowerPoint slide, increase the image size as large as will go, zoom in close and use the drawing tools to trace around them. This produces usable images in just a few minutes.
6. Internet searches will bring up all the images you could ever need or want but they are all protected by copyright law. CreativeCommons.org hosts a search engine that only locates images freely available for re-use, but does not guarantee the results are covered by a Creative Commons license. You will need to locate the original owner of the image and confirm the license rights.
7. There are for-fee services like istockphoto.com where you can buy low-cost royalty-free images. This can become costly but may be worthwhile if you are trying to sell your boss on an important project. Still, be aware of stock photography, which tends to be low-content and easily dismissed by the reader.

Look to your slide title. If your slide is talking about an abstract idea, can you turn it into a metaphor or find an image which might act as a conceptual peg? Again, using the example of software developers in India, the abstract idea inherent in your slide title is that customers are increasingly using free tools online. Brainstorm a little. Does this remind you of anything? You might imagine how customers have stopped using many offline products because free online products are better. You might look for images of a newspaper, a phone book and a roadmap and use these as a conceptual peg to kick off a conversation about how the internet has made a lot of other businesses irrelevant and it is now doing the same to software developer tools.

Use abstract images suggested in your slide title

Concrete images are more effective than abstract images at increasing understanding, recall and agreement. But in practice, it's challenging to find suitable concrete images, which might explain why most PowerPoint slides contain graphs, diagrams, clip art and tables.

The research on abstract images is less promising, because abstract images are less likely to activate familiar mental models, trigger emotions or have an illusion-of-truth effect. But they do have some properties which increase understanding over text alone, and especially for complex ideas.

There are two types of abstract shapes to consider:

1. Representative images

When you need to *summarize complex information* for the reader's understanding, consider a representative image. Representative images are abstract shapes that represent something that is difficult to show as a concrete picture. But they contain important information that illustrates, or expands on, the accompanying text. Examples are graphs, tables and schematic drawings.

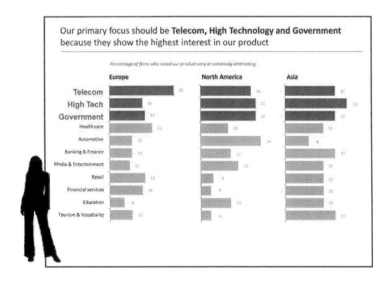

There is not much research comparing the effectiveness of representative images to text. In part, that's because it's only been recently that business managers can easily create charts and diagrams. So the technology is racing ahead of the research. The ASU study, which opened chapter 1, shows a graph was slightly more persuasive than a table, and that an animated graph was significantly more persuasive. The neuroscience article research showed that articles with graphs were less persuasive than articles with pictures of brains.

Representative images increase understanding because they show spatial relationships, such as cause/effect, changes over time, size differences and locations in physical space. It relieves the working memory burden of trying to mentally recreate these spatial relationships which then expose patterns and relationships between data points.

For instance, if I tell try to explain our distribution channel includes a mix of regional distributors (authorized and unauthorized), local distributors (for the B2B, retail and education markets), retailers and resellers (including direct mail), you need to build a mental model in order to hold onto all those details. But a diagram turns those details into a picture where the spatial relationships are clear instantly.

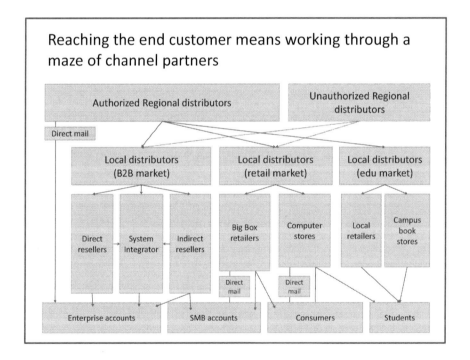

Most importantly, it relieves you of the challenge of holding all those details in working memory. Remember from the last chapter working memory can only hold 3–4 chunks of information at once. Instead, the picture acts as a form of external working memory, freeing you to study different parts of the diagram at your leisure without risk of forgetting something.

There are many types of representative pictures, including charts, graphs and tables. Because graphs and tables are used so extensively in business, we devote an entire chapter to this later in the book.

Other representative pictures are schematic diagrams showing an overview of a system, which are often too complex or too abstract to show with a concrete picture. A Gantt chart may represent different activities and milestone dates, or a process flow diagram may show how to route a customer complaint call to the right person. All these diagrams show complex information that would be too difficult to comprehend as text alone because they put a burden on working memory to build the mental model.

Another type of representative image is *a symbol*, which stands in for a concrete object and is easily recognizable. Some symbols are useful because they quickly summarize a lot of information better than text labels could. For instance, country flags instead of country names, company logos instead of company names, man and woman icons instead of the words "man" and "woman".

Symbols can be powerful when used correctly. They are compact containers that hold a lot of information so if you introduce a few symbols at the start of a slide deck and pack them full of meaning, you can re-use those symbols on future slides.

For example, I often create decks where I talk about different customer segments. I will introduce each segment on its own slide and purposefully include a picture as a symbol to represent that segment. I describe that segment fully and "pack" that symbol full of meaning.

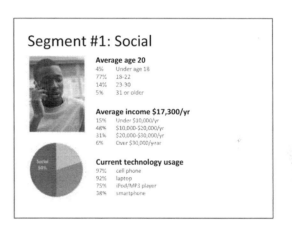

Now, I can re-use that symbol on later slides to summarize a lot of useful information visually for the reader. If there are certain ideas you want to thread throughout your slide deck, consider assigning that idea a symbol so it can be used over and over throughout your deck.

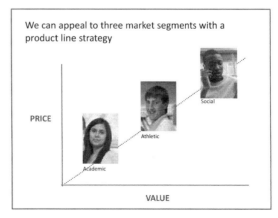

2. Organizational images

If your goal is to *drive a decision making meeting*, consider using a diagram to organize your text. Organizational pictures are abstract shapes that contain and organize text, like process flow diagrams or org charts. For instance, in describing the three sections of the Mindworks Method centered around the reader's question, each composed of four learning modules, I used this diagram to organize the text.

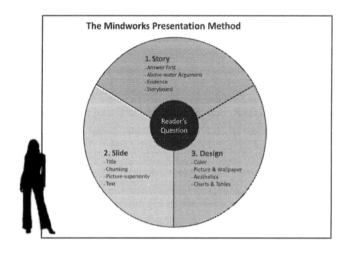

Diagrams like this are very common in boardroom-style slides, but the research on their use is mixed so they deserve special attention.

The scientific term for diagrams is knowledge maps (K-maps). K-maps have been proven useful for organizing your own thinking, analyzing issues and solving complex problems. Mind maps are a form of K-map. K-maps are especially useful for group problem-solving because they make assumptions visible and allow complex problems to be broken into discussion-sized chunks, so if you are driving a decision making meeting a K-map is a great tool.

Meetings that use visuals are more productive than meetings that do not. In one study, 159 business managers were separated into small discussion groups. Half of the groups used a flipchart to manage their discussion; the other half used a computer monitor with visualization software. The researchers wanted to know which groups generated more ideas and were more pleased with the final decision.

What they found is that those who used visuals to guide their discussion generated more ideas and were more likely to reach agreement than those who managed the meeting with flipchart notes. K-maps are powerful because they externalize assumptions where they can be discussed, and a shared understanding can be negotiated. When visuals are not used, everyone's assumptions remain invisible and disagreements can become heated and personal.

But K-maps are not always a great tool for *explaining your thinking to others*, especially if the reader is not very familiar with the topic. K-maps are frequently seen in business slides, but they are often done ineffectively. So let's address what readers need from you in order to understand and use your K-map.

K-maps contain two types of information: *structural* information and *functional* information.

Structural information shows how the information is broken into components and the spatial relationships between the components. Structural knowledge is relatively easy to learn from K-maps.

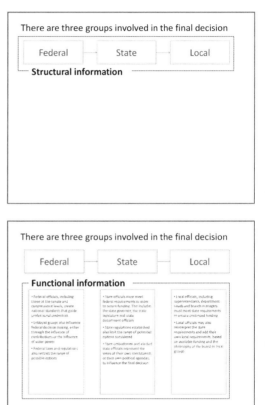

Functional information is the details describing the processes and forces working inside each component. But the functional knowledge is not explicit in the slide. It must be read word by word to be understood. Understanding the functional knowledge *is most critical for problem-solving.*

K-maps are most useful for readers who are familiar with the topic ("experts") because they already know the functional information. Stanford University researchers Barbara Tversky and Julie Heisner found experts learned structural and functional information more effectively from diagrams than from text because they had already acquired the necessary mental models. The K-map just externalized that model. So if you are communicating with people who are already familiar with the topic, then a K-map is more effective than text.

But those who were less familiar with the topic ("novices") learned the structural information equally well from text and diagrams. In addition, they learned functional informational vastly more effectively from text! So if your audience is unfamiliar with the topic, you need to build up their expertise so they can understand your K-map and engage in a productive discussion.

Expertise is built from the ground up; from functional knowledge up to structural knowledge, and not the other way around. Instead of presenting the K-map on slide one, build up the reader's functional knowledge first. Introduce each structure on its own slide and explain it using text descriptions. Then assemble all the structures together in one K-map at the end. Researchers at the University of South Wales (Sweller, Chandler and Ayres, 2002) have studied how to use text and diagrams in education, and they conclude that for novice students it is more effective to teach each structure as an isolated topic and then later show how all the structures are interrelated.

PowerPoint, the Pentagon and the Spaghetti Slide

K-maps are used frequently in the boardroom, but they are often used ineffectively. This case study and slide makeover demonstrate the correct way to use K-maps.

By 2009, the war in Afghanistan had already cost the U.S. $300 billion and the lives of over 1,000 soldiers. That summer, the U.S. government reluctantly approved another $33 billion in war spending, but as the war was going into its ninth year with no clear victory in sight, there was renewed urgency to find a winning strategy.

General Stanley A. McChrystal, leader of U.S. and NATO forces in Afghanistan, was attending one of his many daily briefings in Kabul. In one briefing, this PowerPoint slide was presented, outlining the complex web of issues that made the war so intractable.

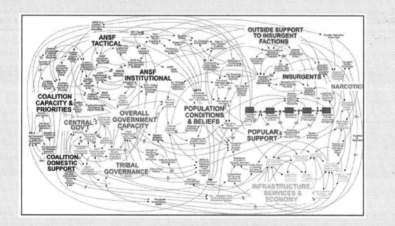

Upon seeing the complex diagram, General McChrystal commented, "When we understand that slide, we'll have won the war." The room erupted in laughter, which often happens when a five-star general cracks a joke in front of his subordinates.

The New York Times used this slide in an article deriding PowerPoint's use in the military. It came to be known as the "spaghetti slide" because it resembled long tangled strands of pasta.

Do you use diagrams like this to illustrate complex issues in the boardroom? Should you? How would you revise this slide to communicate more effectively?

We should salute the Pentagon for using diagrams like this, called K-maps, to drive important decision making meetings. The challenges they face are complex. This diagram helps externalize assumptions, clarify cause/effect relationships and helps depersonalize disagreements and get everyone on the same page so they can move forward and discuss solutions.

If everyone in the room is intimately familiar with all the issues, then this slide is fine. Experts already have functional knowledge. But given the General's comment, and the room's reaction, it's likely some were less familiar than others.

Rather than present this slide all at once, it is more effective to break it into separate structural units and present each on its own slide. Text should be used to describe the contents of each structural unit, and handouts provided, so the audience can build their expertise from functional knowledge up to structural knowledge.

Now that the audience understands the functional details inside each structure, the presenter can pull them all together into a final slide. To assist the reader with chunking, each structural unit can have borders and a distinct color to make them visually distinct.

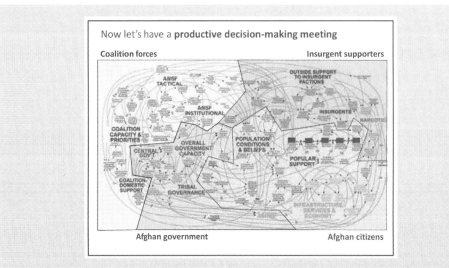

K-maps are frequently used in business, as well they should be because they facilitate good decision making meetings. But there is a right way and a wrong way to introduce them. Introducing everything all at once to unfamiliar readers is overwhelming and ineffective. But building up each structural unit one slide at a time, and explaining the functional knowledge with text explanations, is a more effective way to educate the audience.

The text on these slides is hard to read projected on a distant screen, and is more appropriate used for printed handouts or for reading at a computer. In the next chapter, we focus on the complex issue of text on slides.

Before: Spaghetti slide	**After:** Using Mindworks Presentation Method
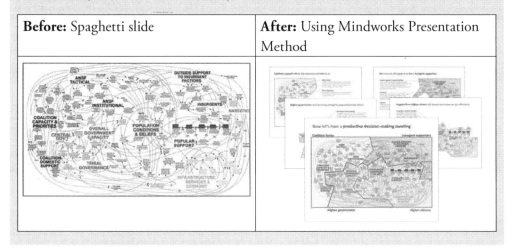	

Another example of organizational images is those abstract shapes that contain text and also convey some meaning in the shape. For instance, a speech balloon is not only a container to hold a quote, but also signifies by its shape that it represents someone's voice.

Bob Horn, a visiting lecturer at Stanford University and author of *Visual Language*, often conducts workshops and asks participants what meaning different shapes suggest to them. Some shapes have a surprisingly consistent meaning to different viewers:

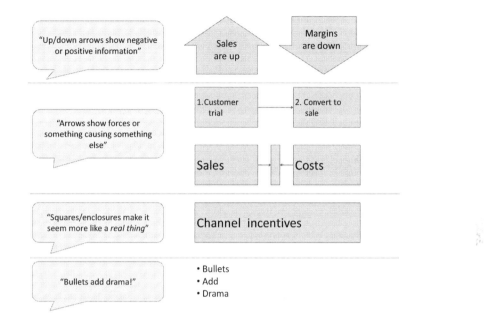

Using squares or enclosures around text is an especially useful way to make an abstract idea seem more concrete. Compare these two slides. On the left, the ideas seem vaporous while on the right the ideas seem like "real things". When you are describing a real thing, and not just an abstract idea, consider putting a shape around it.

What do customers want?

Reliable product

Good price

Fast technical support

What do customers want?

Reliable product

Good price

Fast technical support

This is not an exhaustive list, but just an example of some of the more common organizational images with inherent meaning in the shape. Other examples include checkboxes, checkmarks, stop signs and stars.

There is yet a third type of organizational image called a *signpost*, which has the purpose of calling attention to something and giving the eye a starting place and a path into your material. Bullet points are signposts, because they emphasize to the reader there are, for instance, three points made on the slide. Other types of signposts could be arrows pointing to important data point on a graph or icons placed next to three important points. Signposts are important for directing the reader's eye into your slide and we cover them more in chapter 12 on slide layout.

Creating custom icons

Images courtesy Vectorportal.com

Want to create your own slick-looking custom icons? It's easy! Here's a neat trick suggested by Information & Presentation Designer Magdalena Maslowska (www.hauteslides.com).

1. Create a circle using PowerPoint's Insert > Shape and give it a fill color. You can also add a thick border or drop shadows or other effects. This circle will be the outline for each icon in your set.

2. Find an image in PowerPoint's clip art collection, or online, that is vector art (search "Vector clip art" or visit Vectorportal.com). *Vector* means the image is composed of different shapes that can be ungrouped. To determine if something is vector art, just right click on it and select "Ungroup". (You may need to ungroup it twice).

3. After it's ungrouped, select the shapes you want to keep, delete everything else and fill the remaining shapes with a single fill color. For instance, you could use white as the fill color so the shapes will stand out against the icon's color background.

4. Regroup the remaining shapes and place the newly-grouped image on top of the circle and use the Group command to make them into a single icon.

5. Repeat the process with other vector art to create your own complete custom icon set.

Images used in this book can be seen in color at www.speakingppt.com

A summary of picture choice based on trigger words

It's fascinating to me that Jim Tracey and Walter Starkey required the use of a picture as part of their STOP format. They knew intuitively what research has now proven over the past 40 years: pictures make your message easier to understand and easier to agree with.

To recap, look at the slide title for keywords to suggest the picture that will reinforce your slide's main message.

If the slide title contains nouns, consider using an illustrative image. In particular, if the slide title contains the name of a specific person, or type of person, consider using an image of that person on the slide.

If the slide title contains an abstract idea or the primary purpose of the slide is to persuade the reader, consider using a metaphorical image.

Any time the slide lacks impact, it probably needs a picture. Again, start by looking at the slide title and ask yourself:

> *Is the idea too abstract? Will the reader have difficulty forming a mental image?* It needs a metaphor or conceptual peg, or perhaps an illustrative image if it's discussing something that isn't familiar to the reader.

> *Is the idea too boring?* It needs a concrete image to evoke an emotion. For instance, it's one thing to talk about the devastation of Hurricane Katrina on a slide, but it's completely different to show images of entire city blocks flattened into rubble to make your message impactful.

> *Is the idea impactful but the slide is covered in text?* If you have that much to say, you may need to fully explain each chunk of information on its own slide and then bring it together on the final slide, using symbols to help the reader recall the previous slides.

If the slide title contains a word that describes a spatial relationship, like *growing*, *next* to or *more* consider using an abstract shape or diagram. You can select a diagram from the table below by looking for trigger words in your slide title. For instance, a title like "Higher foreign labor costs has driven down our margins" contains the trigger words *driven down*. Using the table below, you see this suggests a cause-effect diagram.

This list is not exhaustive but a sample of commonly-used diagrams found in business slides. Consider this a foundation of diagrams which are likely familiar mental models for your readers.

In some cases, a single diagram will serve your purposes. But in many cases—likely the majority of cases—you will use some combination of two or more diagrams. For instance, you might want to communicate how one process is better than another process, so will use both a comparison diagram and a sequence diagram.

Type of Diagram	Key Message on Slide	Possible Trigger Words in Slide Title
Cause-Effect	Something leads to something else	*causes, creates, results in, drives, leads to, forces, barriers, hinders, starts with, influence, impacts, affects, explains, results in*
Sequence	Something happens in a certain order	*steps in (a process), starts with, process, first/second, goes through, steps, phases, if/then*
Comparison	Value of something compared to something else	*more/less, most/least, better/worse, best/worst, primary/secondary, top/bottom*
Components	Something is made up of various elements	*made up of, includes, levels, layers, part of, segment, reports to, total, break out, share of, percent of, majority of*
Timeline	Something changes over time or has due dates	*months, quarters, over time, growing, trend, milestone, deadline, increasing/decreasing, trend, in the next, by (date), change in, rise, decline, fluctuate*

Cause-Effect

Trigger Words: *causes, creates, results in, drives, leads to, forces, barriers, hinders, starts with, influence, impacts, affects, explains, results in*

Force Field Analysis

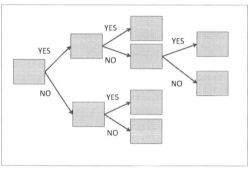

Cause-Effect Chain

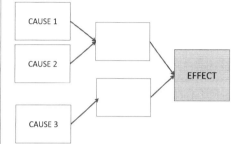

Decision Tree

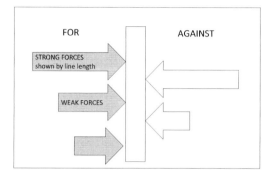

Fishbone Diagram

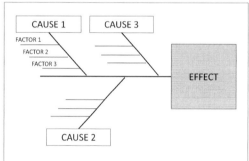

Barriers

Scatterplot

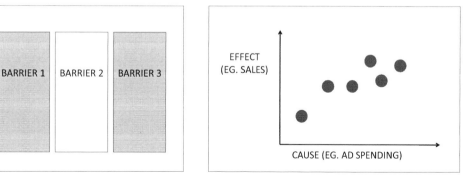

These handouts available for download at www.speakingppt.com

Sequence

Trigger Words: *steps in (a process), starts with, process, first/second, goes through, steps, phases, if/then*

Flowchart

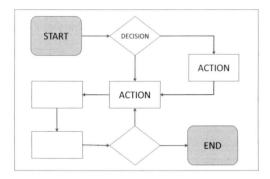

Swim Lanes

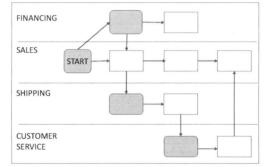

Steps/Staircase

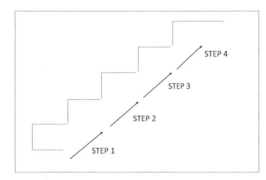

Critical Path

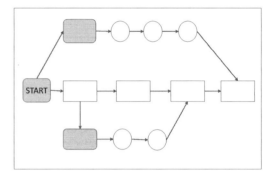

Step Chart

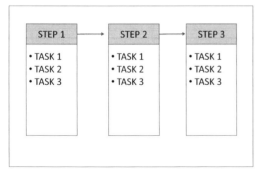

Cycle Map

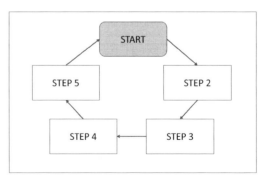

These handouts available for download at www.speakingppt.com

Comparison

Trigger Words: *more/less, most/least, better/worse, best/worst, primary/secondary, top/bottom*

Table (with text or numbers)

	COST	VALUE	TIMING
SEATTLE	Negotiable	High	Small wait
NEW YORK	Firm	High	Long wait
DALLAS	Low	Medium	Immed
WASH, DC	High	Low	Small wait

Grid (with checkmarks or Harvey Balls)

See-Saw

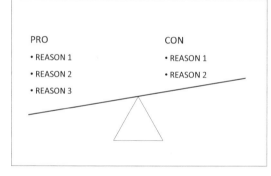

Continuum

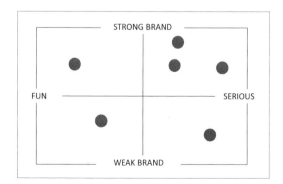

Rating Scale (eg. semantic, Likert)

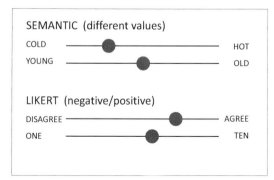

Matrix

These handouts available for download at www.speakingppt.com

Comparison

Trigger Words: *more/less, most/least, better/worse, best/worst, primary/secondary, top/bottom*

Slopegraph

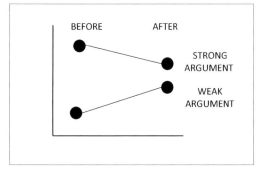

Bubble Chart

Either/Or

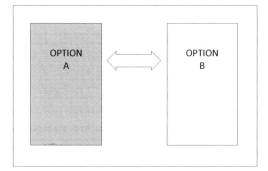

Ranking Chart

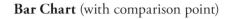

Deviation Bar Chart

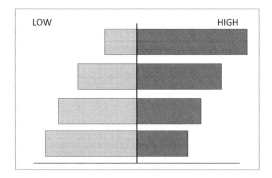

Bar Chart (with comparison point)

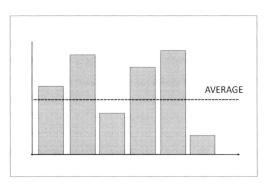

These handouts available for download at www.speakingppt.com

Component

Trigger Words: *made up of, includes, levels, layers, part of, segment, reports to, total, break out, share of, percent of, majority of*

Treemap

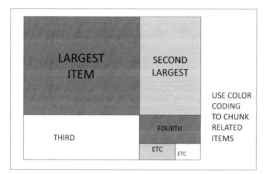

Segment Tree

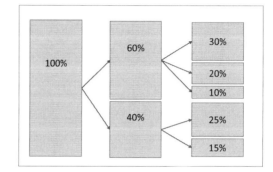

Pie Chart

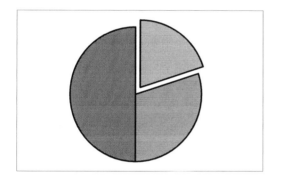

Histogram

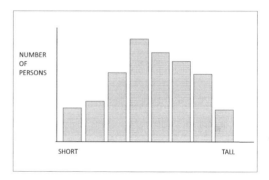

Layers

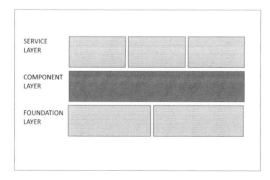

Org Chart

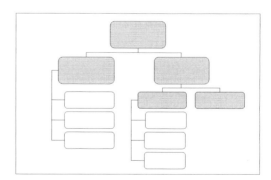

These handouts available for download at www.speakingppt.com

Component

Trigger Words: *made up of, includes, levels, layers, part of, segment, reports to, total, break out, share of, percent of, majority of*

Stacked Bar Chart

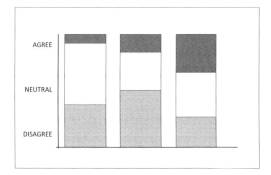

Breakout Chart

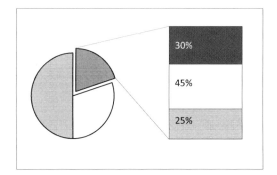

Marimekko Chart

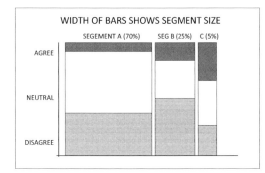

Waterfall Chart

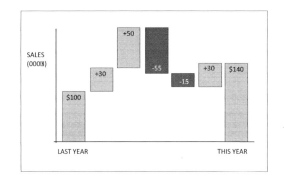

Area Chart: Total

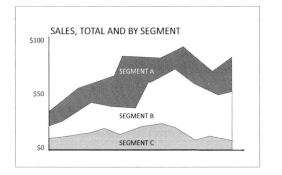

Area Chart: Percentage

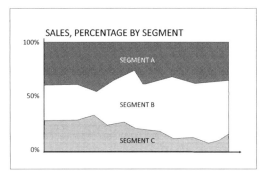

These handouts available for download at www.speakingppt.com

Timeline

Trigger Words: *months, quarters, over time, growing, trend, milestone, deadline, increasing/decreasing, trend, in the next, by (date), change in, rise, decline, fluctuate*

Timeline

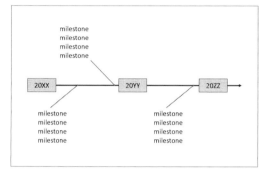

Calendar

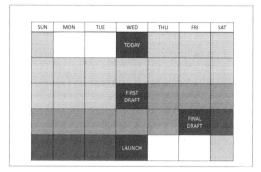

Line Chart (for continuous values)

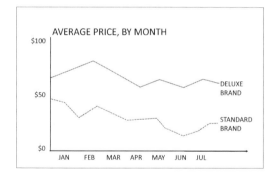

Column Chart (for values unique to that period)

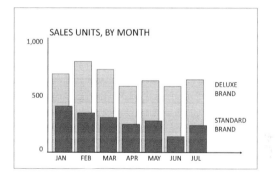

Lifecycle Diagram

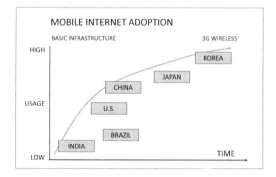

Gantt Chart

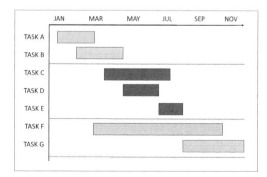

These handouts available for download at www.speakingppt.com

Back to Alex's slide

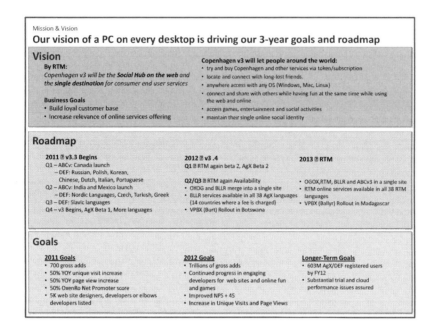

You hold Alex's slide up, rubbing your chin furiously. "I can see you've put a lot of thought into this slide, Alex. There's a lot of good information here. But I don't think people can absorb it all at once. We need to make this easy for the reader. People need some kind of visual they can hold onto while you explain the text to them."

"Let's try to think of a concrete picture that illustrates your message. Let's see. Your slide title says *our vision of a PC on every desktop is driving our roadmap*. The nouns here are *PC on every desktop*. Is that the main message on this slide? Do we need a picture of what it will look like when there's a PC on every desktop?"

Alex mulls, "Maybe I could find a stock photo online."

You agree. "That would make an abstract idea seem more concrete. It would be even better if we had a photograph that came from a real customer, to show our vision in action with some of our early adopter customers, but that may be too difficult to find. Maybe we can find a picture where there are PC's on every desktop, like in a library or a school, and say our vision is already a reality in some places."

"The other trigger word I see here is *driving*. That suggests a cause-effect diagram. We want people to understand our thinking and so this diagram makes it clear what we're trying to accomplish and why we think it will work. I also see the trigger words *3-year,* which suggests a timeline. Perhaps there's a combination diagram we can use to make our message clearer."

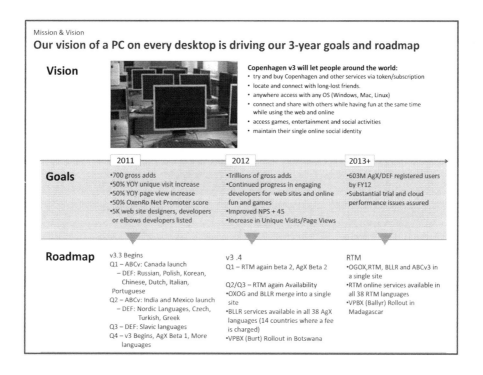

"This slide makes more sense. You've given people a picture they can hold onto while you share your plan, and you've organized the text in a way that makes the cause and effect relationships explicit. We might also want to break this into three slides and introduce the vision on one slide, the goals on another slide and the roadmap on a third slide, then bring them all together. I know that's more work, but it will be easier for the other team to comment on the plan if we take the time to educate them properly."

Before: Wall of Text   **After:** Using Mindworks Presentation Method

Above-water argument

1. When your slide is a Wall of Text, always ask: how can I use the picture-superiority effect to make this slide more impactful? There is 40 years of research showing pictures make it easier to understand, agree with and recall your message.

2. Concrete pictures are more effective than abstract pictures, because they form a conceptual peg that activates a specific mental image, are more likely to trigger emotions and there may be an illusion-of-truth effect native to pictures. Illustrative images literally show what the text is describing and are best for educating the reader. Metaphorical images figuratively show what the text is describing and are best for persuading the audience or making an abstract idea more concrete.

3. Abstract pictures are especially good for illustrating complex spatial relationships. Representative images summarize complex data or pack data into a symbol for later re-use, relieving the load on working memory. Organizational images, like K-maps, organize text into spatial relationships and are excellent tools for decision making meetings. But if the audience is not familiar with the topic, you should build up their functional knowledge one slide at a time before bringing all the components together into a final K-map.

4. Look for trigger words in your slide title to focus on the most important picture to reinforce your main message.

Recommended reading

Imagery and Text by Allan Paivio and Mark Sadoski digs deep into the way the brain processes text and images. This chapter of *Speaking PowerPoint* hardly scratches the surface on the rich research and theory behind visual thinking. *Imagery and Text* covers many other aspects, such as episodic and semantic memory, Schema Theory, the mnemonic value of pictures, how text is converted into meaning through associative and referential connections between text and visuals, and much more. For anyone serious about really understanding how the mind processes pictures, this book is highly recommended.

Visual Language: Global Communication for the 21st Century by Robert E. Horn is an excellent and highly readable primer on the role of pictures in literacy. Pictures have been treated like second-class citizens in the education sector, and Horn's book lays bare visuals as a full language that we have only begun to understand.

Visual Thinking by Rudolf Arnheim is the seminal book on visual thinking. It was ground-breaking in its time when the reigning theory was that people thought in words rather than pictures. It marked a historical shift and a new focus on understanding the role of visual thinking.

CHAPTER 10

Text

Briefing decks, discussion decks and reading decks

THE DEBRIS ASSESSMENT TEAM, made up of engineers from Boeing, NASA and the Johnson Space Center, were frustrated. They were asked to assess the danger to the space shuttle Columbia, which had been hit by a pillow-sized piece of SOFI (spray-on foam insulation) that came loose during liftoff. But their recommendation depended on the exact location and angle of impact and NASA had denied their requests for additional photographs of Columbia's wing while in orbit.

Instead, the engineers were using a crude spreadsheet model, called *Crater*, normally used to assess damage caused by ice crystals no larger than a grape. Crater predicted a two-pound piece of foam striking the wing at 500 miles per hour would tear right through to the wing's aluminum frame. But Crater tended to over-predict damage even using small objects so it was unclear if this prediction was accurate or exaggerated. Again, they needed images of the wing to make a better assessment.

On February 21, 2003 engineers from the Debris Assessment Team gathered in a briefing room to present their findings to NASA management. This was one of the slides discussed during their one-hour presentation, where they admitted they could not show conclusively that Columbia's wing was damaged, and they needed additional visual evidence.

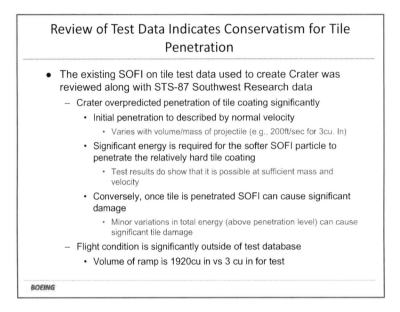

NASA managers were not convinced there was a danger to Columbia and once again declined to take new photographs of Columbia's wing in orbit. It was common for debris to hit the wing during liftoff. Other technical experts advised it was very unlikely that a two-pound chunk of foam could seriously damage Columbia's wing. Maneuvering Columbia to provide a good look at the damaged wing would delay other tasks the astronauts were working on. In addition, NASA managers reasoned, even if the wing was damaged there was no way to repair the craft in orbit.

NASA officials again denied requests for additional imagery and approved the shuttle's re-entry into the Earth's atmosphere. The wing was indeed badly compromised and the shuttle tore apart during re-entry. All seven astronauts onboard were lost.

Afterward, an independent review board looked into what lead to the disaster. They uncovered a complex matrix of reasons—budget cuts, personal agendas, poor decision making processes. But one page of that report was dedicated to this slide, noting how critical information was buried in sub-bullet points and indecipherable to NASA managers.

Bulleted slides like this are common in business. But are bullet points the best way to show text in a boardroom-style slide? How would you modify the text on this slide to make the risk more obvious?

Trouble with text

Text is the most common reason people get into trouble with PowerPoint. Author and trainer Dave Paradi conducts a semi-annual survey to learn what bothers people most about PowerPoint. No surprise, the top three complaints are related to text.

The speaker read the slides to us	69.2%
Text so small I couldn't read it	48.2%
Full sentences instead of bullet points	48.0%
Slides hard to see because of color choice	33.0%
Overly complex diagrams or charts	27.9%

Source: Annoying PowerPoint Survey, Dave Paradi, 2009

Text is the thorniest issue for PowerPoint. Several commentators offer advice like "don't use bullet points" or "only use six words on a slide" or "no more than six lines, six words each line" or "minimum 30 point font." Some commentators advise using pictures instead of text, or pictures with very minimal text.

But is this advice meant for ballroom-style slides or boardroom-style slides? This advice might be fine for a keynote address to a roomful of sleepy conference attendees. But in a boardroom, with the VP of marketing waiting to hear why he should spend $5 million on a custom-built global inventory management system, the commentators have no advice other than "use a text document."

And why the hostility toward bullet points? Does adding a little dot in front of a sentence really render it useless? Instead of reasoned explanations we are presented with ridiculously satirized versions of slides densely packed with bullets. Or dim clichés like "bullets points kill presentations". Or the academically exacting "bullet points can only show linear and hierarchical relationships in a multivariate world".

Is this just personal opinion? What does the research say?

Since text is such a thorny issue, someone must have done some research on this. And, indeed, someone has. Over the past 40 years, educators have done hundreds, perhaps thousands, of studies on how to communicate clearly to students using text, speech and pictures. And we have made new discoveries over the past ten years which tell us, at least in a boardroom setting, where the commentators' advice is correct and when different rules would make you an even more effective communicator.

You will learn, for instance, that the rules for boardroom-style presentations are different than the rules for ballroom-style presentations. And even in boardroom-style presentations, there are different rules for different kinds of presentations:

Briefing decks are presented by a speaker in front of a large, mostly non-interactive, audience. For instance, if you are explaining your marketing plan to a roomful of country managers at the annual conference, the audience is largely passive and the presenter is controlling the pace of the presentation.

Discussion decks are intended for group meetings, where the slides may be viewed projected on a screen, as printed handouts or viewed on a computer screen for remote participants.

These are very interactive sessions, where participants may be flipping through the pages, writing notes and asking questions.

Reading decks are intended for standalone reading. I commonly prepare research reports in PowerPoint and my clients read them standalone at a computer screen and forward them to others in the company as email attachments.

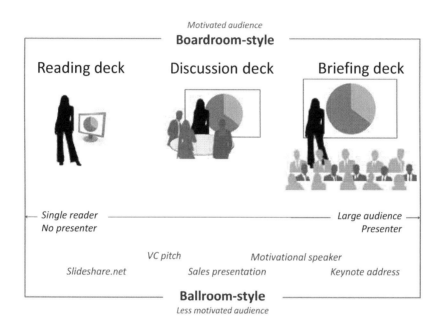

People get into trouble with text because they create a deck appropriate for one situation and try to use it in another. Or they try to take advice meant for ballroom-style PowerPoint and apply it in the boardroom. For instance, have you ever seen a speaker show a slide densely packed with text, then chuckle and say "Well, this is a bit of an eye chart. But anyway…" and continue speaking? This person is using a reading deck for his presentation. And it doesn't work, does it?

Advice that makes you effective in one situation can make you ineffective in another. This chapter summarizes 40 years of research on how to communicate most effectively with text in different situations. And it especially focuses on the newest research published over the past decade.

Because audience presentations are the most common use for PowerPoint, we begin with a discussion of briefing decks.

Briefing decks and the split-attention effect

The most common type of boardroom-style slide is a briefing deck. The presenter will be standing in front of a room and controlling the pace of the presentation. This could include speaking at an all-hands meeting, presenting your marketing plan to a roomful of regional sales reps or even conducting a workshop.

The audience will be largely passive, perhaps taking notes or skimming the handouts, but there will be limited opportunities to interrupt and question the speaker during the presentation. As a practical matter, this usually involves larger groups of perhaps 20 or more persons simply because people become more passive as the group size increases. Speaking to a group of 20 of more persons generally demands a briefing deck.

While these are large-audience presentations, they differ from ballroom-style presentations because the audience is already committed to listening and understanding your argument. This is not a motivational speech or a sales speech, but a business presentation.

The following nine principles, based on hundreds of studies, can help inform how you use text on your slides to communicate effectively.

1. Use slides when you present

The first question is: should you use slides at all when you present? The answer is yes. Slides will make you a more effective communicator and increase your credibility in boardroom settings.

Several studies have found presenters are more effective when they use slides. In a 1986 study by Professor Douglas Vogel, a presenter tried to persuade a roomful of students to attend a time management workshop. When the presenter used slides, students were 43% more likely to register for that workshop than when the presenter used no slides. In fact, when the presenter used no slides, students were *less* interested in the workshop than they were before they heard the presentation.

In 2005, Professors Andeweg and Blokzijl tested whether students learned more when the instructor used slides. Out of six presentations, the two groups which scored the worst on tests were the students who watched lectures without slides. The researchers repeated the study again in 2007 and found the same result—students learned the least when the presenter used no slides.

In a 2008 review of 15 research papers on PowerPoint effectiveness, Kevin Johnson of Nova Southeast University concludes PowerPoint either improves a presentation or has no effect. It was harmful to learning only when used inappropriately, with sound effects, animated text, and graphics not related to the learning material. In all other cases, using PowerPoint either improved learning or had no effect.

The reason is straightforward: slides make your points explicit and provide a structure that helps your audience follow your logic. In fact, learning was improved the most when a below-average presenter used slides, because the audience became even more dependent on the slide content.

In both the Andeweg studies and Vogel studies, the researchers also found that slides increased the credibility of below-average speakers. Above-average speakers' credibility was not enhanced by using slides, but the credibility of below-average presenters grew to nearly match the above-average speaker's credibility scores.

So, the evidence suggests that you will communicate more clearly and enhance your credibility when you use PowerPoint slides, and especially for average and below-average presenters.

What should be on those slides? Text? Pictures? Both? How much text? Should you use bullets? We answer all those questions next.

2. Do not combine extensive text and pictures on a slide

We learned in the last chapter that adding pictures to your slides makes your message clearer and more persuasive. But you should avoid *speaking* and showing a slide with extensive text and pictures because it will make you a less effective communicator. Slides should contain text or pictures with sparse text, but not pictures with extensive text.

For example, imagine you need to brief your executives on sales and market share trends, and discuss some potential solutions. Your audience will understand you up to *twice as well* if you use a text-only slide or a picture slide with sparse text.

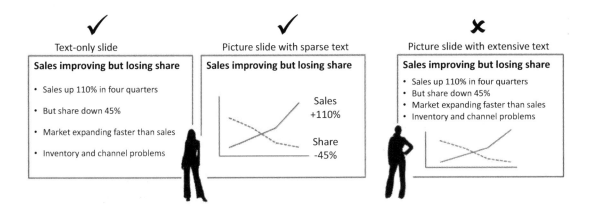

Educational researchers find students learn *less* when they hear and see the same text accompanied by a picture. In 2009, Dr. Chris Atherton, an educational researcher at the University of Central Lancashire, conducted studies with university students. Lecturers taught one group using picture slides with sparse text, while a second group was taught using picture slides with extensive bullet points. Students understood the material more than twice as well when the lecturer used picture slides with sparse text.

A 2006 study by Professors Le Bohec and Jamet also found accounting students learned less when a picture slide contained full sentences versus short bullet points. Students listened to a 30-minute recording of a speaker using picture slides without text, picture slides with sparse text or picture slides with several full sentences. Students learned equally well from the picture slides with no text and sparse text, but learned less when the slide contained full sentences that the speaker repeated.

In addition, the students who saw the full sentences did not believe they could actually perform the accounting steps, which was not heard from the other two groups of students.

Professors Richard Mayer and Roxana Moreno found the same results in their studies. One group of students watched a presentation with speech and pictures. But when the same presentation also included the text of the speaker's words, learning dropped nearly in half! Mayer calls this the *redundancy principle,* where extensive text that is repeated by the speaker's words harms learning when accompanied by a picture.

John Sweller's studies at the University of New South Wales corroborate this. Sweller proposed the Cognitive Load Theory, which says that duplicate spoken and printed text is less effective than spoken text or printed text alone when the presentation includes pictures. That's because working memory becomes overloaded with redundant spoken and written text competing with the picture for limited working memory slots.

There are two explanations for this. One, the split-attention effect, argues that the audience must visually flick back and forth between the picture and text. Holding text in working memory so it can be matched with the picture puts a burden on working memory. But if the speaker provides that text aurally, the audience can inspect the picture without the burden of holding redundant text in working memory.

The other explanation is that "learning" involves attaching new information to existing information, and this process takes place in working memory. When working memory is overloaded with pictures and spoken and written text, it leaves less working memory for the important step of integrating the new knowledge with existing knowledge.

It's important to point out that this refers to pictures that are meant to be studied, like illustrative images or charts. But some pictures, like K-maps or icons that just organize the text on your slides, are not redundant and don't need to be matched with the text.

Study after study finds pictures accompanied by speech and the same text reduces learning. So, to ensure your communications are as effective as they can be, avoid presenting slides with pictures and text. Instead, use a text slide or a picture slide with sparse text, which would include a slide title and short 1–4 word phrases that are closely integrated with the picture.

3. Use bullet points separated by whitespace to add drama, but avoid sub-bullet points

When you use a slide with text, should you use bullet points? By "bullet point", I literally mean the small dot in front of the sentence, rather than the length or grammatical correctness of the sentence. There is a vocal, but largely unsubstantiated, opinion that bullet points should be banned.

But the research says this is simply not true, at least for boardroom-style slides.

Robert E. Horn, who conducts workshops on visual thinking, often asks participants how they react to bullet points. The most common response from audiences? Bullet points add drama!

- Workshop participants say

- that bullet points

- add drama!

There are times we want to add drama to our points. For instance, consider these two lists. One contains bullets points, the other does not. Do you see the difference?

We must increase our co-marketing investments	• We must increase our co-marketing investments
We must provide training and technical support during sales engagements	• We must provide training and technical support during sales engagements
We must provide a differentiated joint value proposition to sales reps	• We must provide a differentiated joint value proposition to sales reps

The list on the left seems like an uncertain set of wispy ideas. They lack concreteness or urgency. The list on the right seems like three tangible things. You can almost feel their weight. In a boardroom-style slide, bullet points can help your ideas feel emphatic and real.

Text also needs to be chunked. You can adjust the line spacing to use whitespace and separate each bullet point into a visually distinct chunk. When the bullets are too close, all the text bleeds together and the audience will have more difficulty finding the separate chunks of information.

• We must increase our co-marketing investments	• We must increase our co-marketing investments
• We must provide training and technical support during sales engagements	• We must provide training and technical support during sales engagements
• We must provide a differentiated joint value proposition to sales reps	• We must provide a differentiated joint value proposition to sales reps

But avoid sub-bullet points. Each bullet point adds drama, but when you litter a slide with indented bullet points, all crying for attention, you create visual havoc. The excessive bullet points become visually noisy and the left indentation makes it hard to chunk. If a bullet point has several sub-bullet points, it may require its own slide.

- We must increase demand gen
  - co-marketing investments
  - partner incentives

- We must provide sales enablement
  - technical training and support
  - sales training

- We need stronger value
  - differentiated joint value prop
  - custom solutions

- We must increase our co-marketing investments and partner incentives

- We must provide training and technical support during sales engagements

- We must provide a differentiated joint value prop and custom solutions

When commentators criticize *bullet points*, I believe they are referring to the misuse of bullet points, which means excessively crowded and with limited whitespace. But bullet points can add drama and concreteness to your ideas. Other ways to accomplish the same thing include placing your text inside shapes, numbering or adding icons next to your text.

4. Use concise or full sentences

When you use bullet points, should you use concise or full sentences? A concise sentence is what we typically think of when we say "bullet point"—a terse, often grammatically incorrect sentence written like a newspaper headline. An example will illustrate the difference:

Full sentence	We should focus our launch activities on the college market
Concise	Launch should focus on college market

The commentators' advice on this appears to favor concise sentences. The "six lines of text, six words per line" advice could be interpreted as six bullet points each six words long, or three bullet points each 12 words long. Other commentators advise using a single sentence of six words—perhaps the slide title—along with some sort of picture.

There have not been many studies testing the effectiveness of concise versus full sentences. What research exists suggests, for text-only slides, full and concise sentences are equally effective because the audience learns most from the speaker and the slides just give the talk structure and allow the audience to study the materials longer.

In the Le Bohec and Jamet study, concise sentences lead to better test scores than full sentences. However, the slides included pictures so there was a redundancy effect that may have contributed to the superiority of concise sentences. Another study found both were equally effective. In the 2005 Andeweg and Blokzijl study, students learned equally well regardless of the length of the sentence. In the 2007 repeat of this study, the researchers found the same results. In fact, when the presenter was below-average, reading from a prepared script and avoiding eye contact or hand gestures, the students were especially dependent on the full sentence slides.

Most of the learning appears to come from the speaker and the slides simply provide structure so the students can follow along. And for average or below-average speakers, full sentences are especially effective because the audience will depend more on the slides than they would for an above-average presenter.

This shouldn't be a license to type long sentences in 12-point font. Andeweg and Blokzijl used 32-point Arial font in their studies, effectively limiting the slide to about four bullet points, each 1–2 lines long when separated by whitespace. In practice, when bullet points become three lines long or more, people are less motivated to read them at all. So use concise sentences to provide structure to your talk or full sentences, 1–2 lines long, if you want the audience to study your message in more detail.

5. Use the speaker's keywords in the bullet point to sync and launch

As the speaker talks through a slide, the audience needs to know which bullet point he is covering. So, bullet points should be short enough, and use keywords, that allow the speaker to easily *synchronize* his speech with the bullet point and *launch* into discussing that bullet point.

Professor David Farkas suggests that bullet points should use the speaker's keywords to assist with this *sync and launch.*

If a speaker begins a new topic saying "Our primary market should be college students" the audience will be looking for keywords like *primary market* and *college students.* Consider two ways to phrase the same bullet point:

• Focus on post-secondary students for launch activities	• Primary market should be college students

The bullet point on the left is logically correct but the audience is lost. They cannot locate the keywords the presenter is speaking. But the bullet point on the right does contain the keywords and the audience can follow the speaker more easily.

Similarly, the bullet point should not be so lengthy that the keywords are lost in the text clutter. Again, if the speaker begins a new topic saying "Our primary market should be college students", which bullet is written so the keywords are easy to locate?

• College students and university students show the highest demand for our premium-priced offerings and should be the focus of the campaign	• Primary market should be college students

So, use short bullet points with prominent keywords to facilitate sync and launch. Farkas notes shorter bullet points also give the speaker more room to extemporize while longer bullets can lock the speaker into covering a specific point. For instance, the longer bullet point requires you defend your recommendation based on market demand. The shorter bullet allows you a longer leash so you can talk about market demand, strategic fit, long-term customer value and so on.

In practice, you may find yourself revising your bullet points as you practice your presentation. A bullet point which is logically correct on paper may feel and sound awkward when spoken. In this case, revise the bullet point to sync with your natural speaking style.

6. Limit your slide to 3–4 bullet points

When commentators criticize bullet points, what they are really talking about is those slides full of bullet points and sub-bullet points, with reduced font sizes that make them inscrutable. Hence, the advice of "minimum 30 point font".

There are two benefits to 30-point font. First and most obvious, it ensures the slide is readable to everyone in the room. But second, it limits the amount of text you can put on a slide to what will fit working memory.

In the Andeweg and Blokzijl studies, the text was 32 point arial font. In the Le Bohec and Jamet studies, the presentation was given on a computer screen and the font was readable. But in both studies, the number of bullet points was limited to about 2–5 points per slide.

The reader can only hold 3–4 ideas in mind at once. So you will want to limit your slide to containing, at most, 3–4 ideas that support your title. There's nothing magic about 30-point font, but in practice it limits your slide to about eight lines of text. Reduce the font and you may try to put too much content on the slide. Even if it's separated by whitespace, more than 3–4 bullet points begins to overwhelm working memory and leads to information overload.

Some people resist this idea, insisting that this is just another example of how PowerPoint dumbs down thinking. *If I have six things to say, and they are all important, then PowerPoint has to accommodate that.*

Well, maybe you do have six important things to say. But when you are trying to sell ideas in the boardroom, you need to simplify. Otherwise, your six important ideas are likely to become lost. Politicians know this principle; they may have 20 ideas for improvement, but when they campaign they stick to three main messages. In the book *Made to Stick*, the authors tell of Bill Clinton's 1992 U.S. presidential election campaign where he stuck to one compelling message, *it's the economy, stupid*, rather than trying to campaign on too many ideas.

Advertisers know that products are complex but selling ideas means simplifying. You see this in taglines where advertisers focus on three ideas at a time, but not more.

"The few, the proud, the marines"   (US Marine Corps)
"Play. Laugh. Grow"   (Fisher Price)
"Food, folks and fun"   (McDonald's)

What happens to these taglines if you try to cram more ideas in?

"The few, the strong, the proud, the patriotic, the marines"
"Play. Laugh. Love. Learn. Grow"
"Food, folks, family, fun and freebies"

It just turns into word soup. The mind can't juggle five ideas at once so the words lose their meaning. A joyous tagline becomes a checklist.

So, perhaps you do have six important ideas you need to tell the reader. But *cramming them all onto one slide defeats your purpose.* You need to find a way to simplify your ideas to 3–4 on a slide. Find ways to collapse a couple of ideas into a larger idea, turn a bullet point with several sub-bullet points into its own slide, or combine like ideas into 3–4 super-sets of ideas.

Overwhelms working memory	**Respects working memory**
1. Reseller incentives	1. Resellers: training and incentives
2. Reseller training	2. Marketing: advertising campaign and social media marketing
3. Advertising campaign	
4. Social media marketing campaign	
5. Back to school promotion	3. Promotions: Back to school campaign and direct mail coupons
6. Direct mail coupons	

Do you see how the list on the left looks like word soup? Rather than emphasize six important points, you have reduced the reader's ability to hold this in memory and extract any meaning. The list on the right contains the same information, but chunked to fit the reader's ability to understand.

This is not a hard and fast rule. There may be times you need to list and discuss individually more than four things, like the eight new features on a competitor's product or the six terms that your sales reps are authorized to negotiate. But, when communicating effectively in the idea marketplace, simplifying ideas gives you an advantage so strive for no more than 3–4 bullet points per slide.

7. Use short 2–3 word phrases as visual cues

While presenting a picture slide, you may have to direct the reader's audience to certain parts of the picture. In this case, use short 2–3 words phrases so you can say something like "If you'll look at the *operating system* layer, you'll notice…"and the audience can quickly find the phrase "operating system" and orient themselves to the correct location on the slide. Although lengthy and redundant text makes your communication less effective, short 2–3 word text phrases on a picture slide are helpful.

In 2008, Professor Richard Mayer re-examined his *redundancy principle* by conducting this study. Students watched a short video narrated by a female voice. One group saw pictures with no text, another saw pictures with short 2–3 word text phrases next to parts of the diagram to direct the audience's attention. Rather than overwhelm working memory, the short text phrases communicated the lesson material more effectively, as shown by student grades.

Several other researchers have tried to measure this effect. Results so far are mixed; some can replicate this effect, others find only weak improvements with 2–3 word visual cues and others find no improvement.

Still, it's important to know that short 2–3 word text phrases on a picture will not harm understanding, and may even improve it. As a practical matter, short phrases also help the presenter direct the audience to attend to different parts of the slide while they sync and launch.

8. If you must present pictures and extensive text

There may be times you simply must show extensive text and pictures together. In that case, here are two proven ways to ensure your communication doesn't suffer:

- Show the picture and text slides separately. In a 2002 study, Professors Mayer and Moreno found students learned better when a presenter showed picture slides followed by text slides, than when the presenter showed the picture and text on the same slide.

- Provide handouts. In the Le Bohec and Jamet study, where concise sentences were more effective than full sentences next to a picture, they conducted a followup study. When the students were allowed to take notes during the presentation, students scored equally well for long and short sentences, reversing the negative effect of speech, text and pictures.

9. Do not animate text to control attention

Some speakers manage the audience's attention by revealing each bullet point as they speak to it. This makes intuitive sense. If you reveal one bullet point at a time, you aren't overwhelming working memory, right?

Mayer studied this and found that, regardless of whether the text was presented all at once or revealed as the presenter spoke, the student scores did not change.

In 2007, Le Bohec and Jamet studied whether the split-attention effect could be overcome by animating full sentence text rather than showing it all at once. And like Mayer, they found student learning was damaged whether the text was provided all at once or animated in as the presenter spoke.

As we covered in chapter 8, the research on animated text is bleak and finds students learn less than displaying all the text at once. The problem is that audiences learn best when they control the pace of the reading. Putting up all the text at once allows them to read and re-read whatever they need, see where the argument is going, and study the material longer.

There may be times animating text makes sense for other reasons, such as to keep the audience in suspense while you reveal the top five complaints among customers. But as a rule, animating text generally makes your communications less effective.

So, to summarize, the nine principles for using text effectively in a briefing deck are:

1. Use slides when you present
2. Do not combine extensive text and pictures on a slide
3. Use bullet points separated by whitespace to add drama, but avoid sub-bullet points
4. Use concise or full sentences
5. Use the speaker's keywords in the bullet point to sync and launch
6. Limit your slide to 3–4 bullet points
7. Use short 2–3 word phrases as visual cues
8. If you must present pictures and extensive text: present the picture slide and text slide separately or provide handouts for note-taking
9. Do not animate text to control attention

So, the commentators' advice on how to use text on slides is supported by research in some cases, but not in all cases. On the other hand, many commentators are talking about ballroom-style presentations where the goal is to inspire and excite a somewhat disinterested audience. Communicating effectively with boardroom-style slides requires a different approach to text based on 40 years of research, some of it published only over the past ten years.

Discussion decks and handouts

The research discussed above assumes the speaker is controlling the presentation's pace. But when the audience can control the pace, then the problem of text and pictures on the same slide goes away completely. That's because the audience has more time to study the text and pictures than they would as a passive audience member.

In fact, communication effectiveness increases in general when the audience can control the pace of the presentation. In 2003, Professor Mayer conducted a study where students either listened passively to a computer-based lecture, or they could control the speed of the lecture, pause it and re-listen to it. Students understood the material 70% more when they could control the pace, and remembered twice as much when they were tested a week later. This effect, called the *interactivity principle*, is a well-established guideline when designing e-learning courses.

A discussion deck differs from a briefing deck in that it generally, but not always, involves a small and interactive group. While you may approach it as a presentation, in reality the audience will interrupt frequently to ask clarifying questions, offer suggestions, share conflicting opinions and so on. Especially if a higher ranking officer in the company attends, the attendees will influence the pace.

In this case, you can modify the rules for briefing decks. In particular:

1. Give people handouts

Showing slides on the wall limits what information people can view. On one hand, this would appear to put you in control of the presentation and focus attention. On the other hand, the handouts allow people to flip forward and backward as needed even as you're presenting a single slide.

Educational researchers find students learn more when they have printed handouts. A 2009 study at Duke University found students scored 73% on short answer tests when they had printed handouts during a lecture and only 66% without handouts. They scored lower even though both groups were given the handouts to study before the test, similar to how business managers may review the slides after the meeting. Handouts will similarly help your audience understand you better.

Some people argue that people will be distracted if they have handouts. But the Duke study proves just the opposite; motivated readers learn more, not less, with handouts. More importantly, if the reader is flipping ahead while you're speaking, it means your message is not very engaging and they are distracted looking for something more relevant to study.

Another argument is the speaker wants to control the pace of the presentation and they lose control when the audience has handouts. I also disagree with this argument. Some in the audience are very familiar with the problem and others will be new to the problem. Finding one pace that meets everyone's needs is implausible. Handouts let them proceed at the pace they need.

In fact, handouts may be better than projecting the slides on the wall for small-group meetings. It's easier to study the slides up close, rather than from 20 feet away, and people can write notes.

Always remember to add slide numbers to your slides. It's frustrating for everyone when someone asks "what slide are we on?" and the slides are not numbered. This advice is obvious, but I've been in too many meetings when this obvious advice was not followed.

The issue of providing handouts is controversial. Some experienced speakers report poor experiences with audiences when they provide handouts and are strongly against them. Others report good experiences. My own experiences have been good, and as an attendee I also like to have handouts so I can bounce around and gather the information I need at my own pace. I've been in meetings without handouts that lacked focus and without handouts I couldn't get oriented again. So my personal bias, supported by research, is to provide handouts.

2. Use slides with pictures and text

When the audience controls the pace, you can use pictures and text on a slide. There is no split-attention effect as long as the audience has enough time to match the text and pictures. Several studies, summarized in a 2002 doctoral dissertation by Huib Tabbers, show the negative effects of using speech, text and pictures together at the same time disappears completely when the reader controls the pace.

3. Limit your slide to 3–4 bullet points

With printed handouts, you can reduce the font size and will be tempted to add more bullet points and sub-bullet points. As long as the slide is legible, there's no reason to stick to 3–4 bullet points, right?

However, do not let this become a license to add more bullet points to your slide. The reader can only hold 3–4 ideas in mind at once. It's easy to overwhelm the reader's working memory and turn your focused message into a muddled mess by adding more bullet points and sub-bullet points. So resist the urge to add more bullet points just because you have more room.

In terms of slide design, a briefing deck or a reading deck work equally well as a discussion deck. That's because the reader can direct their attention wherever it suits them and slow the pace if they need more time or clarity on any item.

So, to summarize, the seven principles for using text effectively in a discussion deck are:

> 1. Provide handouts or distribute a copy of the deck beforehand, so readers can control the pace
> 2. Use slides with text and pictures
> 3. Use 3–4 bullet points separated by whitespace, and avoid sub-bullet points
> 4. Use concise or full sentences
> 5. Use the speaker's keywords in the bullet point to sync and launch
> 6. Use 2–3 word phrases as visual cues
> 7. Do not animate text to control attention

We now talk about reading decks, where there is no presenter.

Reading decks and the selective reading block

Reading decks are read standalone at a computer screen or as printed handouts, without a presenter. The biggest difference is the amount of body text needed. Without a presenter to elaborate, you need to add the speaker's words directly to the slide. Following are the principles for using text effectively in a reading deck:

1. Write bullet points as full sentences

Write the text of your bullet points out as full sentences, not concise sentences. This is first and foremost for the writer's benefit, so you can fully develop, evaluate and refine your own thinking. It's also for the reader's benefit, so they don't need to infer too much from fragmented bullet thoughts.

Bullet points are great for outlining your argument, but poor for developing ideas. Writing is an analytic process. Most writers begin with hazy half-formed thoughts. Writing full sentences helps authors to ramble and take tangents and *find their message*, which they only had a vague notion of when they started. Writing full sentences will help you develop and refine your ideas.

But bullet points block you from developing and refining ideas. Bullets allow you to express thoughts in vague sentence fragments. While a writer might take several paragraphs to flesh out their thinking in a text document, and later realize their thinking is flawed or incomplete, bullet points allow flawed thinking to remain flawed. So use full sentences to develop and refine your ideas.

Readers also need to see your text as full sentences. PowerPoint's defaults encourage authors to write concise sentences that are grammatically incorrect and leave a lot to be inferred. A slide full of concise sentences leads to an overly-terse writing style where the reader must make too many inferences to deduce the slide's message. The bullet points and sub-bullet points are an unnecessarily vague way to present what you would have written in a text document: full sentences.

So, defy PowerPoint's defaults, and the conventions appropriate only for briefing decks, and write in full grammatically correct sentences. It will improve your own thought process and make your ideas clearer for the reader.

2. Use the laws of chunking—3–4 bullets, whitespace and labels

Even though you can write your bullet in smaller font, you should still strive for 3–4 bullet points per slide because of the limits of working memory. Again, this is not a hard and fast rule but follow it if you can and break it knowing that the reader will have more difficulty forming a single coherent idea from 5 or more bullet points.

In addition to separating your bullets with whitespace, remember the law of chunking and use a label to act like a handle on a briefcase to carry your idea into working memory. Especially as you write longer bullet points as sentences or paragraphs, the label becomes an important summary.

There are several ways to add labels to bullet points:

Typical bulleted slide. Notice how difficult it is to chunk and carry into working memory.

Label in front of the bullet. The reader can carry three ideas into working memory using the labels.

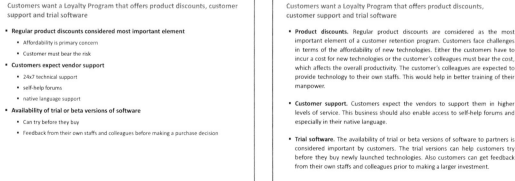

Key words bolded. Try to cast your sentence so the key words are at the beginning, or close to the beginning, of the sentence.

Label above the bullet point. In this case, you can use a smaller font size for the body text.

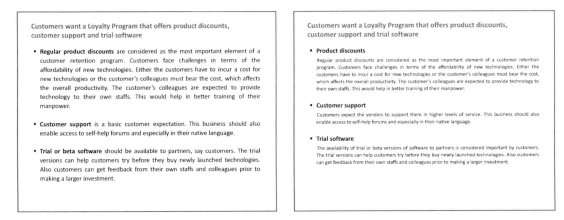

3. Consider using shapes or icons instead of bullet points

The bullet point's main value is acting as a signpost to direct the eye, and make an abstract idea more concrete. But shapes, icons and other graphic elements can accomplish the same thing. Since labels also act as signposts, there may not be much value in using an actual bullet point.

Shapes instead of bullet points

Icons instead of bullet points

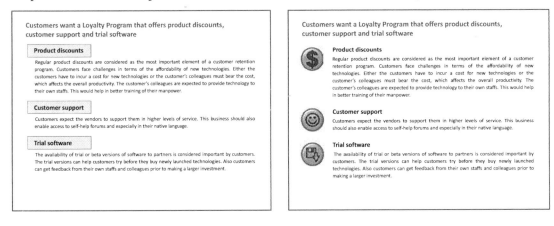

4. Use selective reading blocks

You can and you should use bullet points in boardroom-style slides to add emphasis to your ideas when you use them correctly: written as full sentences, chunked with whitespace and clearly labeled. But there is an alternative that is even better than bullet points: the selective reading block.

Compare the bulleted slide on the left with the slide on the right showing the exact same information using selective reading blocks.

Bullet points

Customers want a Loyalty Program that offers product discounts, customer support and trial software	

- **Regular product discounts** are considered as the most important element of a customer retention program. Customers face challenges in terms of the affordability of new technologies. Either the customers have to incur a cost for new technologies or the customer's colleagues must bear the cost, which affects the overall productivity. The customer's colleagues are expected to provide technology to their own staffs. This would help in better training of their manpower.

- **Customer support** is a basic customer expectation. This business should also enable access to self-help forums and especially in their native language.

- **Trial or beta software** should be available to partners, say customers. The trial versions can help customers try before they buy newly launched technologies. Also customers can get feedback from their own staffs and colleagues prior to making a larger investment.

Selective reading blocks

Customers want a Loyalty Program that offers product discounts, customer support and trial software

Product discounts Regular product discounts are considered as the most important element of a customer retention program. Customers face challenges in terms of the affordability of new technologies. Either the customers have to incur a cost for new technologies or the customer's colleagues must bear the cost, which affects the overall productivity. The customer's colleagues are expected to provide technology to their own staffs. This would help in better training of their manpower.

Customer support Customers expect the vendors to support them in higher levels of service. This business should also enable access to self-help forums and especially in their native language.

Trial software The availability of trial or beta versions of software to partners is considered important by customers. The trial versions can help customers try before they buy newly launched technologies. Also customers can get feedback from their own staffs and colleagues prior to making a larger investment.

The selective reading block looks like a simple idea but it is backed up by 40 years of research and empirical evidence that it leads to better writing and to more understandable and persuasive documents.

Selective reading blocks are based on the well-researched and proven writing method called *structured writing*, which was developed to help readers skim documents and find information quickly, also called *selective reading*.

Structured writing was developed by Robert E. Horn in the 1960's, as a way to improve educational textbooks. In his research, Horn found that textbooks often contained long paragraphs of rambling text where the main message was submerged and difficult to skim. Structured writing starts by respecting the reader's need to limit content to what will fit working memory, and structure it so it is easy to skim and locate information. It also imposes a discipline so the writer is forced to make their message clear, to himself and to the reader.

Structured writing replaces the paragraph with the *information block*. A document can be built page by page using information blocks instead of paragraphs. A casual inspection illustrates how much easier it is to skim and locate information using information blocks versus a typical text document.

Question: Whom should I contact if I have more questions?

Text document

PowerPoint documents require a summative writing style. We will use a style, based on writing styles used by news journalists, website designers and others: write in full sentences, break text into 3–4 chunks of information, use labels to introduce each chunk. For more information you can contact the author Bruce Gabrielle at www.speaking ppt.com	

Information block

Purpose	To explain how to write in a style suitable for PowerPoint
Procedure	1. Write in full sentences 2. Break text into 3–4 chunks of information, presented as sentences 3. Use labels to introduce each chunk
Contact	Bruce Gabrielle www.speakingppt.com

Robert Horn has evolved structured writing into a formal method called Information Mapping™, which has been adopted by organizations around the world including Pacific Bell, Wells Fargo Bank, Nissan and the U.S. Department of Defense. Research shows information-mapped documents are better than text documents to reduce the work for the writer and facilitate selective reading for the audience.

- 50% less time to read

- 80% less time to find information

- 50% reduction in word count

Both the STOP format and structured writing are based on the insight that writers often use paragraphs to ramble and go off-tangent and lose their focus. Both methods were developed during the 1960's as a way to discipline the writer's focus and help the reader locate information more easily. Both methods work by placing limits on how much information the writer can present and the use of clear labels to enable selective reading.

I use the term *selective reading block* because information blocks have a very specific definition in business documents. In Information Mapping, there is a formal taxonomy of 40 types of information blocks, like "Purpose", "Procedure" and "Contact". Selective reading blocks are not limited to 40 types and may be any word or phrase. To avoid confusion, and to reinforce the focus on the reader's needs for clear but brief labels, I use the term selective reading block rather than information block.

Why does the selective reading block work? Because it's how busy executives deal with information overload.

Business readers do not want long text documents. Instead, they practice *selecting reading*: skimming long documents, looking at headers and stopping to read intently when they find a section that interests them. In one study by Professor Luuk Lagerwerf, researchers observed executives reading two proposals. Executives spent the most time with the executive summary, skimmed the middle of the proposal looking at conclusion paragraphs, and then intently studied the cost section.

These business readers had two versions to study: one a typical text document, and the other augmented specifically with introductory and conclusion paragraphs to facilitate selective reading. Executives preferred the second one 2-to-1. More importantly, when it was augmented for selective reading, the executive was more likely to study the cost section, indicating higher inclination to move onto making a purchase decision.

In a similar 1997 study, researchers observed Dutch politicians reading lengthy text documents. Like the business executives, the politicians only read 23% of a text document, skimming the headings to locate areas of interest and then reading that section intensively.

There is growing awareness in the news industry that readers do not have a lot of time to spend with long narratives and so journalists are looking for alternative story formats to present information in short bite-sized pieces.

Recently, the Poynter Institute conducted research to find alternatives to full-text news articles. They tested three versions of a news article: a mostly-text story, a mix of text and graphics and a mostly-graphic story with brief text annotations. After reading each article, people were tested to see how much they understood. The story that performed the best? The graphic one with annotated text.

Business readers also are time-pressed and readers want your help making your document easy to selectively read. Selective reading is one way executives deal with information overload, which has always been a problem in business but is getting worse as technology increases the amount of available information but not the available hours. We are swamped with incoming email and meeting invitations. We can find almost any information we want on the internet. We have more ways to collect data, and more tools to analyze it and spit out reports. And, thanks to productivity software and email, we can more easily produce reports and share them across the hall or across the world. Selective reading blocks summarize information in a way that readers want it and that helps them move onto making a decision.

By adopting the selective reading block as an alternative to the bullet point, we can approach a text-heavy slide with the following principles in mind:

1. Full sentences. Develop your thinking and communicate clearly using full sentences

2. Limited. Write in 3–4 selective reading blocks per slide, the limits of working memory

3. Visually distinct. Use whitespace or borders to visually separate each chunk of information

4. Labels. Use a brief and meaningful label to introduce and summarize each selective reading block

Selective reading blocks differ from bullet points because they allow skimming the labels to locate information, and body text is moved to the side to be studied as appropriate. These two slides contain the exact same information. But the selective reading block is easier to skim, and the body text is moved off to the right and doesn't need to stretch the entire width of the slide.

Bullet points

Selective reading blocks

Customers want a Loyalty Program that offers product discounts, customer support and trial software

- **Regular product discounts** are considered as the most important element of a customer retention program. Customers face challenges in terms of the affordability of new technologies. Either the customers have to incur a cost for new technologies or the customer's colleagues must bear the cost, which affects the overall productivity. The customer's colleagues are expected to provide technology to their own staffs. This would help in better training of their manpower.

- **Customer support** is a basic customer expectation. This business should also enable access to self-help forums and especially in their native language.

- **Trial or beta software** should be available to partners, say customers. The trial versions can help customers try before they buy newly launched technologies. Also customers can get feedback from their own staffs and colleagues prior to making a larger investment.

Customers want a Loyalty Program that offers product discounts, customer support and trial software

Product discounts	Regular product discounts are considered as the most important element of a customer retention program. Customers face challenges in terms of the affordability of new technologies. Either the customers have to incur a cost for new technologies or the customer's colleagues are expected to provide technology to their own staffs. This would help in better training of their manpower.
Customer support	Customers expect the vendors to support them in higher levels of service. This business should also enable access to self-help forums and especially in their native language.
Trial software	The availability of trial or beta versions of software to partners is considered important by customers. The trial versions can help customers try before they buy newly launched technologies. Also customers can get feedback from their own staffs and colleagues prior to making a larger investment.

The selective reading block in this example contains text. But it could just as easily contain a graph or a picture or bullet points or whatever content is needed. It is based on 40 years of research into how business readers want to skim materials and a proven method that has been adopted by companies around the world.

5. Use category labels for reference documents; summary labels to surface your line of reasoning

Labels are an important part of selective reading blocks, for three reasons: they act as signposts, they enable selective reading and they help surface your above-water argument.

First, labels act as signposts into your slide. *Signposts* is an important principle in visual design because the reader needs a starting point and a path through your document. Eye-tracking studies show that when we are reading something online, like a website, our visual path starts in the upper-left corner, grazes across the top, drops down and makes another shorter horizontal pan and then skims down hugging tightly to the left margin. This is known as the F-path.

Creating selective reading blocks

To create selective reading blocks, use the table tool in PowerPoint. The default table in PowerPoint 2007 gives you colored cells and 18-point font. Instead, select the table style with no borders and no fill and change the font size to a smaller size. Then, add horizontal borders. This will ensure your selective reading blocks are aligned attractively and you can resize them quickly later.

Images used in this book can be seen in color at www.speakingppt.com

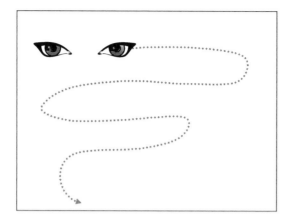

Placing your labels along the F-path locates them prominently on the slide for the reader. A predominantly horizontal alignment or a predominantly left-aligned vertical alignment is most convenient for the reader who wants to skim and locate specific kinds of information.

Vertical labels. This is often good for reference materials, like training documents, so the reader can quickly skim the different topics covered on the slide and decide which sections to read fully.

The top to bottom arrangement subconsciously suggests the top idea is more important than the bottom idea, so arrange your most important idea on the top where practical.

Horizontal labels. The symmetry makes this visually pleasing and appears to give equal importance to each topic, but it can be more difficult to accommodate on a slide if some selective reading blocks are larger than others.

You will need to decide how much label text you want to write. Do you want a brief category label (eg. market segments) or a summary label, that communicates your main message (eg. Our primary market segment is college students)?

Category labels are concise and easy to skim. But no clear message emerges unless you also read the body text.

Category labels are most appropriate if the reader is motivated to read all the body text, like in a reference document.

Category labels also work well in a discussion deck, where you want to use the label as a visual cue to direct the reader's attention but you will verbally elaborate on the label.

Summary labels are more verbose and less easy to skim but they surface your slide's *above-water argument* for the reader to understand and evaluate.

Summary labels are most appropriate if you goal is to persuade, because they surface your line of reasoning clearly.

Your choice of label depends on how much you want to surface your above-water argument on the slide. If your goal is to persuade the reader, a summary label makes your reasoning most explicit. But if the slide is informational, such as a reference document or a status update, category labels allow the reader to skim the slide's contents and pick out the information they need.

Surfacing your above-water argument also helps you inspect and refine your own thinking. Is your above-water argument sound? Is it complete? Is it clear? Here is your chance to refine your own thinking by writing out summary labels.

It's often helpful to start with a category label, like "product discounts", and then ask yourself *what about product discounts*, just as you did to find the above-water argument for your entire deck. This forces you to make a point on the slide, rather than just sort data.

For reading decks, labels are important signposts into the rest of your slide. They give the eye a place to land and help the reader understand your above-water argument or locate information quickly.

6. Use large label fonts to encourage skimming, small label fonts to encourage reading

Do you want the reader to study the body text? Then use the same font size for the label and the body text. Or, if you just want the reader to skim the labels and ignore the body text, use a larger font size for the label. Eye-tracking studies on news websites find when the headline is larger than the article text, people skim the headlines. But when the headline and body text are the same size, people are drawn into reading the article.

Label font larger than body text font.
The reader will skim the labels and ignore the body text.

Label font same size as the body text font.
The reader will read the body text.

7. Consider different strategies to manage excessive body text

What if you have more text than will fit on a slide? The STOP format is based on the insight that it takes on average about 500 words to fully articulate and support a topic statement. A PowerPoint slide can hold 500 words but it doesn't leave much room for pictures. And if you're going to fill a slide with 500 words, it may not offer much more advantage than a text document.

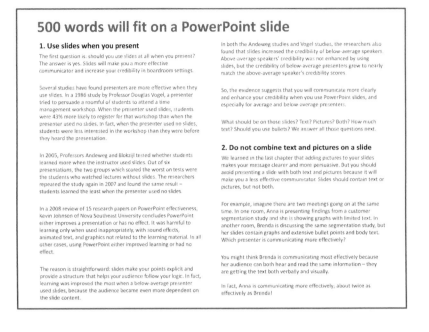

If you find yourself with this much text, ask yourself (or your reader): does my reader want all this detail? If the answer is yes, then a text document may be the answer.

But maybe not. Jim Tracey and Robert E. Horn both faced the question of how to discipline your text to fit the strict limits of their respective formats. We can modify their advice for PowerPoint slides:

a. Summarize your text more. Your text may be rambling or offering irrelevant details. Rewrite or cut out sentences that do not support that summary label.

b. Break into additional slides. Are you are trying to cover too much on one slide? Ask yourself the spaghetti-and-cake question from chapter 8: *does all this information need to be on the same slide?* If not, respect your reader's cognitive capacity and give one or more selective reading blocks its own slide.

c. Sequence your slides. If the spaghetti-and-cake test tells you all this information needs to be on the same slide, cover each selective reading block extensively on its own slide, then bring them all together on one summary slide. A modification of this is to introduce half of your information on one slide, then use a "continued" slide to introduce the rest.

d. Add a sidebar. If you need extensive body text on the same slide, you could break your slide into two sections: one with the central message and diagram and another section for body text. This second section can be divided with a border and color, to clearly distinguish it from the rest of the slide.

Images used in this book can be seen in color at www.speakingppt.com

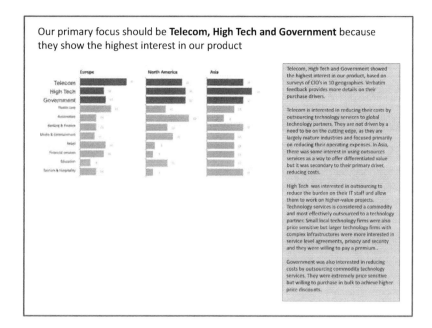

e. Use a separate body text slide. You could introduce four selective reading blocks briefly on one slide, then add a second slide that is optional reading, composed only of body text. Use a two- or three-column format, because about 8–12 words per line is most comfortable for the reader. And repeat the labels exactly as they appeared on the previous slide, to help the reader synchronize the body text with the right selective reading block.

Slide 1: briefly introduced slide

Slide 2: 500 words of body text

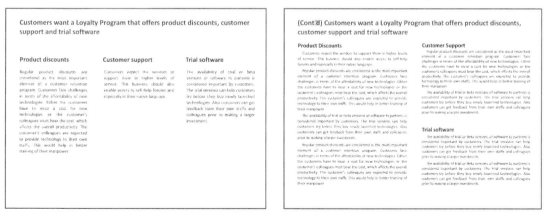

This assumes the reader wants the additional details, so you probably want to use this sparingly in a PowerPoint document. If you find yourself writing a lot of body text slides, that may be an indication that a text document would be better.

f. Add text to the notes section. In theory, it makes sense to add a lot of body text to the notes section. But in practice, it becomes a chore for the reader to visually inspect the notes section and the slide at the same time. And because of the split-attention effect, it is more challenging to understand materials when you have to bounce back and forth between a block of text and another element like a picture or a selective reading block, holding the information in working memory like water in a pail and hauling it over to the other information so they can be matched.

Still, there are times you can add additional text to the notes section, such as footnotes explaining how certain calculations were made or a list of websites where the reader can go for more information. It's important to direct the reader to look in the notes section as readers will not assume there is additional body text there.

g. Insert a comment. Professor David Farkas of the University of Washington suggested an interesting solution which was to insert a comment on a slide. The comment appears as a small unobtrusive box but when you click on it, or hover over it, a window pops up and provides lengthy body text. This works for a reading deck but not for printed handouts or a briefing deck. Also, you cannot see the comment box when you are in presentation view.

h. Add spoken notes. Since spoken text plus pictures is so effective, theoretically you could insert an audio clip of your body text. I've never seen this done but PowerPoint does have a feature that makes it as easy as point-and-click (Insert > Sound > Record Sound).

So, to summarize, the seven principles for using text effectively in a reading deck are:

1. Write bullet points as full sentences
2. Use the laws of chunking—3–4 bullets, whitespace and labels
3. Consider using shapes or icons instead of bullet points
4. Use selective reading blocks
5. Use category labels for reference documents; summary labels to surface your line of reasoning
6. Use large label fonts to encourage skimming, small label fonts to encourage reading
7. Consider different strategies to manage excessive body text

So the next time you create a text-heavy slide don't just fill in the default bullet point template. Research shows how to communicate text most effectively for briefing decks, discussion decks and reading decks. Handle text poorly and you'll end up on Dave Paradi's semi-annual survey. But handle it well, and you will differentiate yourself for your clear and persuasive boardroom communication.

Back to the NASA slide

The critics may be right that, in the case of the Columbia disaster, the engineers should have provided their recommendations in a text document. But maybe not. They were asked to meet the NASA managers for one hour and present their recommendations. It was an important meeting and they needed to be persuasive. The NASA managers were already skeptical the foam strike caused any damage and had already denied three requests for additional photos. So the engineers needed to be brief and persuasive and drive a focused discussion.

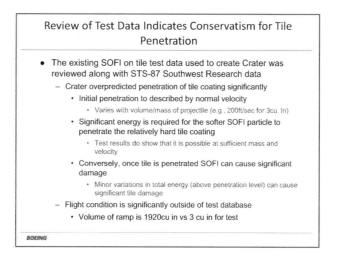

The bulleted slide was not effective. Looking at this slide, no clear argument emerges. NASA managers could not know what to focus on because so much text was crammed onto the slide.

Let's consider their argument. The engineers were unsure how badly Columbia was damaged because it depended on where, and at what angle, the wing had been struck. The foam was just two pounds, but it struck Columbia at about 500 miles per hour. If the foam had glanced off the heat-resistant tiles that covered the wing's surface then the damage was likely insignificant. But if it had struck directly onto the leading edge of the wing at full speed, it could have caused serious damage. They needed to visually examine the wing and were asking the Department of Defense to take additional pictures of the Columbia in orbit with their high-powered cameras.

First, the slide creator needs to clarify the overall slide message in the title: "We need additional photos of the wing in-orbit."

We next need to decide: is this a briefing deck, discussion deck or reading deck? The engineers were invited to present to a roomful of NASA managers so let's assume it's a briefing deck. There are several principles we need to follow:

- Limit to 3–4 bullet points per slide

- Use keywords to help with sync and launch

- Use concise or full sentences

- Chunk bullets with whitespace and avoid sub-bullets

What are the 3–4 bullets on this slide? If we study this slide and summarize each set of bullets and sub-bullets, the above-water argument has now been surfaced:

- Crater over-predicts penetration in general, and in this case predicts damage that is deeper than the coating on the leading edge of the wing

- Significant energy is required to penetrate the hard coating on the edge of the wing

- Once the wing edge is damaged, a spider-web of cracks can spread across the wing and result in severe wing damage

- The foam that struck Columbia is 600 times larger than the largest projectile we've ever modeled

They are basically saying *we don't really know because the model has never been used for anything this large.* Now we can see the argument is poorly ordered and incomplete. What they really want to say is:

- Crater predicts SOFI penetrated through to aluminum frame

- But these results are inconclusive; the SOFI that hit Columbia is 600 times larger than anything in the Crater database

- Damage could be insignificant if it hit the heat tiles, or critical if it penetrated the coating on the wing's leading edge *(currently missing from this slide)*

- We need photos so we can visually confirm one of these scenarios *(currently missing from this slide—now promoted to the slide title)*

That gets us a bulleted slide like this, which surfaces our above-water argument clearly without becoming lost in text clutter.

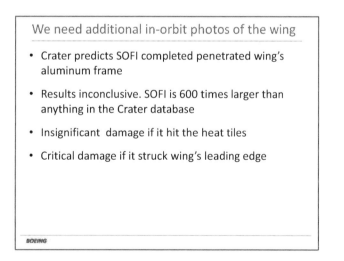

Some of these sentences seem too long to easily facilitate sync and launch. We only need the bullets to structure the presenter's talk and briefly surface the above-water argument. The second and third bullets should be shortened and, by thinking about the keywords the speaker will use to sync and launch, could be rewritten like this.

Now we have a wall of text and, as we learned in the last chapter, we might consider adding a picture to give this presentation more impact. But adding a picture will actually make us less effective in a briefing deck. We will be more effective if we create a picture slide and introduce it before moving to the text slide. If you look at the slide title, the nouns are *photos* and *wing*. One option is to use an illustrative image of Columbia's wing showing the best case and worst-case scenarios, and what additional photos they need.

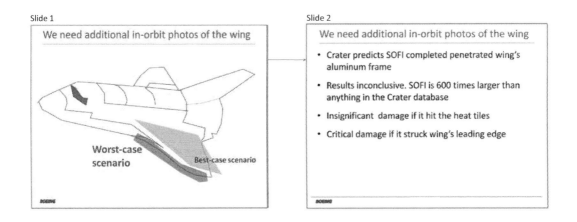

This slide can also be used as a discussion deck because the speaker will provide the body text through their speech. But it does not act as a good reading deck because it lacks the necessary body copy to explain each bullet point. We can convert this into a reading deck by following these principles: use selective reading blocks with a summary label that surfaces the slide's above-water argument, write in complete grammatically correct sentences, and combine the text and picture on the same slide.

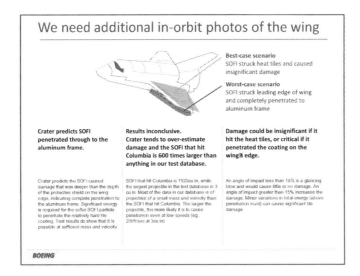

Bullet points hurt the engineers' argument. The bullet points were not presented so they were easy for the NASA managers to understand nor easy for the NASA engineers to sync and launch. Their text slide was not an effective way to communicate and persuade because they tried to combine the detail of a reading deck with the structure of a briefing deck. And that rarely works.

To be completely fair, the Debris Assessment Team had been turned down three times for additional photos because they could not produce conclusive evidence the wing was damaged. On the other hand, the NASA managers did not ask for equally conclusive evidence the wing was *not damaged*. It was this backward logic that caused the managers' over-confidence and was primarily what lead to the Columbia disaster; not the engineers' unclear communication.

Before: Using bullets and sub-bullets

After: Using Mindworks Presentation Method

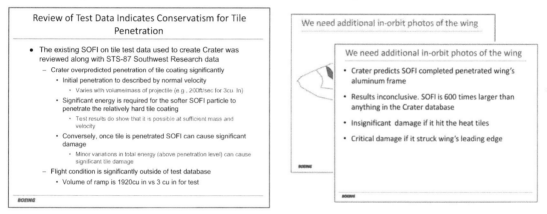

Above-water argument

1. Overwhelming the audience with text is the main PowerPoint complaint. There are different rules for briefing decks, discussion decks and reading decks based on 40 years of research. Some of the most important research has only been published in the past decade.

2. Briefing decks can overwhelm the audience's working memory when spoken text, written text and pictures are presented together. Instead, limit your slide to 3–4 bullet points, written as concise or complete sentences and use keywords to help you sync and launch. Present text slides and picture slides separately.

3. Discussion decks involve a more interactive audience. Provide handouts or an electronic version of your briefing deck or reading deck, to give them control over the pace of their own learning.

4. Reading decks can include bullet points or selective reading blocks. Write summary labels to surface your above-water argument or category labels to assist in selective reading. If there is too much body text for the slide, consider strategies like writing more briefly, adding a body text-only slide or adding a sidebar.

Recommended reading

Multi-Media Learning by Richard E. Mayer describes dozens of studies showing how learning is harmed when educators combine speech, text and pictures.

Mapping Hyptertext by Robert E. Horn is his ground-breaking introduction to the imperfections of text documents and the superiority of structured writing in general, and Information Mapping in particular, as a writing aid and to facilitate selective reading.

How High Can It Fly by Robert E. Horn covers the research that demonstrates the superiority of structured writing over typical text documents.

SECTION THREE

DESIGN

Criticism #3: Amateurish use of color and design

Boardroom-style slides are often filled with decorative elements: garish colors, drop shadows, background images, three-dimensional charts. Sure, it looks amateurish. But does it really matter?

It turns out that graphic design is critically important. You may be hurting your chances to sell ideas if you don't understand some of the basic principles of graphic design.

Attractive slides help put your reader in the right frame of mind and more likely to agree with you. But use decorative elements clumsily and you can make your slide look cluttered and unprofessional and make the reader more negative toward your message.

Slide aesthetics clarify your message and invite the reader to spend more time with your slides. Poor slide aesthetics repel readers and reduce their willingness to spend time with your slides.

Attractive slides enhance your professional image. You feel more proud to share your work when the slides look visually pleasing.

Slides aesthetics are critical for selling ideas in the boardroom. That's why consulting firms take their slide aesthetics so seriously.

But there is a right way and a wrong way to approach slide aesthetics.

You don't need to become a graphic designer. But you do need to learn some basic principles of how to use color, layout, alignment and decorative elements to enhance the persuasive power of your boardroom-style slides. Don't worry; the principles are intended for left-brain business managers, even those with no graphic design skills at all. They are practical, easy to implement and you will see improvements in your slides right away.

This section covers:

Color: How to use color intelligently to make your slide look more professional, easier to understand and more persuasive.

Picture and Wallpaper: Lead the reader's eye through the slide. Determine what is important on your slide and needs the reader's attention and what can be subdued.

Aesthetics: Attractive slides are easier to agree with than unattractive and cluttered slides. Learn the importance of alignment and what accidental decorative elements to be on the lookout for.

Charts and Tables: Do not just copy and paste Excel charts into your slides. Learn how to modify them so they support your message and turn your data into a story.

CHAPTER 11

Color

Use color to increase interest

Y OU ARE SCROLLING THROUGH THE SLIDES produced by your product launch marketing manager, Grace, reviewing the launch timelines for the next release of your Copenhagen product. But you have a headache. The background of each slide is a rich forest green, the text a grinning yellow, the title is purple with a drop shadow, the shapes are a fruit basket of colors.

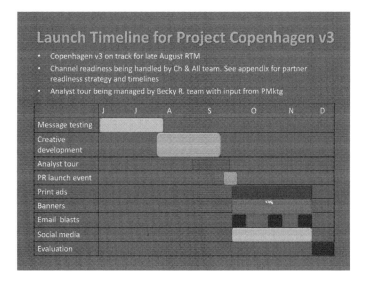

It takes a long time to read through the slide—once, twice, three times. But the slide makes you fidgety and it's hard to focus. Everything seems to be crying out for your attention and you need to work hard to focus on one thing at a time. You wonder *if I'm re-reading this slide three times, is everyone else also wasting time reading these slides two or three times?*

Could your team be more effective communicators and partners? What would be your advice to Grace?

Color is convincing

John George is a former gang-member now in prison for killing an elderly man and his wife by throwing them off the side of a roadside cliff. He towers 6 feet 6 inches tall and weighs over 300 pounds. He has tattoos up and down his arms, back and chest, and even two crosses tattooed on his cheeks. His eyes are as empty and chilling as the muzzle of a shotgun.

John is a dangerous prisoner. Most of the other inmates steer wide of him but occasionally John explodes and attacks other inmates with whatever weapon is handy: an iron bedpost, a broom handle or his bowling-ball-sized fists. This brings a swarm of prison guards down on him like an avalanche.

And what do they do with John to calm him down? Do they inject him with a tranquilizer? Does he talk to a psychologist about his feelings of rage? Is he strapped to a cot until he cools down?

No. They take him to the pink room.

The pink room is a special cell created especially for prisoners like John. It is painted bubble-gum pink, or *Baker-Miller Pink* to be exact, a specially-mixed color proven to have a calming effect on disruptive and aggressive inmates. Confined in the pink room, people become subdued in minutes, stop shouting and banging on things, and often even cry or fall asleep.

Baker-Miller Pink is effective; some studies have found even color-blind and some blind persons are soothed by it. Baker-Miller Pink is so effective that at least 1,500 hospitals and correctional facilities in the U.S. now have a pink room for calming unruly inmates and patients.

College football even has a rule that the visiting team's locker room must be the same color as the home team's, after some complaints that visiting teams were given pink locker rooms, presumably to sap their aggressiveness.

The restaurant industry also knows the physiological effects of color. Fast-food restaurants use warm colors like red, yellow and orange to stimulate customers' appetites and make them fidgety enough to not linger too long in the seating area. More upscale restaurants use cool colors like blue, green and purple, which have a calming effect that encourages patrons to relax and linger over drinks and dessert. When Burger King changed its uniforms to blue and green, colors that suppress appetites, sales declined significantly.

Scientists believe color affects us both psychologically and physiologically. Psychologically, it reminds us of experiences and the accompanying emotions: blue-green reminds us of the calming ocean, green reminds us of nature, black reminds us of the dark and mysterious night.

But color also affects us physiologically. Color is essentially light rays with a specific wavelength and frequency. Light is absorbed by the eyes, but also the skin. Warm colors like red and orange cause the heart rate to accelerate. Cool colors like blue and green make the heart beat slower. Orange makes people hungry. Yellow can be stimulating but too much yellow can make people irritable. Some doctors even use colored light to treat depression and disease.

Because it affects our moods, color can be one of the most powerful elements on your boardroom-style slides *when used correctly.*

A 1994 study demonstrates the persuasive power of color. Researchers Joan Meyers-Levy and Laura Peracchio showed print advertisements to university students. Some of the ads were black and white, some were mostly black and white with color highlighting and some were full color.

In almost all cases, students felt significantly more positive toward the product advertised when the ads had color of any kind; attitudes were most negative toward the product when it was advertised in black and white. The researchers repeated this study twice and the results were the same.

There was only one exception to this finding. When the ad was complex and the reader was highly motivated to understand it, the full color ad generated the most *negative* reaction. Students preferred instead the color highlighted ad or the black and white ad. This was confirmed both times they repeated the study.

This is an important caveat, because most of your boardroom-style slides will be important to the reader with somewhat complex content. So color can be used to make the reader more positive toward your message. But excessive color can make the reader more negative to your ideas.

Color makes a message more convincing because persuasion is improved by appealing to emotion. As we discussed in chapter 5, we are heavily influenced by our emotional brain. Emotion influences logic more than logic influences emotion. Study after study finds that color affects emotions, usually positively.

In *Moving Mountains*, one of the finest books ever written on stand-up presentations, author Henry Boettinger had this to say about persuading an audience:

> "Emotions and beliefs are masters; reason their servant…At the least, reason excuses; at the most, it restrains its master."

It's no wonder, then, that color can affect how willing people are to agree with your message. A report entitled *The Profit of Color* from the Color Marketing Group highlights research findings on the persuasive power of color:

- using color in advertising outsells black and white by 88%

- color accounts for 60% of the acceptance or rejection of an object and is a critical factor in the success of any visual experience

Because it affects our emotions and physiology, color increase the reader's motivation to read your slide. In fact, color will make readers *twice as likely* to spend time with your slides. Consider some research on how color improves the amount of time readers spend with your slide:

- using color in a printed piece increases readership by up to 80% and readers pay attention up to 82% longer (1)

- color visuals increase willingness to read by up to 80% (2)

- using color can increase motivation and participation by up to 80% (2)

- a color image sustains interest for up to 300% longer than an identical black and white image (1)

- people are 55% more likely to pick up a full color piece first (1)

1. The Color Marketing Group, "The Profit of Color"
2. 3M Corporation "The Power of Color in Presentations" in monthly newsletter "Meeting Guides"

Slides that are all black and white are fatiguing, but color adds energy to slides that keep readers interested longer. A casual inspection shows how the same slide is more energizing when you add color.

Black and white: people are less motivated to read and less emotionally affected

Color: people are more motivated to read and their emotions are affected positively

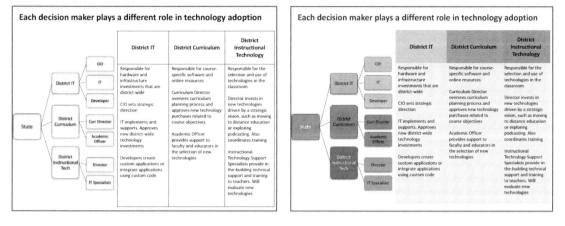

Besides making readers more motivated to read your slides, color helps readers understand your message better and remember it longer. Consider some additional statistics on color and comprehension:

- information is communicated up to 70% more quickly and 77% more effectively when color is introduced (1)

- color enhances learning and improves retention by more than 75% (2)

1. The Color Marketing Group, "The Profit of Color"
2. 3M Corporation "The Power of Color in Presentations" in monthly newsletter "Meeting Guides"

The research indicates that color is a powerful tool to increase visual interest, comprehension and persuasion. You can probably feel the difference in your own energy when you look at a color slide. Just as you should always strive to use a picture on your slide, you should always strive to use color.

Intelligent color uses

Color should be used on every slide, to add visual interest that attracts and holds a reader's attention and makes them more open to agreeing with your ideas.

You should strive to use no more than 3–4 colors on each slide. Just as working memory can manage 3–4 chunks of information; it can also manage 3–4 colors.

A 1997 study at the University of Iowa tested how many colors could be held in visual working memory. Participants were shown an image of 1 to 12 colored blocks for one-tenth of a second, then a blank screen for another second, then a second image with colored blocks for two seconds. They were asked if the second image was the same as the first image, or if one of the colors was different.

When the screen contained one to three blocks, participants' answers were nearly perfect. At four blocks, accuracy began to decline, then fell off drastically at five or more colored blocks. Researchers concluded visual working memory can hold 3–4 separate colors comfortably. A visual display with more than four colors simply overwhelms working memory with too many distinct elements.

An old graphic design rule also recommends three colors. Graphic designers subscribe to the 60-30-10 rule, which says that a pleasing combination of colors uses 60% of one color to set an overall mood, 30% of a second color to add contrast and visual interest and 10% of third color to add accents and a touch of elegance.

Based on the limits of visual working memory, and this simple graphic design rule, a slide should be limited to 3–4 distinct colors, plus a neutral color like gray for the text.

There are three things to think about when selecting which elements to add color to:

1. What are my information chunks? One important use of color is grouping items. Recall in chapter 8 we discussed the Law of Similarity. You can use color to pull items together into one chunk of information and separate them from others. For instance, if I make a blue line on a graph I will also make the label for that line blue.

2. What do I want to emphasize? Color can also be used to attract attention to the main points on your slide. There will be many things on each slide: text, images, titles, shapes. Color can be used to highlight what's important. This is such a critical concept we cover it extensively in the next chapter.

3. What meaning do I want to convey? Color can be used to encode meaning. The most obvious example is using the traffic light colors green, yellow and red to indicate project status. Red will be used frequently on slides to indicate areas for concern. You might use company colors to indicate your company and competitors on a chart.

The correct way to use colors is to meet the reader's needs for clarity and visual interest. So when is color just decorative?

1. When it interferes with chunking

2. When it draws attention to the wrong things

3. When it accidentally conveys the wrong message

4. When there are more than four colors on the slide

Consider what happens when you apply colors purely for visual interest without an understanding of its consequences.

1. Interferes with chunking

The slide is attractive with a creative "checkerboard" approach to coloring the various elements different shades of blue. But the aesthetics have become the focus of this slide and the reader has lost the ability to easily see 3–4 chunks of information.

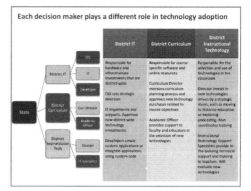

2. Draws attention to the wrong things

This slide uses color for the table borders and as a fill color of the table cells, attracting the eye away from the org chart on the left. The reader has to spend extra time re-orienting themselves to the important parts of the slide.

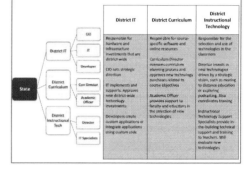

3. Conveys the wrong message

In this slide, your heart starts racing at the sight of three red boxes. Is there danger? Why is one box green and other boxes yellow? Does that indicate status? The reader will try to interpret the meaning of the colors and can be confused if the meaning doesn't match the message.

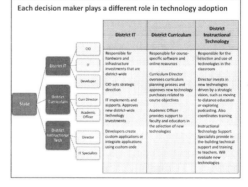

4. More than four colors

This slide contains seven colors, plus black text. The mind struggles to understand which chunks of information go together and where they should focus. Does it feel like there is too much information on the slide? That's because working memory can only hold four things at once and must keep dropping other things.

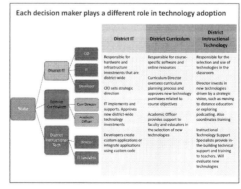

A more purposeful way to use color on this slide is to use no more than 3–4 colors to chunk information, direct attention to the most important elements and convey some meaning. Consider this improved slide:

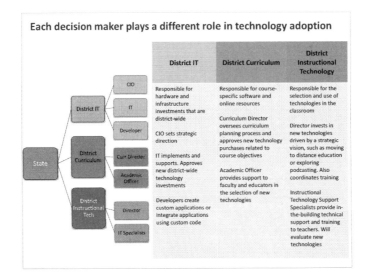

Notice a few other things about this slide:

- there are three colors on this slide plus black/gray which makes it energetic without becoming overwhelming

- the colors in the org chart match the colors in the table, so the eye can easily group the corresponding information

- color is only used to reinforce the main message—"each decision maker". The box labeled "State" is gray because the state is not one of the decision makers discussed on this slide

- there is no unintended meaning in the slide colors

So, use this manager's checklist to ensure you are using color most effectively on your slide, and not just using it for decoration.

Manager's color checklist
1. Is there more than 3–4 colors, plus a neutral text color?
2. Does the color interfere with chunking?
3. Does the color draw attention away from the main message?
4. Does the color send the wrong message or generate the wrong emotion?

Images used in this book can be seen in color at www.speakingppt.com

Which colors should you use?

Many persons select colors by opening PowerPoint's color picker menu and choosing something at random, based on how they are feeling. *Let's see, how about this blue? No, maybe a bit darker? Hmmm…what about orange?* They choose colors by whim.

Instead, you should choose colors with a purpose: to make the reader feel more positive toward your slides, which will make your ideas easier to agree with. Remember our discussion in chapter 5 on evidence. It's not enough to have a strong logical argument; winning people emotionally is just as important, if not even more important, and the right colors can help you put your audience in the right frame of mind.

Rather than randomly scrolling through the color picker every time you need to add color to your slide, create a standard color palette that you use over and over again.

Here's an example of the color palette I use for all my slides.

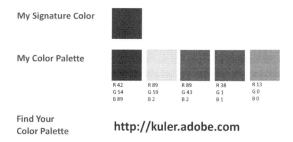

My Signature Color

My Color Palette

R 42   R 89   R 89   R 38   R 13
G 54   G 59   G 43   G 1   G 0
B 89   B 2   B 2   B 1   B 0

Find Your Color Palette   **http://kuler.adobe.com**

The signature color is the most important color in this palette. This is the color you'll use most commonly for things like slide titles, text labels and graphs. Your slide will have a consistent and professional look if you use your signature color to unify all the slides. This should be a relatively dark color so it can work as text or shapes. Light colors like orange and yellow don't work well as slide titles and labels.

The other colors will be your accent colors, which you'll use for the slide background, shapes, charts and other visual elements. Because these accent colors harmonize with your signature color, you can confidently add these colors to your slide and maintain an attractive and professional look.

You will want to make sure your color palette includes some shade of red. Red is used commonly in boardroom-style slides when you want you suggest bad news, such as a graph showing declining sales or a project report showing which deliverables are behind schedule.

Creating a personalized color palette has three advantages:

1. Saves you time. Typically, slide creators are selecting colors as they build slides. They open the color menu, browse through the list of available colors and experiment with different colors. But this is inefficient. You will waste considerable time experimenting with and

rejecting color combinations. By creating a standard color scheme you get your work done faster by re-using the same proven colors every time.

2. Slides will be visually pleasing. The colors will harmonize well. Especially in the left-brain business world, some of us are not very good at selecting attractive color combinations. An estimated 8% of U.S. men and about 0.4% of U.S women are color-blind. If you are one of these folks, you will have difficulty seeing colors accurately and selecting colors that are attractive together.

3. Builds your credibility. Consistent colors throughout a slide communicates a subtle message that the slide creator is disciplined and purposeful. Consulting firms use consistent colors in their PowerPoint decks to increase the reader's confidence in their capabilities. Selecting a wide variety of colors for your deck will give it a haphazard look—lime green on one slide, forest green on another, a jarring purple introduced on slide three, which reflects poorly on the slide creator.

It's a bit outside of the scope of this chapter to get into color theory and how to select a color palette. Thanks to technology, you don't need to learn color theory to select a pleasing color palette. Just go to your favorite search engine and type "color scheme" and you will be presented with dozens of websites which will help you generate your color palette.

The way you do this is by selecting your signature color first, then generating a color palette that harmonizes well with that signature color. How do you select your signature color? Select something relatively dark, because you'll use it for text and it needs to be readable. And choose something that most people will find pleasing.

A 2004 University of Georgia study asked students to look at colors and rate whether the color made them feel positive, negative or neutral and to explain their rating. Two-thirds of colors generated a positive emotion, one-third generated a negative emotion and just a handful generated no emotion.

The most popular color was green; 96% of students said it made them feel positive. The least popular color was gray with 90% of students saying it made them feel more negative.

Most positive reactions		Least positive reactions	
96%	Green	24%	Green-yellow
94%	Yellow	19%	Black
82%	Blue-green	7%	Gray
80%	Blue		
76%	Red-purple		

%students who said the color made them feel more positive. University of Georgia, 2004

One of the most interesting things about this study was the reason students gave for their ratings. They talked about how colors reminded them of personal experiences and the accompanying feelings. Green was popular because it reminded students of the calm experience of watching nature and trees. Yellow reminded them of the sun, flowers and the summertime. Gray was least popular, and made people feel depressed, because it reminded them of bad weather, rain, fog and cloudy days.

If we feel more positive toward colors that remind us of pleasant experiences, then one way to select your signature color and color palette is to pick colors from a picture you think your audience will find pleasing.

For instance, if you work in a company in San Diego, you might choose a color palette that reminds people of the San Diego Chargers football team, with navy, gold and powder blue. Assuming your audience has learned largely positive feelings for that team, the colors could subtly influence them.

There is a website that will let you upload a picture and automatically generate a color palette based on the colors in that picture.

- go to http://kuler.adobe.com

- select Create > From an Image

- select Upload and locate an image on your computer

- Kuler will create a color palette for you, which you can modify to be brighter, darker and so on using the options in the left navigation bar

- you will need to register for an account to save this color palette

- once saved, click on the "slider" icon to see and edit the color values

- write down the RGB values (mix of Red, Green, Blue) for each color

- go into PowerPoint and create your own color palette using these RGB values

- in PowerPoint 2007, go to Design > Colors > Create New Theme Colors

- to change a color, click on it and select More Colors…

- enter the RGB values and click Okay

- repeat for each color in your palette

After Kuler generates your color palette, select one of the darker colors as your signature color (called "base color" at the Kuler website). This will re-order all the colors and allow you to experiment further to find a set of colors that work well with your signature color.

When you select your signature color, remember that colors have meaning. I use dark blue as my signature color; it's contemporary but still conveys authority. I deal primarily with technology companies and research shows readers associate the colors blue and gray with technology. These colors are also versatile enough for bar charts and line graphs. I can make most of the chart elements gray and highlight the important elements with dark blue.

Color meaning is learned based on experiences and so meaning varies by culture. White is the color of purity and brides in the West but the color of funerals in the East. Yellow is the color of cowardice in Europe, but the color of courage in Japan and the color of prosperity in Egypt. In China, red is the color of good luck but the color of mourning in South Africa. When choosing colors, consider if your audience may interpret the meaning differently than you intended.

Many people select colors primarily for aesthetic value. There's nothing necessarily wrong with that; adding color of any kind increases visual interest in your slide. Using blue to chunk three elements is just as effective as using red or purple or pink. Drawing attention to an important point on your slide can be done with a red box, a black circle or an orange triangle.

But selecting your colors purposefully can make them more persuasive by generating positive feelings, so it's not a decision that should be made too casually. A custom color palette reduces the number of decisions you need to make and helps ensure each slide is attractive and professional-looking automatically and enhances your credibility.

Contrast

There is too much to learn about graphic design to cover in this book. And it's not necessary for you to become a graphic design expert to create clear and professional-looking PowerPoint slides.

But there is one principle you should learn if you want to use color well and make your slides pop: *contrast*. Oops! I mean…

Contrast is the secret to eye-catching PowerPoint slides. Using a harmonious color palette makes everything work well together. Harmony is pleasing, but you want your slide to pop! Contrast emphasizes the differences, not the similarities.

First, good contrast makes your slides more readable. For instance, black text on a white background has high contrast and the text will be readable. But gray text on a green background has low contrast and the reader will struggle to separate the text from the background.

Second, contrast will make your slide pop! Robin Williams, graphic design expert and author of *The Non-Designer's Design Book* calls contrast one of the four most important principles for pleasing design. The most important advice she gives is: Don't be a wimp. If you want contrast, don't make it *kind of* different; make it *really* different.

The key is to look for *strong* contrasts, not *slight* contrasts. Be bold! Be daring! Colors can be contrasted based on their hue, saturation and brightness.

1. Hue. Hue is the graphic design term for what we commonly call *color*. Red, blue and green are all hues used on your computer monitor. Mixing these different colored lights creates additional hues. Red and green light mix to create yellow. Green and blue light mix to create cyan (light greenish-blue). Red and blue mix to create magenta (violet). Gray is a special color. It is created by mixing all of the hues in equal amount.

You can arrange the hues based on their proximity to the colors that created them to make a color wheel.

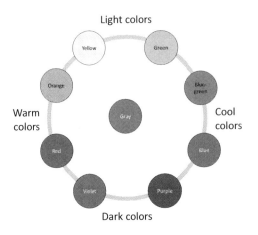

Hues that are farther away on the color wheel have higher contrast than hues that are close. For instance, yellow and purple have high contrast because they are on opposite sides of the color wheel, but yellow and orange have low contrast because they are composed of similar colors.

Warm and cool colors. Hues with a lot of red are called warm colors; they are energetic and seem to advance on the page. Hues with a lot of blue are called cool colors; they are calming and seem to recede on the page. You can roughly divide the color wheel in half based on whether they are predominantly warm or cool colors.

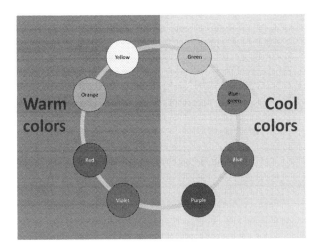

Contrasting a warm and cool color, like red and green, has higher contrast than contrasting two warm colors, like red and yellow.

Dark and light colors. Hues with more blue/red reflect less light and are called dark colors. Hues with more yellow/green reflect light better and are called light colors.

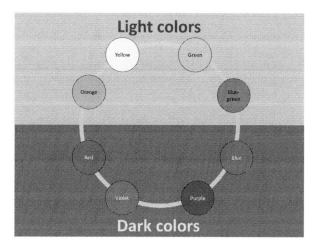

Contrasting dark and light colors, like blue and green, has higher contrast than contrasting two dark colors, like blue and purple.

In the last section, you created a color palette which contained a limited number of hues. You will want to ensure your palette includes a mix of warm and cool colors, as well as dark and light colors, for maximum contrast options.

2. Saturation. While contrasting hues gives maximum contrast, when the hue is too pure it leads to a very vivid contrast, almost cartoonish. Bright reds against gleeful oranges and clownish purples looks more like a kindergarten art project than a serious business document.

You can modify the purity of each hue by reducing its saturation. A pure hue is 100% saturated, which means it contains its color and nothing else. For instance, 100% red contains red and no other color. By reducing the saturation, other neighboring colors mix and change the color closer to gray. At 0% saturation, the color turns to gray.

Reducing a color's saturation essentially dulls the color and makes it more smoky. A slightly smoky blue is more professional-looking than a 100% saturated vivid blue. If you find your slide colors look too vibrant and gleeful, your color saturation is probably too high.

Colors work together best when their saturation is equal. Research by Gerald J. Gorn found colors with higher saturation make the reader more excited, so if your goal is to excite the reader you will want to use relatively high saturation levels. It's usually not a good idea to use colors that all have 100% saturation because the effect is too vivid, but there may be times you want that vivid effect. Small areas of 100% saturated color can offer nice contrast, like a small shape on a large background.

You can adjust saturation levels in PowerPoint 2007's color picker. Just click on the shape or text you want to adjust and select Format > Shape Fill (or Text Fill, Line Fill) > More Colors. That will bring up the color picker.

Go into the Custom tab and you will see a square with a rainbow of colors. Hues are arranged left to right, starting with red, orange and yellow and proceeding to blue, violet and purple and then back to red again. The saturation is indicated from top to bottom. 100% saturation is at the top of the box and 0% saturation is at the bottom, where all colors converge toward gray.

The currently selected color will be indicated by a cross on the color picker. You can adjust the hue by moving the cross left and right. You can adjust the saturation by moving the cross up and down. Just click in the center of the cross and use your arrow keys to move the cross along. Or, just click on a new spot in the color picker box.

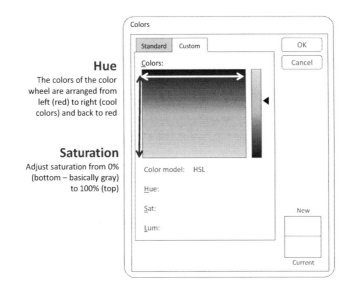

You can double-check the exact saturation level by selecting the *Color model* pull-down menu and select HSL (Hue, Saturation, Luminosity). The exact saturation value is found in the Sat field. If you find your colors don't harmonize well, one easy correction is to double-check the saturation levels and enter the exact same value for each color.

3. Brightness. A hue can be made darker by adding black to it, or lighter by adding white. For instance, you can take the color blue and add some white to make powder-blue or add some black to make navy. These three blues have different levels of *brightness* (also called *luminosity*).

In graphic design language, blue is the *hue*, powder-blue is the *tint* and navy is the *shade*. The hue is the color you start with. Making it lighter by adding white makes it a blue *tint*. Making it darker by adding black makes it a blue *shade*.

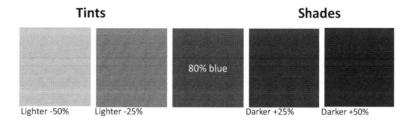

Adding tints and shades is one of the easiest ways to increase the contrast of your colors. Don't contrast colors in some narrow band of brightness, because the contrast will be too subtle. Contrasting shades against tints pops more.

Light colors do not make good shades. Adding black to yellow or orange makes them look muddy and contradicts their nature to reflect light. On the other hand, dark colors will make good tints.

Brightness can be adjusted in the color picker, using the slider on the right side of the color box. Slide the bar toward the top to create tints and slide it toward the bottom to create shades. Like saturation, you can check the exact brightness value by going into the color picker, choosing HSL from the Color model drop-down menu and look at the value in Lum (luminosity).

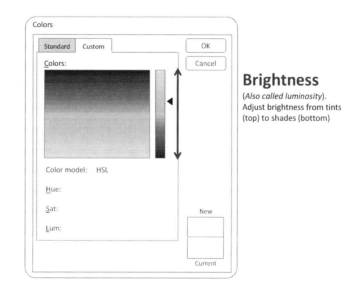

Brightness
(*Also called luminosity*).
Adjust brightness from tints
(top) to shades (bottom)

We've now discussed three ways to contrast colors, using hue, saturation and brightness. The main point to keep in mind is to look for strong contrasts, not weak contrasts. Let's quickly recap the advice in this section:

- contrast warm and cool colors

- contrast dark and light colors

- avoid 100% pure saturation; it looks too vivid and cartoonish

- try to maintain equal saturation levels for your colors; they will harmonize better

- contrast tints and shades; avoid tints and shades in the same narrow brightness value range

And, of course, contrast is highest if you contrast colors based on dark/light, warm/cool and brightness all together. Again, you can really make your slide pop if you go for extreme differences rather than modest differences.

Moderate contrast: Colors with moderately different brightness levels. It looks pleasing but the contrasts are subtle rather than strong.

High contrast: The same colors with extreme differences in brightness. Note how the colors stand up on the page and look more professional.

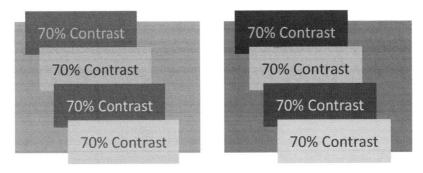

There will be times you want to reduce contrast on your slide. For instance, you may have a pie chart with five slices but three of those slices are very small. Rather than giving each pie slice a different color, you might use a different color for the two largest pie slices, but make the three smaller pie slices different tints of blue. That avoids adding too many colors to a slide only to accommodate relatively insignificant information chunks.

In particular, text needs at least 70% contrast with the background to be easily readable. That means you either want dark text on a light background or light text on a dark background.

So what is better? In terms of readability, research says light text on a dark background is more readable and less taxing on the eyes, especially light green on a dark green background because green has been shown to be the most restful color for the eyes. This might suggest you want to create a color background and light text.

But boardroom-style slides with too much color will make people feel more negative toward your ideas, so you should avoid dark backgrounds. They make the reader work too hard to understand your slide's message. And the more complex your slides, the more you should avoid dark background colors.

In the Meyers-Levy-Peracchio study that opened this chapter, you learned that color makes people feel more positively toward your message. But as the message became more complex, color actually made people feel more *negatively* toward the product being advertised.

An important part of the research was how they tested the ad on students with high motivation to read (by telling them they were one of just a few students whose opinions counted) and those with a low motivation to read (by telling them their scores would be averaged with hundreds of others). This design is important; it allows us to understand how color affects readers with a high interest in your message, the conditions for boardroom-style slides, versus unmotivated audiences, the conditions for ballroom-style slides.

Unmotivated readers felt most positively toward ads with color highlighting and full color, for both simple and complex ads. That's because they were not motivated to carefully study the message and were only responding to the peripheral cues, like how attractive the ads were.

For motivated readers, the results were a bit different. For simple slides, they also responded most positively toward the color ads, and especially the ads with color to highlight the relevant parts.

But for complex slides, motivated readers were most positive toward the highlighted ads or the black and white ads. They were most negative toward the full color ads.

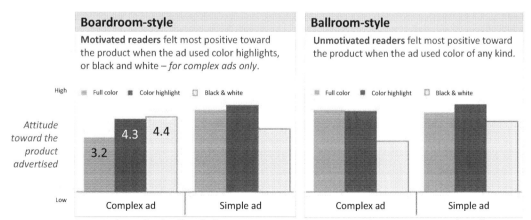

Source: Understanding the Effect of Color, Joan Meyers-Levy and Laura A. Perracchio, 1994, Experiment 2 (n=166)

The researchers concluded that color uses up valuable working memory and the more complex your message, the more selectively you need to use color, especially for motivated readers. For simple ideas, or unmotivated readers, the distraction is not large enough to matter. But for motivated readers and complex ideas, too much color will make people feel more negatively toward your proposal.

That's why boardroom-style slides, with complex information and a motivated audience, should use less color than a ballroom-style slide. This doesn't mean using black and white, but just using color selectively. One way to remove excess color is to avoid using a dark color for the slide background.

I recommend a white background, which is consistent with what business readers expect in a serious business document. I also recommend that text should be gray, not pure black. One hundred percent black text on a white background can be unpleasant and makes a slide look too severe. Reducing the text to gray quiets it down and allows it to support the other colors, rather than compete with them. You still want the text to have good contrast with the background so it's easy to read. I find 75% black is a good color for text.

Alternatively, you could use a light color tint for the background and a slightly darker gray text; like a 10% tint and 85% gray text. Many consulting firms believe a light-colored slide background makes their slides look more professional and credible. You will want to use a tint of one of the accent colors from your color palette so it harmonizes with the other colors you use.

Ballroom-style slides contain less text and the reader is less motivated, so you can use more colorful backgrounds to make them feel positively toward your message.

Use the *squint test* to check that your slide has enough contrast. Close your right eye and then squint your left eye. Or, convert your slide into grayscale. In PowerPoint 2007, go to the View tab and select Grayscale in the Color/Grayscale menu. Can you still see the contrast on the slide? If not, then the contrast is too subtle.

Selecting color is part science and part art. This chapter describes basic color theory but in the end, trust your judgment. If colors don't look good to you, they probably won't look good to others.

Color is powerful and persuasive and will make readers want to spend more time with your slides. But over-use or misuse of color interferes with your clear message and can make the reader feel more negatively toward your ideas. A good PowerPoint communicator will master some of the basic principles of using color on slides.

Back to Grace's slide

Because there are more than four colors, you suspect there may be a problem on this slide. You use this slide as an opportunity to coach Grace on how to use color effectively by going through your manager checklist.

> *Does the color break up the chunking?* Yes, there is virtually no chunking happening on this slide. Everything is its own chunk of information.
>
> *Does the color direct attention incorrectly?* Yes, there is virtually no focus here. Every color is dark and shouting for attention. The eye has no place to land.
>
> *Does the color convey unintended messages?* Possibly. The bright red box might be signaling danger. The bold green background might be signaling all is well.

To fix this slide, you need to ask "what is the main message on this slide?" That should be written in the title. That will tell you what you want to highlight, and will naturally lead to identifying the 3–4 chunks of information.

Let's say you and Grace decide the point she wants to make is September 7 is the launch date. For the next three months, the focus will be creative development. Then September to November will be focused on post-launch activities. Great, the first thing you do is ask Grace to rewrite the slide title to emphasize that message.

Now you look at the slide and consider how to highlight September 7, with some activities happening earlier and some later. You can break this chart into three chunks, using colors to group them: pre-launch activities, launch activities and post-launch activities. You treat the launch, September 7, with a reddish color to suggest excitement without using a pure red which might suggest danger. Then you similarly use color to chunk the other two time periods. We use green for the first chunk to signal things are on track and blue for the last period, a calming color that generates positive feelings and signals there is nothing to worry about. This mix of green, red and blue also contrasts dark and light colors and warm and cool colors.

You use tints for the table's background colors and shades for the colored bars to increase contrast and make the slide look professional.

You simplify this further by removing the color background and incorporating the bullet points directly into the timeline. Now you've used color purposefully to chunk information and direct attention to the launch date, while using a warm color to suggest excitement during the launch.

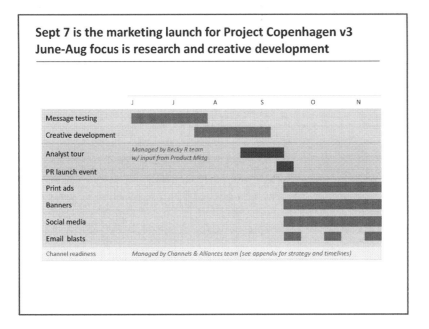

Now color is not just decorative, but serves a purpose for the reader. It helps the reader quickly understand the slide while making it more pleasing and so more persuasive. And by paying attention to contrast, Grace has produced a slide that enhances her own professional image.

Before: Colors selected on a whim   **After:** Using Mindworks Presentation Method

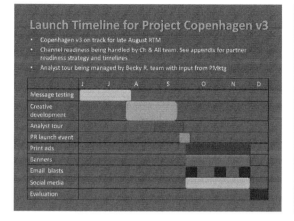

Above-water argument

1. Color increases reader interest and positive attitudes toward your message. It's a critical aspect of creating slides that are clear, interesting, professional-looking and convincing.

2. Use 3–4 colors to chunk information, highlight key points and convey meaning. Purely decorative color is probably okay as long as it doesn't interfere with chunking, highlight the wrong information or send an unintended message, but use the manager's color checklist to see if color could be working harder for you.

3. Adopt a custom color palette to use in all your slides. It will save you time creating slides, give you harmonious colors that will be visually pleasing and a consistency to your slides that enhances your credibility. A color palette based on a pleasing image may also affect the reader's mood positively.

4. Use contrast to ensure your slide is readable and eye-catching. Contrast warm and cool colors, and dark and light colors. Try for extreme differences in brightness to add pop! Avoid colors with 100% saturation, which makes them too vivid. Avoid over-use of color, like dark backgrounds, on slides with complex information. Aim for 70% contrast in text against the background and use the *squint test* to double-check your contrast allows good readability.

Recommended reading

The Non-Designer's Design Book by Robin Williams is written for the artistic novice and is perfect for the left-brain business manager. This crash course in the critical principles of pleasing graphic design is an easy read and a handy reference.

Slide:ology by Nancy Duarte and *Presentation Zen* by Garr Reynolds are two of the better books on PowerPoint slide design, including how to use color and contrast for designing ballroom-style presentations, like keynote addresses or sales presentations.

Color, Contrast & Dimension in News Design from the Poynter Institute is an online interactive lesson demonstrating how to use different types of contrast. The instructional material is beautifully designed and the interactive lessons lets you experience the effects of different color choices and contrasts. http://poynterextra.org/cp/colorproject/color.html

CHAPTER 12

Picture and Wallpaper

Manage the reader's visual path

Y OU ARE PREPARING TO PRESENT your product roadmap at an upcoming all-hands meeting, to educate a team of 50 marketing staff. You've asked your direct report, Grace, to create the roadmap slide. This is what she shows you.

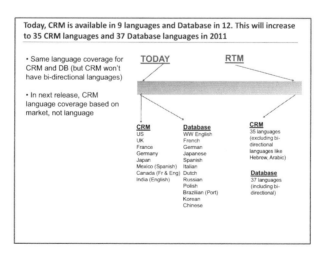

The slide title is clear, but the content seems disorganized with text and diagrams both competing for attention. You know that presenting this slide to a room requires minimal text, perhaps 2–3 words for visual cues only. If Grace intends this to work as a reading deck or discussion deck later, you'll also need to subdue any other text as much as possible, perhaps by moving it off the visual path.

Even so, there is just a little information on this slide but for some reason your eye doesn't know where to land. What are you supposed to look at first? Your eyes seem to scrabble around, looking for a starting point.

Is this slide ready to present? What is your advice to Grace?

What's the Picture?

If everything on your slide is important, then nothing is important.

Your slide will contain a lot of content: pictures, text, diagrams, arrows and so on. But you need to be purposeful about how you arrange elements on the slide, so the reader can see what is important right away and not be distracted by everything else on the slide. When everything is treated as equally important, the reader will have trouble finding a starting point and a path into your slide.

Map shock is the term used to describe the feeling of being disoriented when looking at a complicated visual, such as a complex subway map, where everything is presented as equally important. The reader describes this as not knowing where to start or how to navigate through the complex information. The reader becomes frustrated, discouraged and gives up trying to understand.

It would be fair to say that complex slides create a similar reaction—*PowerPoint shock*. This is similarly caused by the eye not knowing where to start on a slide or how to navigate through it. The more common term for this is "Death by PowerPoint" where you are presented with a slide that is so complex and poorly organized the reader doesn't know where to start and how to navigate into the content, becomes disoriented and frustrated and gives up trying to understand it.

Map shock!

PowerPoint shock!

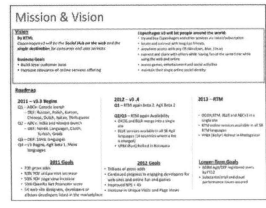

PowerPoint shock causes the reader to ask:

What am I looking at?

Where do I start?

How do I move through this slide?

If they cannot find answers to these questions, they simply give up. Your message has failed.

The solution to PowerPoint shock is to provide clear guidance to the reader how to navigate through the slide. You do this in two ways: by determining what is the focus of your slide, and by providing a clear starting point and visual path through the slide content.

Let's first discuss providing a focus for your slide. For instance, in this text block, what are the four ways to make a message more clear?

> **Information design is the antidote to information overload. The designer needs to understand how attention works, and especially the difference between top-down and bottom-up attention. Intelligent use of color, size, layout and other graphic design elements can make a message more clear.**

This text block is frustrating to read because there's no way to quickly find the information you want. Instead, you need to read through the entire text block until you stumble upon the information you are looking for.

Okay, let's try again using a different text box. What are the four ways to make a message more clear?

> Information design is the antidote to information overload. The designer needs to understand how attention works, and especially the difference between top-down and bottom-up attention. Intelligent use of **color, size, layout and other graphic design elements** can make a message more clear.

Do you see how much easier it is to understand when the writer highlights the critical pieces for the reader and subdues the less critical pieces?

In this example, we have reduced most of the text to 75% gray, except for the important text, which is 100% black and bolded. We have done two things to make the message more clear: we've *highlighted* the important content, and we've *subdued* the less important content.

I call this the principle of *Picture and Wallpaper* and it's one of the most critical things you can do to make your slides clearer and differentiate yourself from other communicators. The *Picture* is the part of the slide you want the reader to pay attention to. It's the main message or data on your slide. The *Wallpaper* is everything else on your slide that provides the context or the supporting details, but does not need to capture the reader's attention immediately.

In the field of information design, this principle is called *information hierarchy*. Information overload is not caused by too much information, but too much information that is poorly organized. The antidote is information design: organizing complex information so that the reader can navigate it easily and find what they need. Information design has been practiced for hundreds of years by map makers, medical illustrators, highway sign designers and others who need to simplify complex visual displays.

When designing a slide, you should ask *What is the Picture*? Where do I want to direct the reader's eye? Asking this question is a good discipline; it forces the writer to have a clear point they are trying to make.

Consider this simple business graph. What is the main message the reader should take away?

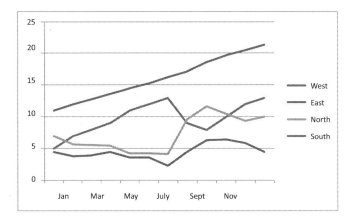

You're not sure, are you? There's a lot going on here. This graph contains *information* but it has not been *designed* to communicate a clear message. There is no focus; no *Picture*. Everything is equally important. The reader will spend a long time on this graph trying to determine what needs his attention and what message he should take away.

Now, what's the main message in this graph?

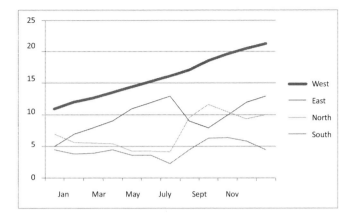

This is the exact same data, but now the writer is trying to deliver a clear message: sales are increasing in the Western region. He has directed the reader's eye instantly by asking *What is the Picture* and then using information design principles to emphasize that line.

But equally important, he has reduced the width of the other three lines, subduing them and making them easy to ignore. They have become Wallpaper; context on the graph and not the graph's focus. Determining what is Wallpaper is just as critical as determining what is Picture.

Let me repeat that: subduing the Wallpaper is just as important as highlighting the Picture. Remember our discussion of contrast in the last chapter. By reducing some content's prominence, it increases the contrast between the Picture and Wallpaper and helps the reader instantly know where to look and what message to take away.

Using the same data, we can tell a completely different story, just by selecting different content to make the Picture and turning everything else into Wallpaper.

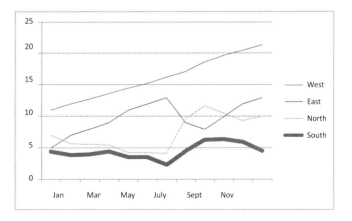

Complex slides are often a clue that the slide designer didn't know what they were trying to say. They poured data onto a slide, but didn't do the hard analytic work to figure out what message they were trying to convey. Forcing yourself to ask *What is the Picture* is a good discipline to become a better communicator. If you don't know what the Picture is, your reader will not know either.

One of the most important things you can teach your staff is to highlight the main message on each slide. Rather than letting them present a ton of data on a slide that takes the reader forever to sort through, you should constantly ask your staff to make a point on each slide.

The question you should always ask is: *What's the Picture?*

Use location, color and size to highlight the Picture

The Picture is the main point of the slide. It is where you want the eye to go and what you want the reader to understand. There may be a lot of detail on the slide, but you want to focus the reader's attention primarily and initially on the Picture.

The rest of the data is also important, that's why it's on the slide at all, but primarily to provide context and supporting details. The Wallpaper *frames* the Picture and provides the necessary background, but it is not the main point of the slide.

There are four ways to draw attention to the Picture: color, size, whitespace and location. You can use more than one of these principles at the same time to really draw attention to the Picture and subdue the Wallpaper.

1. Color

You learned from the last chapter that some colors seem to advance toward the reader and some to recede. Colors which advance are good Picture colors because they draw attention. Colors which recede are good Wallpaper colors because they settle quietly into the background.

Warm colors like red and orange make good Picture colors. Cool colors like blue and green make good Wallpaper colors.

Dark shades make good Picture colors while light tints make good Wallpaper colors. Gray is an especially good Wallpaper color because it is easy to ignore and harmonizes well with any other color. That's why it's a good practice to use a dark shade of any color for slide titles and labels to draw attention to your slide summaries, but use 75% gray for body text to make it recede into the background.

For instance, consider these two slides. The slide on the left uses a dark color to highlight one of the lines and its text label, and gray to subdue the other lines and their text labels. The chart on the right uses the default colors in Excel for the lines and text labels. On which slide does your eye know where to start?

Dark color for the Picture and gray for the Wallpaper. The bottom line attracts attention.

Default colors for the chart lines. There is no clear message.

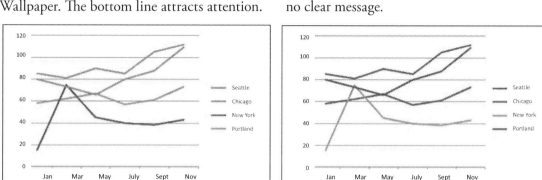

2. Size

Large items attract more attention than small items. Large fonts are seen before small fonts, thick lines before thin lines and large shapes before small shapes.

For instance, you might have a line graph with each of the lines labeled. You can attract attention to the most important line by using a thicker line width and increasing the font size of its text label. Similarly, you can subdue the other lines by making them thinner and reducing the label text size.

Other ways to increase the size of text is to bold it or use all capital letters. Other ways to reduce the perceived size of text is to use italics. I use 75% gray text in italics for footnotes because I want them to recede on the page but still be readable if needed. Similarly, when I place unimportant annotations into diagrams, I use gray italic text, to reduce its perceived importance.

Larger fonts and line width. Notice the annotated text in italics, which appears to whisper.

Same size fonts and line widths. The eye cannot tell which part of the graph is important.

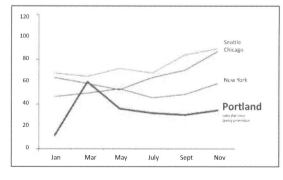

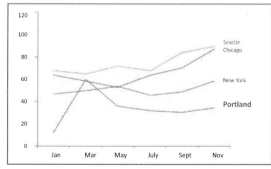

3. Whitespace

The eye is drawn to large expanses of whitespace and tends to avoid cluttered spaces. You can attract attention to a part of the slide by designing it in a cushion of whitespace.

Extra whitespace cushions the Picture word, helping it stand out from the other lines

Crowded whitespace. Text competes for attention by crowding the whitespace

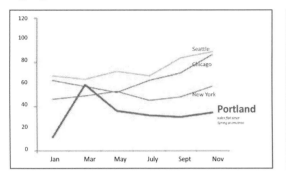
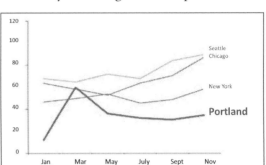

4. Location

There are certain parts of the slide the eye looks at first. Especially on a computer screen, eye-tracking studies show readers start in the upper-left corner, scan horizontally and then read down hugging the left side of the screen. This is called the F-path, which we introduced in chapter 10.

The top left quadrant of the slide is the called the *optical center*. When we are looking at a slide, we don't look right at the middle of the slide. We look slightly up and to the left because, in the western culture, we are taught to reader left to right and top to bottom. Just like gravity, your eye is drawn naturally to look at the optical center. Advertisers often place attention-grabbing elements in the optical center to capture a reader's interest.

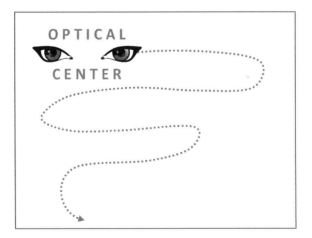

Images used in this book can be seen in color at www.speakingppt.com

You can make your Picture prominent by moving it into or near the optical center. At a minimum, try to move it to the top half of the slide, which will give it prominence because it gets read first.

It's not always feasible to do this, because elements may not easily be moved to the optical center. And for simple slides, color, size and whitespace may be sufficient. But if you can move information into the optical center, it will make the reader look at it automatically.

Picture highlighted using the optical center. Note this also uses font size and whitespace effectively.

Optical center left blank. The Picture is still highlighted because the slide is simple.

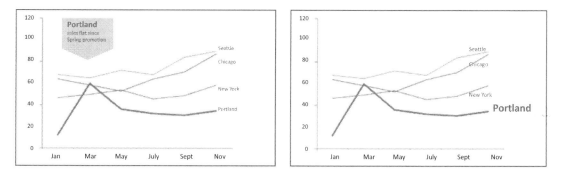

The eye also tends to hug the left side of the slide, especially when viewed on a computer screen. So important content should be placed more toward the left margin and less important content toward the right margin. For instance, when you are presenting two options for the reader to consider, place the superior option on the left side of the slide and the inferior option on the right. They reader will automatically view the superior option first. When they look at the inferior option, it will be with a slight bias for the first option and an evaluation that is sensitive to the inferior aspects of the second option.

Strong. Recommended option is closer to the left margin so it is seen first and the idea on the right is considered inferior.

Weak. Moving an idea toward the right margin weakens it; the eye is drawn to the content closest to the left margin.

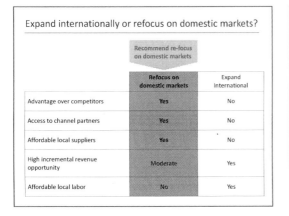

In practice, I like to start out designing my entire slide as Wallpaper, and then determine where I want to focus attention. Then I can use the design principles we covered in this section to increase attention on the Picture and subdue the Wallpaper.

Picture	Wallpaper
Warm colors	Cool colors
Shades	Tints
Large fonts, bold	Small fonts, italics
Thicker lines	Thinner lines
Surrounded by whitespace	Surrounded by content
In optical center	Away from optical center
Left side of slide	Right side of slide

Highlight the Picture with text

In order to direct attention, it's important to understand how attention works.

Think of attention like a surly bouncer guarding a nightclub entrance. Attention decides who gets into the club and who has to wait in line. This nightclub is *working memory*. There are only four slots available in working memory and attention decides who gets in and who stays out, so attention has a couple of rules it follows.

The first rule is called *top-down attention*. Here, attention is consciously looking for very specific kinds of information to make a decision. If you are on the invite list, attention lets you into the club. If you're not on the list, you wait outside.

The second rule is called *bottom-up attention*. He is looking for certain things that catch his eye. They aren't on the list, but he will let them into the club anyway: celebrities, beautiful people, his own friends. So you can get into the club even if you're not on the list.

An example will illustrate the point. Imagine I am driving on highway 405 north, near my office, looking for the next exit. My gas tank is low and I'm actively looking for the exit sign and the location of the gas station, which is not familiar to me. I have a lot of things I could be paying attention to: the traffic around me, the speedometer, the time, the music on the radio. But I can't process all of it; my most immediate need is gas so I'm looking for the next exit. This is top-down attention. I am paying attention to things I don't normally pay attention to because I need to solve a problem.

Suddenly, a police siren wails behind me. My eyes flick to my speedometer. *Was I speeding?* Then they dart to the rearview mirror. I see the pulsing red lights and a police car rocketing past two lanes over from me. I breathe a sigh of relief that I'm not being pulled over. This is bottom-up attention. I was alerted by the loud siren and then the red flashing lights. This also triggered top-down attention: looking at my speedometer.

We covered bottom-up attention in the last section of this chapter: using color, size, whitespace and location to attract the reader's attention subconsciously.

Top-down attention is captured with text that indicates what you want the reader to pay attention to. That's why the slide title is so important; it tells the reader exactly what to look for. Research shows that people look at an image differently, based on the accompanying text. Using the same picture of a model lounging on a sports car, people spend more time looking at the car if the headline says "Become a Formula One driver" and more time looking at the model if the headline says "Become a fashion model".

When you ask yourself *What is the Picture*, the answer should be found in your slide title. If it isn't, you probably need to rewrite your slide title or rethink what you want to highlight on the slide.

That's also why labels are so important; they direct top-down attention to certain content on your slide, and summarize that content.

The placement of the labels is also important; you want them to appear before the images and body text.

For instance, in the slides on the left, the labels appear before the images and body text, so the reader's top-down attention is activated first. They will understand the message relatively quickly. The slide on the right reverses this, showing the images before the labels, so the reader is unsure what to pay attention to at first. They must read the text then go back to the image a second time to process it correctly.

Strong. Text before content. Top-down attention is activated and the reader knows what to look for.

Weak. Content before text. Reader is puzzled by the content and needs to read the text then look at the content again.

Placing the text before the content also moves it high on the slide and toward the left margin, the two parts of the slide where the eye wants to go first.

Sometimes you need several text blurbs to highlight different parts of a diagram or chart. In that case, you can use *call-outs* for both top-down and bottom-up attention. Call-outs can also be useful if the Picture is difficult to move into the optical center, or is otherwise difficult to highlight with color, size or whitespace.

Call-outs are text blurbs placed in a prominent location, often near the optical center, which point to some place on the slide and summarize the main point. They can also use large bolded text in colorful boxes surrounded by whitespace. In this way, they activate top-down attention as well as bottom-up attention.

Consider this slide, using a call-out located on the top half of the slide and near the optical center. This placement activates top-down attention by placing it high on the visual path and links those thoughts directly with the relevant places on the line graph.

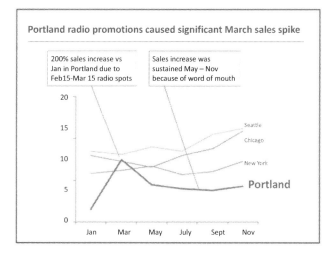

There is one more important point to make about attention: it tends to focus on small areas at a time. Attention has been said to operate like a spotlight. When it focuses on one area, it forgets what it just saw in another area. Or, if has to hold what it just saw in working memory while sweeping its spotlight to another area.

So placing two pieces of content far apart taxes working memory. This is the split-attention effect, which we covered in chapter 8 and chapter 10. Placing them close together, so they can both be viewed at the same time, frees up working memory and makes it easier to understand.

So, to ensure the reader gets your message, push call-out information as close to the content as possible.

Call-outs integrated with the content make it easier for the reader to understand. Everything can be seen in attention's "spotlight".

Call-outs far from the content make it more challenging for the reader. Working memory must hold information from two parts of the slide.

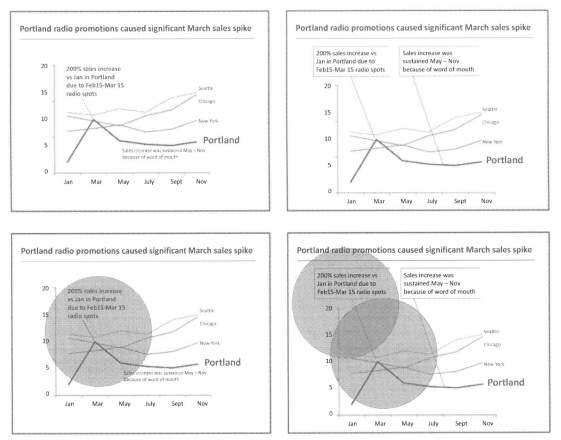

Using transparent colors is another good way to highlight content in a crowded place. You can place a shape on top of some content to highlight it without blocking it. In PowerPoint 2007, go into the Fill Color menu and select "More Colors". On the Custom tab, at the bottom, you'll find the Transparency slider. Move that slider to about 60% to create a shape you can place over content in a crowded place.

Another smart tip is to create a custom shape, rather than standard circles and ovals, and fill the custom shape with transparent color. This can often give your slides a distinctive and professional appearance. In PowerPoint 2007, go to Insert > Shapes and select the tool that looks like a stubby boot.

Custom shapes and transparent color

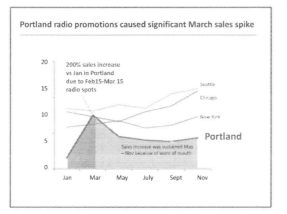

Standard ovals and transparent color

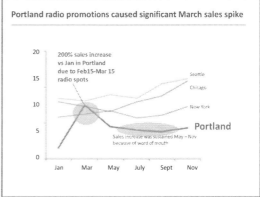

Direct the eye through the slide with a visual path

Highlighting the important information and subduing the supporting details helps to reduce the clutter on complex slides and emphasizes the main message. This is half the battle to combating PowerPoint shock.

But you also have to think about the visual path the reader will take on the slide. Where will they start their journey? How will they move through the rest of the slide?

You want the reader to start with the slide title, which activates top-down attention and directs the reader to your important content. The reader starts in the optical center, which is just a bit lower than where the title starts. You will need to use graphic design techniques to draw the eye up to the title from the optical center. Some options are:

- use the largest font on the slide for the title

- use a background color that separates the title from the rest of the slide

- place a brightly colored line under the title

- use a bright color for the words in the title

- place a box around the title

- I like to use a technique called the *toothpick* — a brightly colored ornamental line pointing at the title like a thin directional arrow. I have seen other slide designers use brightly colored rectangles or other bright shapes. But the purpose is the same—to draw the eye up to the title

After the reader has read the title, you want to move them through the rest of your slide. We've talked about way people view content on a computer screen as the F-path, starting in the optical center, skimming across the top, dropping down and hugging the left margin. If you can fit your content in a generally left-to-right or top-to-bottom orientation, the eye can easily skim it and the reader will become oriented easily.

But sometimes the content fits awkwardly on a slide, and a strict left-to-right or top-to-bottom orientation is not possible. In fact, you may want to direct the reader from the bottom up, or right to left, or even bounce them to different parts of the slide. There are several ways to direct the reader in a non-conventional visual path:

- *number* the different elements so the reader follows them in a particular order

- use *arrows* to direct the reader from one element to another

For instance, here's a slide showing different layers of technology a company can buy to build a website or web application. The main message is that developers can start with the basic platform layer and add more components to create more advanced applications.

But the platform layer is at the bottom of the slide! And there's no obvious way to move it to the optical center. We want the reader to start at the bottom and read up the slide.

You can direct them through the slide in the order that will best deliver the message by numbering the visual path for them. Here, I've highlighted the bottom layer and numbered the layers from one at the bottom to four at the top, shifting each layer over away from the left margin to suggest a staircase moving upward. I've also added an arrow to reinforce the direction I want them to read. Note that the content is virtually unchanged; all that is changed is the design.

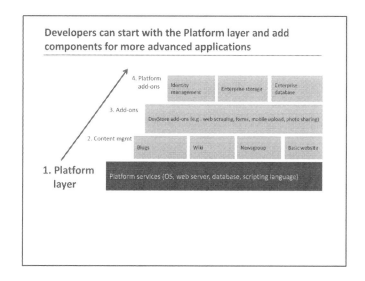

Numbering can be especially useful as visual cues for briefing decks. The presenter can direct the audience to "Notice number one is our platform layer" and readers will have an easy cue to locate their place on the slide.

Too often, slide creators dump information carelessly onto a slide based on where it will fit, rather than where the reader's eyes will go. The result is a confused arrangement where the reader feels lost and confused, creating PowerPoint shock. A little care in organizing your slide can avoid this and make it easy for the reader to pay attention to the key points you want to make.

Back to Grace's slide

You and Grace review the current slide and agree the slide layout is confusing for the reader, causing PowerPoint shock:

1. There's no clear focus on the slide. All the text is black, the timeline uses attractive colors and nothing is consciously emphasized.

2. The optical center is wasted on bullet points that do not contain critical information.

3. There's no clear starting point for the reader and no clear visual path.

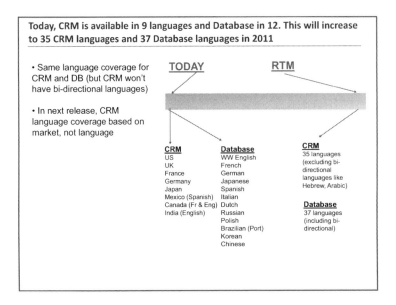

What is the Picture? You and Grace agree that the main point you want to highlight is there are nine languages available today and there will be 35 languages available in the next release. These summaries should go high on the slide, near the optical center if possible, using larger font sizes and perhaps whitespace to make them stand out. You also want these two blurbs to be close together, so the reader can compare them easily.

What is the Wallpaper? The data is the actual timeline and the languages that will be available. These can be studied at the reader's leisure but don't need to be highlighted. The text can be 75% gray so it doesn't compete for attention. You can also integrate the two low-priority bullet points on the left directly into the timeline as footnotes, using italics.

What is the visual path? By removing the stray bullet points, you can now stretch this timeline to cover the entire width of the slide, ending up with a predominantly left to right arrangement. There's no need to number the visual path because it is intuitive, but you decide that adding an arrow helps the visual path and also signals the move from this release to the next release.

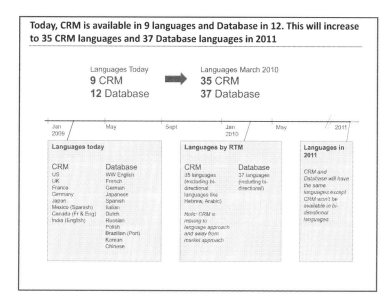

This slide is easier to read and understand because the reader starts reading in the optical center, can see the above-water argument high on the slide and can drill into the details waiting patiently below and not calling for attention. The details are more meaningful because the slide title and summary labels activated top-down attention.

Before: Information organized haphazardly   **After:** Using Mindworks Presentation Method

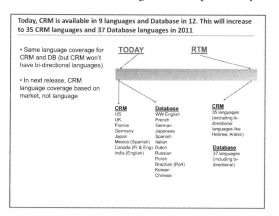

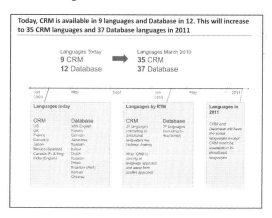

Above-water argument

1. Decide what is *Picture* on your slide and what is *Wallpaper*. Lack of focus on a slide causes information overload, or what might be called *PowerPoint shock*. This is a feeling of being disoriented when looking at a complex slide, not knowing how to navigate into the content and a feeling of being frustrated and discouraged. The solution to *PowerPoint shock* is to give the slide a starting point and a visual path.

2. Highlight the Picture with dark colors, size, whitespace and location near the optical center or high on the slide. Subdue the Wallpaper with muted colors/grays, smaller size and less prominent position. Using design techniques attracts bottom-up attention.

3. Text attracts top-down attention. Use the slide title and summary labels before the content. Use call-outs to attract both top-down and bottom-up attention and integrate your call-outs close to the content because of the split-attention effect.

4. Lead the eye through the slide by positioning information on the visual path, which is an F-path on a computer screen. Use graphic design to draw readers up to the slide title first. Decide on a predominantly left-to-right or top-to-bottom layout or else number the elements if you need to use an unconventional visual path.

Recommended reading

Books by Edward Tufte like *Envisioning Information* and *Beautiful Evidence* will introduce you to the challenge of creating maps, train schedules and other information rich materials. Though Tufte is a vocal critic of PowerPoint, he has influenced many authors with his theories about the data-ink ratio, just-noticeable difference and other principles of communicating complex data in print.

Information Dashboard Design by Stephen Few. While Tufte's books can be too academic for some readers, Few's principles are practical and clearly illustrated. This book covers how to design information dashboards, not slides, but the principles of displaying complex information elegantly and highlighting the information that needs attention is the foundation for this entire chapter. In particular, his illustrations of bad information dashboards will make you laugh at first, until you realize how you make the same mistakes on your own slides.

The Information Design Handbook by Jenn and Ken Visocky O'Grady is an attractively laid out and highly readable introduction to the principles of information design, including how the eye works through information graphics, map shock and the importance of providing clues to help orient and direct the reader.

The Information Design Workbook by Kim Baer covers some of the history of information design and the key principles. It provides many examples of good information design which can deepen your understanding and spark your own creativity.

CHAPTER 13

Aesthetics

Attractive slides are easier to agree with

I**T'S LATE. Y**OU ARE WAITING FOR your direct report, Maria, to email you the marketing deck you wanted to review prior to your meeting with the product management team tomorrow. Maria sends you an email at 9:55 p.m.: *I need another hour. Almost done!*

So, she's working from home, you think to yourself. That's good, you suppose. Or is it? Your spouse has been politely nagging you for months to focus on the family in the evenings, and not on work. You go upstairs to watch an hour of TV then come back to your office to check email again at 11 p.m.

Still no deck.

You wander upstairs and start cleaning up the kitchen, wondering what is taking Maria so long. A half hour later you wander downstairs and check your email. There it is! You hurriedly open the deck and start skimming the slides you'll show the product management team tomorrow showing your marketing approach.

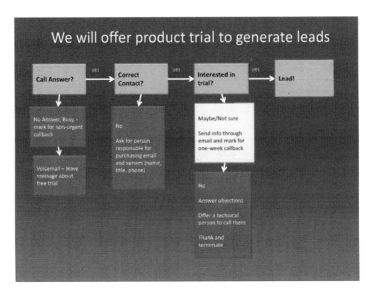

The slides look slick, with many colors and artistic effects. But for some reason, the design is overwhelming the message. It takes effort to ignore the ornamental effects and focus on the meaning.

You glance again at the clock on your computer—11:40 p.m. Is this what Maria was working on all evening? Is this a good use of her time? Your time? Is this slide okay to present to the product management team tomorrow?

What is your advice to Maria?

Attractive slides are easier to agree with

Does it matter how attractive your slides are? On one hand, experts like Edward Tufte advise you remove as much ink as possible that isn't data. Information designers also say *design, don't decorate*. Their mantra is to not add visual elements unless they add meaning.

On the other hand, there are others who say aesthetics increase visual interest and emotional engagement. Educators, for instance, know that adding some humor to a lesson can liven up an otherwise dry lecture. Those who design software interfaces agree that attractively designed buttons are more inviting to use than buttons designed only to be functional.

So, does it matter how attractive your slides are?

It turns out that slide aesthetics are more important than we might realize. As we've discussed several times in this book, winning approval is about more than presenting logical facts; it also involves winning people over emotionally. Pleasing aesthetics leads to positive emotions which in turn affects how the reader thinks.

Consider this text block. How willing are you to support this recommendation?

> It is recommended that we expand our marketing into the university segment. The audience is large (7.7 million students in the United States) and our competitor is making plans to launch a marketing campaign at the beginning of their next fiscal year.

The text is readable but it takes some effort. Now, let's look at the same recommendation presented differently.

> It is recommended that we expand our marketing into the university segment. The audience is large (7.7 million students in the United States) and our competitor is making plans to launch a marketing campaign at the beginning of their next fiscal year.

This text takes less mental effort to read. Compare how this text block makes you feel versus the first text block. Do you feel more positive? Has your willingness to support this idea changed?

In a 2008 study at the University of Michigan, researchers found students were 50% more likely to agree to do something, like begin an exercise routine or prepare a recipe, when the instructions were provided in an easy-to-read font. Hard-to-read fonts required more mental effort leading to more negative feelings and more reluctance to comply.

This mental effort is called *processing fluency*, or *cognitive fluency*, and the principle is simple: the easier it is to mentally process something, the more positively you feel toward it and the more likely you are to agree to it.

Researchers believe that when we feel pleasure from seeing something visually attractive, we subconsciously believe we also like the idea we are reading. Similarly, when we feel frustrated that we have to work extra hard to understand something, we subconsciously assume the idea is frustrating us or it will be more difficult to do something. We mistake the feeling for the thoughts.

In 2001, Professors Winkielman and Cacioppo showed students pictures—some easy to process and some more difficult—and measured how much students smiled. Students not only felt more positive toward the easy-to-process pictures, but the researchers also found those pictures activated the smiling muscles more than harder to process pictures. The effect was not just psychological, but actually physical!

In 2006, researchers at Princeton University gave students a list of fictitious company names and asked which companies were likely to be successful. Companies with easy-to-pronounce names were rated as likely to be more successful than those with hard-to-pronounce names.

The same researchers studied new stocks on the stock market and found that stock prices did actually increase faster in the week after their IPO for companies with easy-to-pronounce names. Difficult-to-pronounce names take more mental effort, make people feel more negative, which makes them feel more negative toward the stock and more unwilling to purchase it.

In a 2007 study, students were asked to choose between two mobile phones based on written descriptions. When the description's font was easy to read, 84% of students could make a decision. When it was hard to read, only 59% could make a decision. Again, forcing the reader to exert extra mental effort made them more negative and less likely to accept any of the options.

Studies like these show us that slides that are easy to process generate more positive feelings which then translate into higher willingness to agree with your ideas.

The principle of cognitive fluency also applies to aesthetics. What makes something visually pleasing? This question has been discussed and debated for centuries, but researchers find that objects which are considered attractive are also rated high for cognitive fluency. That is, the easier it is to mentally process an image, the more attractive we consider it.

Consider these two displays.

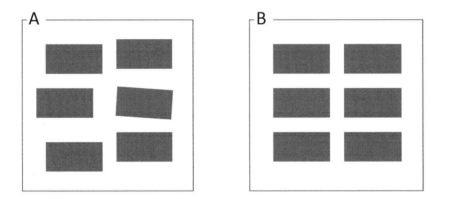

Figure A takes more mental effort because there are more angles that need to be processed. It also looks sloppier and less visually pleasing. It might even make you feel slightly annoyed. Figure B has the same number of blocks but is arranged to reduce the mental effort to process it. It also looks more attractive and may generate a more pleasurable feeling for you.

Can you make your slides so cognitively fluent that everyone will support your ideas? Maybe. But perhaps it's just as important to reduce the amount of clutter on your slides that reduce the cognitive fluency. In most cases, this means *removing rather than adding elements*.

It is impossible to cover all the principles of good aesthetics in this book, and it's likely you do not have an interest in learning all these principles. Still, there are some simple principles of aesthetics you can follow to improve the cognitive fluency of your slides and so their attractiveness. We have covered several of these principles in other parts of the book.

Amount of information. Slides that are too complex take excessive mental effort and reduce cognitive fluency. We covered how to limit information to what will fit working memory in chapter 8.

Grouping information. When content is brought together in groups, it reduces clutter and requires less mental effort to process. We covered this in chapter 8 on chunking and in chapter 11 on using color for grouping.

Color and contrast. Colors with high contrast are easier to distinguish and read and require less effort than colors with low contrast. We covered contrast in chapter 11.

Good figure-ground. The eye likes to see something prominent and something else in the background, rather than having everything compete for attention. We covered this in chapter 12 on Picture and Wallpaper.

Alignment. Alignment is an important part of slide design which we'll cover next in this chapter. As you can see from Figures A and B above, poor alignment looks sloppy and will reduce cognitive fluency, make readers more negative toward your message and so less likely to agree.

Good alignment is one of the simplest things you can do to make your slides more aesthetically pleasing and so make your proposals easier to agree with. We cover that next.

Alignment

In order to create slides so attractive it would make a consultant jealous, double-check there is good alignment.

All objects on your slide should line up with at least one other object. Objects that are floating in space, not aligned with anything else can add clutter to your slide, reduce cognitive fluency and make your slides look less attractive. Whenever you want to make your slides look more attractive, start by fixing the alignment.

Consider this slide, which we saw in the last chapter. It just seems *off.* That's because I reduced the cognitive fluency of this slide by putting several objects out of alignment. The title is center aligned, so it doesn't line up with anything. The text box in the optical center is now a bit higher and doesn't align with anything else. The gray rectangles below the timeline have different lengths so they no longer line up with their neighbors. The right margin is narrower than the left margin. Several lines of text no longer align with each other.

Today, CRM is available in 9 languages and Database in 12. This will increase to 35 CRM languages and 37 Database languages in 2011

Languages Today
9 CRM
12 Database

Languages March 2010
35 CRM
37 Database

Jan 2009 — May — Sept — Jan 2010 — May — 2011

Languages today

CRM
US
UK
France
Germany
Japan
Mexico (Spanish)
Canada (Fr & Eng)
India (English)

Database
WW English
French
German
Japanese
Spanish
Italian
Dutch
Russian
Polish
Brazilian (Port)
Korean
Chinese

Languages by RTM

CRM
35 languages (excluding bi-directional languages like Hebrew, Arabic)

Database
37 languages (including bi-directional)

Note: CRM is moving to language approach and away from market approach

Languages in 2011

CRM and Database will have the same languages except CRM won't be available in bi-directional languages

It is so easy to fix this slide by ensuring every element lines up with at least one other element.

Today, CRM is available in 9 languages and Database in 12. This will increase to 35 CRM languages and 37 Database languages in 2011

Languages Today
9 CRM
12 Database

Languages March 2010
35 CRM
37 Database

Jan 2009 — May — Sept — Jan 2010 — May — 2011

Languages today

CRM
US
UK
France
Germany
Japan
Mexico (Spanish)
Canada (Fr & Eng)
India (English)

Database
WW English
French
German
Japanese
Spanish
Italian
Dutch
Russian
Polish
Brazilian (Port)
Korean
Chinese

Languages by RTM

CRM
35 languages (excluding bi-directional languages like Hebrew, Arabic)

Database
37 languages (including bi-directional)

Note: CRM is moving to language approach and away from market approach

Languages in 2011

CRM and Database will have the same languages except CRM won't be available in bi-directional languages

To check the alignment, turn your gridlines on. These dotted lines help you line elements up so they can share a common invisible border. In PowerPoint 2007, go into the View tab and click the Gridlines checkbox.

Images used in this book can be seen in color at www.speakingppt.com

I cannot tell you how valuable it is to have your gridlines on while you are composing slides. It gives your slides an air of precision and discipline. And you'll produce eye-catching slides in less time because you place each element correctly the first time, and don't need to resize and move elements later.

Good alignment also makes your entire deck look more consistent. From one slide to the next, consistent alignment ensures all elements share a common structure, with the title starting in the same place, similar margin sizes and so on. When you fudge the placement and alignment of elements from slide to slide, it appears less professional. Elements will seem to jump as the reader moves between slides. In contrast, when you use good alignment, elements will seem to show up in the same place from slide to slide.

The most important thing with alignment is to create invisible lines that hold the slide together. Titles aligned on the left help create that invisible line along the left margin of the slide. Avoid center-aligned titles; they create an invisible line down the middle that doesn't align with anything else.

Today, I always work with my gridlines turned on. It lets me create slides perfectly aligned the first time rather than having to come back later and straighten things up.

Stop decorating if the reaction is *cool design!*

What about decoration on slides? By decoration, I mean content that doesn't add meaning but simply adds visual interest. Decorative elements can include drop shadows, beveled edges, gratuitous color gradations, textured fills, background images and other visual confections.

Information designers follow the rule: design, don't decorate. Among information designers, there is a difference between *design* and *decoration*.

Design adds meaning. Design is for the *reader's* benefit: to organize information, add meaning and highlight important content to make it easier for the reader to locate the information. Good design is also pleasing to the eye so adds visual interest as a secondary benefit. We covered the principles of design in the last two chapters.

When things won't line up

Don't you hate it when you want to line up, say, two boxes but each movement is this big jerky step that moves it either too high or too low? How can you just nudge it a hair up or a hair down?

Here's a neat trick. Hold down the ALT key while dragging the shape. This will allow you to adjust the location a hair at a time. This also works when trying to resize a shape. Zoom in using the slider in the lower right corner for really precise alignment.

Decoration adds no meaning. Decoration is at its heart self-expression. That doesn't necessarily mean decoration is harmful to your design, but it primarily satisfies the writer's needs, not the reader's needs.

So if decoration doesn't add meaning, should it be avoided completely?

The surprising answer is no, you shouldn't avoid decoration. Decorative elements can increase visual interest, which increases emotional engagement, makes readers more motivated to listen to your ideas and can influence their decisions positively. The challenge is to use decoration to increase visual interest but not distract from your message.

A humorous Tide commercial illustrates the point. Tide's commercial, which aired during the 2008 Super Bowl, shows an eager job candidate being interviewed. He is wearing a white shirt with a coffee stain on the breast pocket. While he waxes on about his background, the white-haired interviewer is stunned when the coffee stain begins to speak.

As the job seeker continues discussing his candidacy, the stain shouts some unintelligible gibberish even louder. The interviewer is more fascinated with the strange talking stain than he is the job candidate, who continues talking blissfully unaware of the distracting noises made by his coffee stain. While the job candidate is trying to convey his important message and convince this company to give him a job, the coffee stain is ruining his chances. Tide's message: silence the stain.

Like the hapless job candidate, you may also have unintelligible content mumbling on your slides and competing for the reader's attention. When this content finds its way onto your slide accidentally, I call them *mumblers*. It's okay to use these mumblers on your slide if they aren't competing for attention. But you should at least become aware of them so you can decide whether you want them on your slide or not.

Some mumblers find their way onto slides without us being aware. Often, after we create a slide, we feel dismayed that it's not pretty enough or not professional enough. And so we start adding ornamentation to try to dress it up. But we are not designers and inexpert attempts to dress up our slides may actually do the opposite.

Edward Tufte, author of several books on information design, provides a useful concept for removing *mumblers* from your slides: the data-ink ratio.

Consider that every drop of ink on your slide either provides useful information (data) or is just decoration. Decoration is not necessarily bad. In some cases it adds energy to your slides. But too much decoration starts to compete with the data, just as the obnoxious coffee stain competes with the job candidate.

Consider a slide like this. The slide designer has added a lot of decorative touches to add visual interest. But is this easier to read because of the decoration? Or is the decoration making it harder to read their message?

What percent of the ink on this slide is data? 10%? 5%? Less? Is there any ink you can take away without removing data?

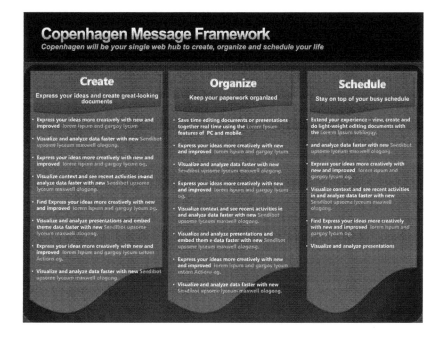

Recall the importance of Picture and Wallpaper. The more ink you have on a slide that shouts for attention, the harder it is for the Picture to be noticed. If you have several noisy elements on your slide shouting for attention, you make it harder for the reader to know what is the Picture.

I know in my workshops that participants do not like the advice to remove decorative elements from their slides. I remember after one workshop, a participant approached me to thank me for the instruction. Then asked me where is the best place to download backgrounds for PowerPoint slides.

The impulse to decorate dies hard.

Designing PowerPoint slides is ultimately an artistic task. Some of us are good artists; many of us are not. But design is a deeply personal act. Just as we all have our own writing style and speaking style, we all have our own design style. And we want to express ourselves through our work.

I once had the pleasure of discussing this with Nancy Duarte, author of *Slide:ology*. I asked her how much decoration is too much for a business slide. Her response was insightful. She pointed out that PowerPoint is one of the few creative outlets available to many of us. It's natural, even healthy, to express ourselves a little bit through color and ornamentation. We are, after all, not just mindless number-crunching machines, but human beings with emotions and passions and dreams. If PowerPoint can enrich us, even a little, by giving us a safe outlet to express our creative selves, we should try to accommodate this.

I think this is an important insight. It's easy to give the advice to remove anything that doesn't add meaning. But human behavior is more complex. We need to find a balance between what is ideal and what is personally acceptable.

Perhaps the best guideline is it's safe to add decoration up until the point it distracts from your message. But how do you know when the decoration is starting to become a distraction?

If you look at your slide and think *cool design!* your decoration is starting to be more noticeable than your message. That's the point where you should start thinking about what mumblers you can remove.

Remove accidental mumblers

Below, I list some common mumblers which can be replaced with more subtle alternatives. I encourage you to consider removing them from your slides completely. If you use them, use them consciously and only if your first reaction isn't *cool design!*

Large areas of dark saturated colors. Vivid colors have a tendency to advance and call attention to themselves, competing with the text for attention and interfering with readability. Replace these with muted colors or tints.

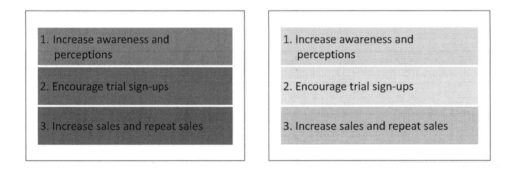

Drop shadows, reflections, 3-D effects and other ornaments meant to dress up your slide. These play no role in communicating your message and just add flashy distractions. They often look amateurish and self-conscious as well. If you use them, apply them with restraint to the Picture element of your slide to help direct attention.

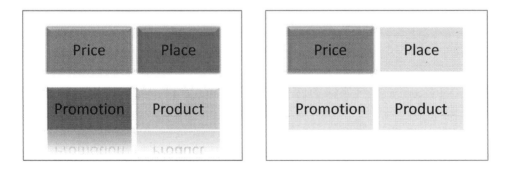

Images used in this book can be seen in color at www.speakingppt.com

Heavy lines and borders around shapes. It's rarely necessary to put heavy borders around shapes and they can interfere with the readability of the text. Light thin borders, or even no borders, look more elegant. Use left alignment for headers and text; it creates an invisible left border in the reader's mind that makes a dark border unnecessary.

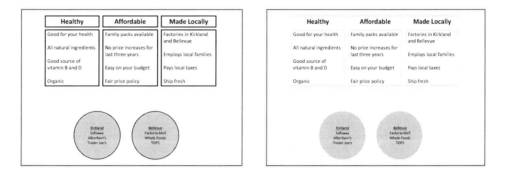

Gratuitous use of photographs and clip art. Visuals can enhance instant understanding and have an emotional impact. But they can also be used as decoration, such as putting clip art of Christmas trees in the corner of your slides explaining a Christmas promotion or photographs as backgrounds on charts to liven up the data. Instead, let the data stand on its own.

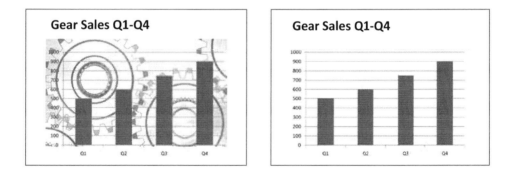

Background images and templates. They often look slick, and can be used when they are quiet and subdued. But busy background images can compete for attention with your clear content and some background templates can overlap with the text and images on your slide, making them needlessly harder to read. Instead, go for a simple white or tint background.

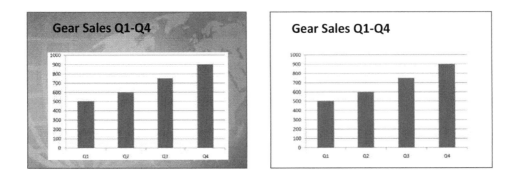

BFA's (Big Fat Arrows). Like any shape, large arrows only need the lightest outline around them. Make your arrows as small and as light-colored as possible. Muting your arrows allows the reader to focus more on the content, with subtle arrows to guide them to the next message. Large full-bodied arrows can become focal points unnecessarily.

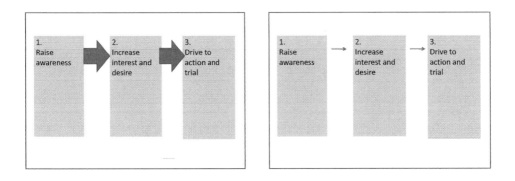

Colored backgrounds are sexy and seduce us with their attractiveness. But they also tend to focus the reader's attention on the aesthetics rather than the message. When you present a slide you want the reader to think *good idea, what will it cost to implement this* and not *cool slide, pretty colors!* Also, knockout letters (light letters on dark background) are harder to read because the background moves forward and the light-colored text recedes.

The goal of the background is to provide a contrast for the text to stand out on. Light colored backgrounds are fine, and are often used by big consulting companies like McKinsey, but dark text on white has the best readability.

Gradations of color and textured fills. On some slides, for no reason, you will often find colors that fade from dark to light or from one color to another or texture fills. The purpose is clearly to ornament an otherwise straightforward visual. But the gradations do not provide any meaning. Stick to solid colors without gradations.

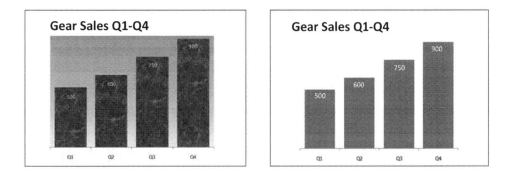

Design is often a question, not of what else to add, but what else to take away. You can increase the cognitive fluency of your slide by always being on the hunt for mumblers. Can you make this line smaller? Lighter? Does this box need a border? What else can you take away?

When I conduct workshops, I often get this question: *if I remove everything that isn't data, then what about corporate logos in the footer?*

My opinion is that the corporate logo in the footer serves no purpose for your reader. But if the logo is small and located at the bottom of the slide, it's easy to ignore. Still, I am increasingly not placing my company logo on slides I create for clients. It uses up valuable screen real estate and sometimes bumps self-consciously into content on the slide. If you work for a large company, it may not be in your power to decide whether or not to include a logo. But at a minimum, you should move it to the bottom of the slide and minimize the size.

None of this advice is to say that these ornamental effects cannot be attractive and add visual interest to a business slide. But just use them purposefully, not accidentally, and stop if the reaction is *cool design!*

Of course, the simpler the slide, the more you can put decorative elements on it to liven it up. I will often use saturated colors and emotional images on the title slide and section headers. It does add visual interest to a PowerPoint deck and doesn't disrupt the message if the slide is simple enough. Ballroom-style slides are less complex than boardroom-style slides and can accommodate more decorative elements.

And what happens to our overly-artistic slide when we remove all the mumblers: color backgrounds, beveled edges, reflections and gradated color?

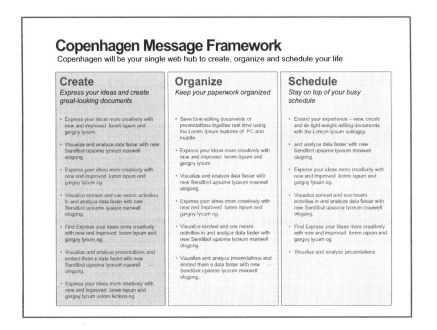

The slide is clearer for the reader once the mumblers are removed. How much clearer? Unfortunately, we don't have a thermometer that can give us that answer. It lacks the seductive detail of the original version but it has high cognitive fluency which makes it aesthetically appealing while still being readable.

I'm aware that, as a market researcher, part of the value I offer clients is the ability to deliver the final report in an attractively formatted PowerPoint deck. This isn't just a nice perk. The client has spent tens of thousands of dollars, sometimes hundreds of thousands of dollars, and the final report is what they will use to help drive change in the organization. I take slide aesthetics very seriously.

Back to Maria's slide

Your first reaction to the slide is *cool colors!* That's a sign the decoration is competing with the message and you might want to remove some mumblers from this slide.

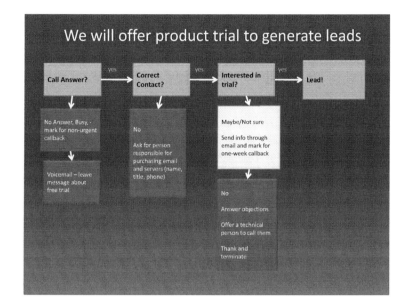

What is the Picture? You decide you want to highlight the top row of the diagram, taking a customer from a successful contact to a qualified lead. You will want to use darker colors to highlight that section and lighter tints for the lower boxes in the diagram. You can even keep the drop shadows on the top row of boxes to increase the visual interest of the Picture.

You can also reduce the extra decoration by turning the color background to white, removing the bevel effects on the shapes and reducing the size of the arrows to more of a whisper.

The alignment is also poor on this slide, with the title center-aligned and several boxes poorly aligned so they look sloppy on the slide. You turn on the gridlines and align the boxes with their neighbors. Then finish by aligning the title left.

Just a few minutes later, you have this slide.

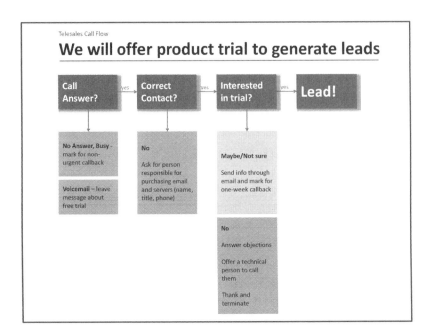

You recognize this slide lacks the seductive quality of the original slide. But this slide does have higher cognitive fluency which makes it easier to read and more likely to elicit agreement. The original slide put form over substance. But you knew what mumblers to be on the lookout for and made a conscious decision to remove most of the decorative elements from the slide.

Before: Low cognitive fluency   **After:** Using Mindworks Presentation Method

Above-water argument

1. Cognitive fluency means how much mental effort you need to exert to understand something. Attractive slides use principles that increase cognitive fluency and make people more likely to agree with your suggestions. Slides with low cognitive fluency are harder to process, and make people more negative and so less likely to agree with your ideas.

2. Work with your gridlines on. Alignment is one of the simplest ways to increase cognitive fluency and ensure slides look attractive. Every element on a slide should line up with at least one other element. Left-aligned slide titles help create an invisible line along the left margin.

3. It's okay to use some decoration if it doesn't distract from your message. But if your first reaction is *cool slide design* your decoration is competing with the message.

4. Be aware of potential mumblers like large areas of dark saturated colors, background images, thick lines, color gradations and ornamental effects like drop shadows and beveled edges. It's okay to use them purposefully, and in a restrained manner, but beware of them finding their way onto your slides accidentally.

Recommended reading

The Non-Designer's Design Book by Robin Williams is written for the artistic novice and is perfect for the left-brain business manager. This crash course in the critical principles of pleasing graphic design is an easy read and a handy reference.

Slide:ology by Nancy Duarte approaches slide design from a graphic design perspective. Her book is a gem for showing non-artistic slide designers how to simplify and beautify slides.

Presentation Zen by Garr Reynolds teaches the use of simplicity and restraint in graphic design. Garr has an excellent sense of design and artistry and illustrates how to use decoration and design to complement, not compete with, your message.

Any book by Edward Tufte, including *Envisioning Information* and *Beautiful Evidence* will introduce you to the challenge of creating maps, train schedules and other information rich materials. Tufte has influenced many authors with his theories about the data-ink ratio, just-noticeable difference and other principles of communicating complex data in print.

CHAPTER 14

Charts and Tables

Use charts to tell a story

YOU AND YOUR DIRECT REPORT, Julia, are preparing to present your marketing recommendations to your general manager. Julia has just completed a market research project to learn which industries would be most interested in your new product. Here is the slide she is planning to present.

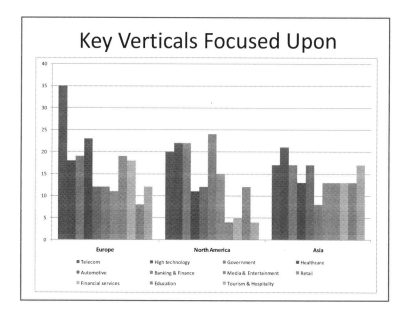

You study this slide for a long time, trying to match the colors in the legend to the colors in the chart. It takes a lot of effort, and since you just learned about cognitive fluency, you're concerned the extra effort will make your general manager more negative toward Julia's conclusions.

Is there a better way to present this data? What is your advice to Julia?

Find the story in the data

There is a story locked in every chart. The data tells the story of declining customer satisfaction or increased competitive activity or emerging customer needs. The data is pointless if it doesn't explain something going on in the world that needs your attention—a story. Your job as a business communicator is to listen to the data and then help others see the story.

Excel doesn't know the story. Excel creates dumb charts based on the default settings. If you copy and paste a chart from Excel into PowerPoint, the story will remain locked in the data. The reader will have more difficulty understanding your important message. Well-designed charts also look more professional and visually pleasing, increasing cognitive fluency and making people more receptive to your suggestions.

This chapter tells you how to display charts and tables so they tell a story and look professional. A discussion of charts is also a capstone to many of the design principles we've covered including chunking, Picture and Wallpaper, color and mumblers.

To begin, let's consider a typical chart created with Excel's default settings. This is data on what is important in selecting a company email system. I have changed nothing; simply copied and pasted it from Excel. What is the story?

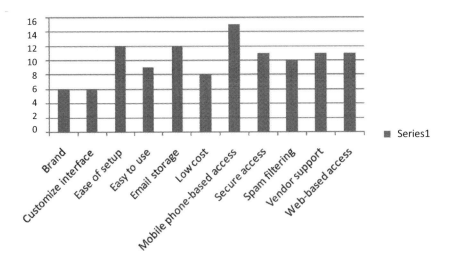

There are four reasons the story is buried in this chart:

1. Most important, there is no Picture. Everything is equally important so the eye does not know where to focus

2. There are a ton of mumblers on this chart

3. The data is sorted alphabetically and is not organized, or chunked, in a meaningful way

4. The colors are random, not informative

This chart tells no story. Perhaps the slide creator doesn't even know what story they want to tell and is just dumping data onto the slide hoping the reader can figure it out.

We can pull the story out of this slide by following the principles we've discussed in this book.

1. Mumblers

Telling a clear story in charts begins by removing distractions. You can remove the horizontal lines running through the chart area. The y-axis is divided every two units when every four units would be sufficient for showing approximate values. All the text on the x- and y-axes can have a smaller and lighter font, to make them recede more. The revised chart below removes distracting mumblers.

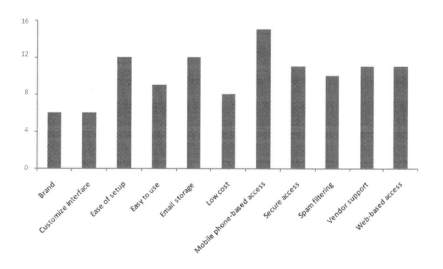

2. Chunking

There's unnecessary whitespace between the bars, pushing them apart and making it difficult to chunk all this data. The rule of thumb is that the space between the bars should be 50% of the width of each bar. I personally prefer 30%.

We can also organize this information from highest to lowest, to find the most relevant groupings. Note we put the largest value on the left, where the eye naturally wants to read first. Now we have:

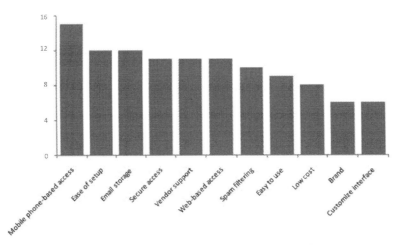

3. Picture and Wallpaper

We aren't sure yet what the story is, so we can reduce the entire chart to Wallpaper. We do that by changing the bar colors to gray. We can add color back in later, which we will choose with purpose, when we know the story.

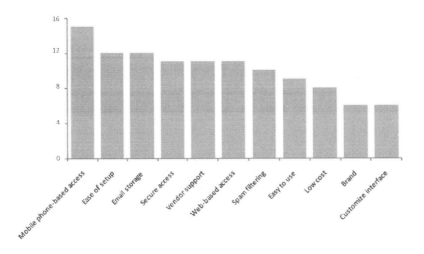

Images used in this book can be seen in color at www.speakingppt.com

We have now created a neutral and uncluttered canvas where we can tell the story, by treating some elements as Picture and directing the eye there. But what is the story? Perhaps I want to say something as simple as "The three most important things to customers are mobile-phone based access, ease of use and email storage." I can do that by highlighting only the relevant bars on this chart.

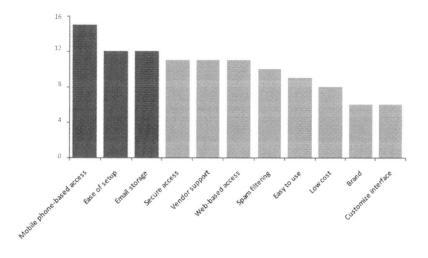

I am always on the lookout for mumblers and want to keep simplifying this chart. I wonder if I can remove the y-axis completely and simply add the numeric value labels directly to the bars. In this case, an alternate way to reinforce the Picture is to make the numeric values on the highlighted bars larger than on the gray bars.

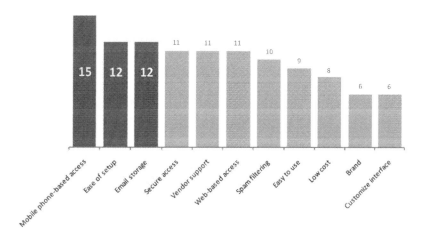

4. Color

I selected gray for the Wallpaper because gray recedes and also harmonizes well with any color. And I selected a blue from my color palette for the Picture bars so the slides would have a consistency throughout the deck. I did not just settle for Excel's default colors.

Using the principles of chunking, Picture and Wallpaper, mumblers and color can help you present a clear story to the reader and add flair to dreary Excel charts. It's much easier to present the data on the right to an executive than the data on the left, because the reader knows exactly what message you are trying to communicate and is less likely to reach a different conclusion than you intended.

No story using Excel defaults   **Clear story** using Mindworks Presentation Method

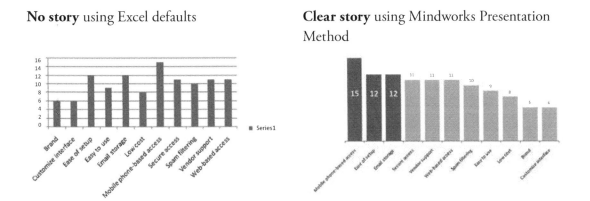

Recap:

1. Start by removing mumblers. Common mumblers are horizontal lines and excessive numbering along the y-axis. You can also reduce the font size of axis labels and use a gray font to make the axis labels recede.

2. Arrange the data into groups, or chunks, by ordering them highest to lowest. Or find some other natural way of clustering the data into groups. Reduce the spacing between bars to 50% or less.

3. Turn everything into Wallpaper by selecting a neutral color, like gray, for all the bars.

4. Determine what is the Picture on your chart and use color and placement to bring focus to those chart elements.

Reversing Excel defaults

To remove unnecessary whitespace between the bars	• right-click on any bar in the series • select Format Data Series • in the Series Options menu go to Gap Width and enter a lower value. The rule of thumb is 50% but I personally prefer 30%
To remove the horizontal lines	• click on any line and press delete
To change the color of the bars	• click once on any bar to select the series • go to Format on the ribbon • select the Fill sub-menu to choose a new fill color
To change the numbers on the y-axis	• right-click on the y-axis • select Format Axis • in Axis Options select "Fixed" for the Major Unit and enter the new number in the text box • you may need to modify the maximum value and the minimum value as well

The power of horizontal bar charts

When the bars are oriented left to right, as in the above examples, it is called a column chart. Column charts are appropriate when the data naturally reads left to right, like any measure that changes over time.

But an even more versatile chart that people don't use enough in business is the horizontal bar chart.

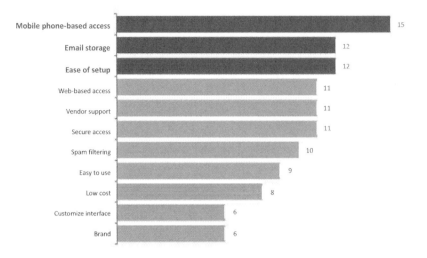

The horizontal bar chart has a number of advantages:

- it communicates high-to-low instantly

- you can write lengthy labels next to the data

- the labels are now positioned in the optical center where you can highlight key pieces of data

- you can use small multiples to put several data series next to each other across the width of the slide

Small multiples is a term coined by Edward Tufte, indicating putting a number of graphs next to each other so the eye can easily dart about and compare data points. By arranging horizontal bar charts side by side, you can remove the label from all but the first bar chart and present a lot of information in a compact space.

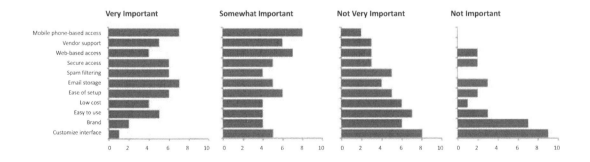

It's important to sort the order of the bar chart into descending order, so you can communicate quickly. I've seen many bar charts—horizontal and vertical—where the data is sorted alphabetically or randomly. Whoever created that chart missed an opportunity to communicate instantly, and instead they forced the reader to sort the data.

Sorted alphabetically. This chart has no meaningful order and so no story

Sorted high to low. The reader automatically knows what is important

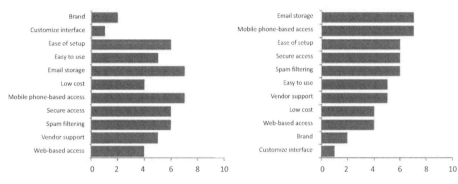

Often, you will have horizontal bar charts that are further broken into additional data series. For instance, when measuring the importance of different components of a company email system, you may have asked customers to rate each item on a four-point scale from not important to very important. By default, Excel will give you this chart:

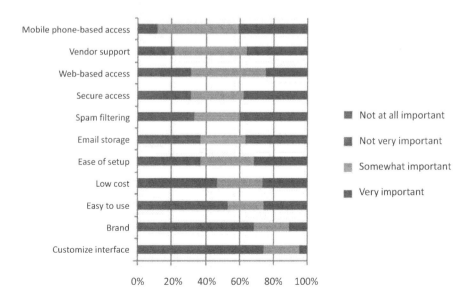

This is called a stacked horizontal bar chart, because the different data series are represented as bars and stacked on top of each other.

Working with multiple data series introduces a new challenge: what to do with the legend. In previous chapters we talked about the split-attention effect. Related items should be integrated close together. The default legend in Excel puts the legend off to the right, so the reader has to keep looking back and forth to understand the color coding. The legend is also arranged top to bottom while the stacked bars are arranged left to right, making it even harder for the reader.

It's easiest for the reader if the legend is seen before the data, in close proximity to the data and ordered in the same way as the data. In this case, I move the legend to the top of the chart, ordered left to right. I have also removed the vertical rules mumbling on this chart, and reduced the font size and font color on the x- and y-axes and for the legend names. I've also adjusted the gap width between the horizontal bars to 30%.

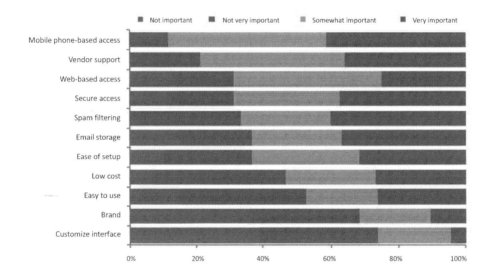

Now we need to start thinking about our story and which elements we want to treat as Picture and Wallpaper. By default, stacked bar charts come with vivid colors that distract the eye. You will want to reduce the visual clutter by subduing the colors.

There are two extreme values on this chart: *not important* and *very important*. You can assign each of them a distinct color, such as green for very important and orange for not important. Why not red for the low value? Because red attracts attention and suggests trouble; I don't want my message to be misunderstood by an unnecessarily alarming color.

The intermediate values—not very important and somewhat important—can be lighter tints of those extreme colors. This allows the intermediate values to recede and allows us to examine the extreme values. We are also using colors selected from our custom color palette.

Images used in this book can be seen in color at www.speakingppt.com

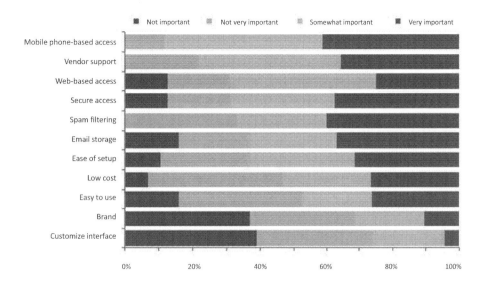

I will sometimes use "no fill" as one of the colors, or a light gray tint, to create more contrast between the high and low values. The reader can infer the missing value easily.

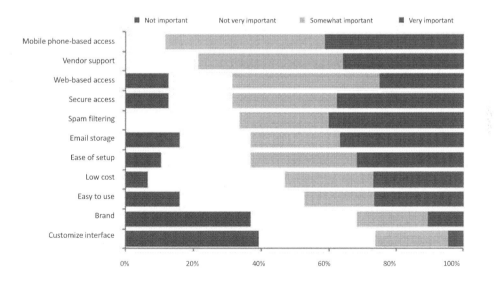

We can now better see the magnitude of the high values versus the low values. The problem is the high values don't have a common baseline for easy comparison.

But there is another way to present this information by creating a common baseline for the high values: a deviation bar chart. You will want to manually add a vertical rule to indicate the new baseline, and to complete the aesthetics, adjust the legend so the labels align with the bars they represent.

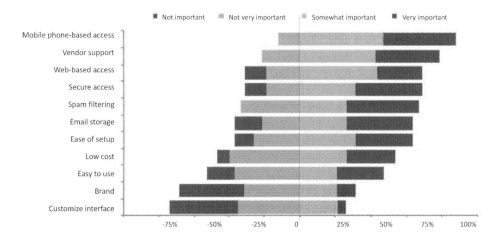

Now the data is arranged so the story is emerging. But what is the story? Perhaps you decide that the most important features are related to email access: mobile-phone based access, web-based access and secure access. Add some elements in the optical center, such as arrows pointing to the relevant bars, to complete your story.

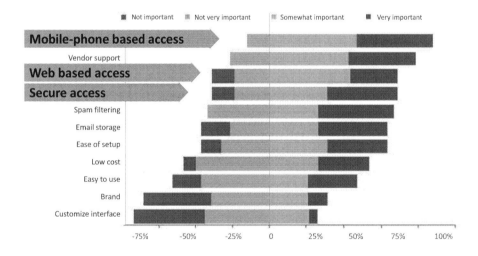

Did you also notice, for the lowest bar on this chart, that I closed the gap that used to exist to the right of the y-axis? I did this by making a copy of the chart, cropping out the whitespace and then piecing them together like a puzzle. I often find Excel's charts aren't flexible enough for my purposes and I need to cut them up and re-assemble them in PowerPoint. You may need to zoom in to precisely align the pieces for this type of detailed work.

Images used in this book can be seen in color at www.speakingppt.com

How to create a deviation bar chart

Deviation bar charts cannot be created automatically in PowerPoint. You need to add a fake column on the negative side equal to the sum of the two positive values, and a fake column on the positive side equal to the sum of the two negative columns. Leave the column name blank (actually, use a space for the column header, as Excel ignores columns without a column header). Now fill these two fake bars with "no color" and remove the line color.

Notice that I've also expanded the legend so the labels align better with the colored bars, especially the "somewhat" label which is now aligned with the common baseline. Notice also the x-axis is inaccurate because it counts the blank cells in the calculation. You will need to delete this from the chart and create your own x-axis manually.

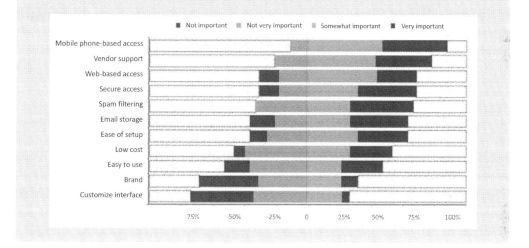

Line Graphs

Like column charts, line graphs are commonly used to show change in quantity over time, like sales, supplier costs or market share. Line graphs work better than column charts when you have more than two data series, or there's a lot of variation in the data that might not be instantly clear in a column chart.

Let's say your company has four product lines: Hardware, Software, Services and Maintenance. You want to produce a report showing how sales have trended over time. The default settings in Excel will produce this line graph:

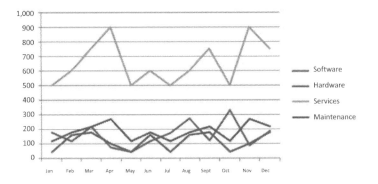

Most of the same rules apply to correcting the Excel defaults in line graphs: remove the horizontal lines, minimize the fonts in the y-axis and convert text into Wallpaper.

The labels should be located immediately next to each line, typically at the end of the line or integrated into the last part of the line. Remember whitespace pushes elements apart, so ruthlessly drive out whitespace between the label and the line. Using the same color for the label text and the graph line will help chunk them together. Excel does not have a way to do this automatically, so you will need to delete the legend and add the line labels manually.

It's possible for the lines to overlap and so the graph becomes noisy, making it difficult to see the differences in the data. For instance, in this example, sales of Maintenance, Software and Services overlap with one another, making it difficult to compare.

One solution is to show the data as four separate line graphs, using the principle of small multiples. You may want to keep the horizontal lines, to help compare values across different graphs, since they are no longer super-imposed over each other.

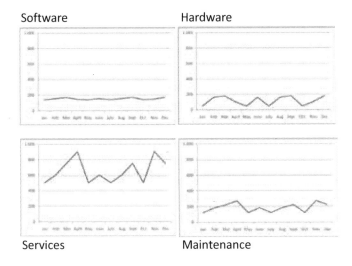

There may be times your line graph has more than four lines. Remember the Rule of Four: once a chunk of information has more than four units, the brain cannot hold it all in working memory. So try to keep line graphs to four data series, or consider breaking them into separate line graphs.

Here's an extreme example of a cluttered line graph, with eight data series. It's impossible to tell what kinds of patterns there are.

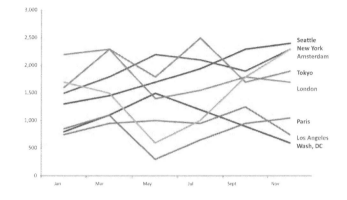

This will be easier to view if it's broken into two separate line graphs. Group the data in some logical way and that supports your message. Don't just group them into two random groups of four.

Here, I've separated the data into U.S. cities and international cities. Now the reader can more easily see the data trends I want to point out. In fact, I'm going to highlight the data trends I want to focus on and use a wider line width. Now it stands out clearly.

Copying and pasting Excel graphs

When you copy a graph from Excel, don't just paste it into the slide using Control-V. This will paste it as a graph still linked to the original data. If you change or delete the original data, even accidentally, the graph will also change.

The best way to paste it is as a Windows Metafile. This preserves the image's sharpness and it looks very professional. To paste, press Control-Alt-V and a window will open. Scroll through to find Windows Metafile. This will save it with a border around the graph. I personally don't like the border and use the cropping tool to remove it.

The only problem is you can't change the colors of the bars, the text, or anything else. It's just a picture. If you want to be able to manipulate the chart after you paste it, then paste it in a "vector" format (basically means in an editable format). Press Control-V and then select the drop-down menu that appears in the lower right corner and select "Excel chart (entire workbook)". In addition to being editable, the image also has no border around it and the background is transparent.

Pie charts

Pie charts are the junk food of data visualization. They look delicious but contain very little nutrition. Consider this pie chart, plotting sales in four sales regions: West, North, East and South. The default settings in Excel give us this.

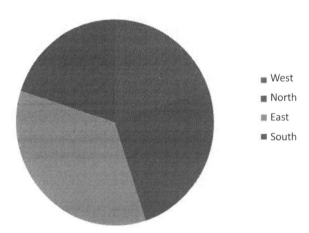

There is a lot wrong with this pie chart, and you already see all the mumblers: saturated colors, meaning arbitrarily encoded in the colors. You also see the labels are separated from the pie chart and the reader's eye needs to keep flicking back and forth to interpret the data. These are easy to fix.

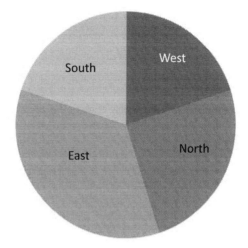

But what does this tell you? The reader can see that East plus North are about 60% of the pie. But is North the same size as East? Are sales in the East twice those of the West or is that an optical illusion? People are not very good at comparing sizes of two-dimensional objects like pie slices. Compare this pie chart with this horizontal bar chart. Which one communicates more clearly?

The reader gets very little information from a pie chart at first glance. Even after studying it, it's difficult to make accurate size assessments

Bar charts communicate more information instantly and are easier for the reader to make accurate size assessments

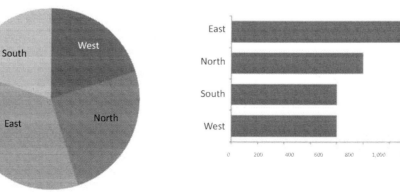

The only real advantage of pie charts is its ability to quickly convey *this adds up to 100%*. Many experts agree that pie charts are only valuable when there are just 2–3 pie slices or when one pie slice is vastly larger than all the others combined.

In that case, use the following rules to make best use of the power of pie charts:

- if possible, move the Picture to the top left corner of the pie chart. For instance, if your main point is that 30% of customers are dissatisfied, order the pie slices so that 30% slice is the upper-left slice, situated close to the optical center

- if possible, order the slices so the smallest slice is in the upper-right, at the one o'clock position and the slices become progressively larger

- if you have more than 2–3 pie slices, try to group your pie slices by using a single color with different levels of brightness (tints and shades) rather than giving each pie slice its own color

- label each pie slice with its name and numeric or percentage value

- use the principles of Picture and Wallpaper to highlight the important pie slice using darker colors and larger font sizes, and using smaller font sizes and subdued colors for the remaining pie slices. Moving one pie slice out of the pie chart also draws attention to it

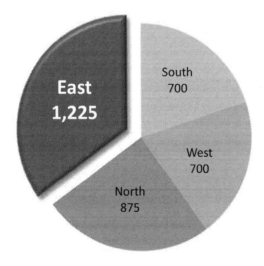

Pie charts should not be dismissed entirely. There have been some beautiful pie charts that communicate a message clearly and attractively, even by experts who do not generally support the use of pie charts. But consider first the story you are trying to tell. If the story is "this group is much bigger (or much smaller) than other groups" then a pie chart will tell that story. But when precise measurements are needed to tell the story, bar charts tell that story better than pie charts.

Setting your own defaults

Want to re-use the settings from a favorite chart? Just save that chart as a template and apply it to other charts in the future.

To save it as a template
1. Click on the chart you want to save as a template
2. Go to the Design tab, and click on Save as Template
3. Make sure the Charts folder is selected, name your chart template and click on Save

To apply that template to a new chart
1. Select the Excel cells containing the data for your new chart and go to the Insert tab
2. Click on ANY of the chart types and click on All Chart Types at the bottom of the drop-down list
3. Click on the My Templates folder in the top of the left navigation box
4. Select the template you want to apply. If you don't see the chart names, hover over the icons and the names will appear

For more help with chart templates, search in Excel's help menu for "Reuse a favorite chart by using a chart template".

Tables

Charts are useful for summarizing data and highlighting patterns. But there will be times you want to show the raw data instead of a graph.

Tables pose a special challenge because they contain a lot of data that puts a burden on the reader to quickly absorb it all and locate the interesting data points. Especially if you are presenting a table on a slide, the reader will have difficulty quickly locating the data points projected on a screen 30 feet away. You can help the reader get to the point more quickly if you'll use the laws of chunking, Picture and Wallpaper and mumblers to clean up your tables and make them instantly understandable.

For instance, let's say you want to show the results of your product research but in a tabular format. You might create a table that looks like this.

	Not important	Not very important	Somewhat important	Very important
Customize interface	9	8	5	1
Brand	7	6	4	2
Easy to use	3	7	4	5
Low cost	1	6	4	4
Ease of setup	2	5	6	6
Email storage	3	4	5	7
Spam filtering	0	5	4	6
Secure access	2	3	5	6
Web-based access	2	3	7	4
Vendor support	0	3	6	5
Mobile phone-based access	0	2	8	7

There's too much data here for the reader to absorb at once. What is the story in this data? Let's say your story is "Customers are most interested in email storage, mobile phone-based access and ease of setup." Now, how do we set that story free?

1. Remove mumblers

The excessive lines on tables interfere with readability and you can usually begin by removing all the lines. It's a best practice to include a leader line every 3–4 rows, just to help the reader keep their place when reading across wide tables. The column headers are also mumblers because the data is what is most important, not the labels. The column header font sizes, just like the x-axis font sizes, can be reduced so they are readable but not calling for attention. Similarly, all the data can be turned gray. You want it to recede so the data you highlight will stand out.

	Not important	Not very important	Somewhat important	Very important
Customize interface	9	8	5	1
Brand	7	6	4	2
Easy to use	3	7	4	5
Low cost	1	6	4	4
Ease of setup	2	5	6	6
Email storage	3	4	5	7
Spam filtering	0	5	4	6
Secure access	2	3	5	6
Web-based access	2	3	7	4
Vendor support	0	3	6	5
Mobile phone-based access	0	2	8	7

2. Chunking

Organize the data in some meaningful order such as highest to lowest. Whitespace pushes elements apart, so adjust any excessive whitespace such as the gap between the first column and the data columns.

	Not important	Not very important	Somewhat important	Very important
Mobile phone-based access	0	2	8	7
Email storage	3	4	5	7
Ease of setup	2	5	6	6
Secure access	2	3	5	6
Spam filtering	0	5	4	6
Vendor support	0	3	6	5
Easy to use	3	7	4	5
Web-based access	2	3	7	4
Low cost	1	6	4	4
Brand	7	6	4	2
Customize interface	9	8	5	1

3. *Picture and Wallpaper*

When using tables, it's a good idea to turn all the data into Wallpaper using gray text and then use color, bolding and font size to focus on the Picture. That helps the data recede into the background, except for the data you want the reader to focus on.

You also want to move the most relevant information into the left-most column. That way, the reader sees it before any other data. The story you want to tell is there are some product attributes that are highly important to customers and some that are very unimportant. In this case, we want to arrange the columns from *very important* in the first column to *not important* in the last column.

	Very important	Somewhat important	Not very important	Not important
Mobile phone-based access	7	8	2	0
Email storage	7	5	4	3
Ease of setup	6	6	5	2
Secure access	6	5	3	2
Spam filtering	6	4	5	0
Vendor support	5	6	3	0
Easy to use	5	4	7	3
Web-based access	4	7	3	2
Low cost	4	4	6	1
Brand	2	4	6	7
Customize interface	1	5	8	9

Now you've created a neutral canvas to paint your Picture on. Using the laws of Picture and Wallpaper, there are many ways to highlight the relevant data points: font size, color, enclosures, call-outs and so on.

I find the Law of Enclosure works very well in tables, either by placing a border around the relevant data point or by using a fill color for the relevant cells. I find color and font size is often not distinct enough to call attention as quickly as the Law of Enclosure.

Option 1: Cell fill color

	Very important	Somewhat important	Not very important	Not important
Mobile phone-based access	7	8	2	0
Email storage	7	5	4	3
Ease of setup	6	6	5	2
Secure access	6	5	3	2
Spam filtering	6	4	5	0
Vendor support	5	6	3	0
Easy to use	5	4	7	3
Web-based access	4	7	3	2
Low cost	4	4	6	1
Brand	2	4	6	7
Customize interface	1	5	8	9

Option 2: Border around table cell

	Very important	Somewhat important	Not very important	Not important
Mobile phone-based access	7	8	2	0
Email storage	7	5	4	3
Ease of setup	6	6	5	2
Secure access	6	5	3	2
Spam filtering	6	4	5	0
Vendor support	5	6	3	0
Easy to use	5	4	7	3
Web-based access	4	7	3	2
Low cost	4	4	6	1
Brand	2	4	6	7
Customize interface	1	5	8	9

Helping the audience think in concrete pictures is especially important when you're presenting statistics. Most statistics are difficult to visualize. If you are presenting statistics and they lack impact, think about how you can make them more concrete.

People can relate to things if they can imagine them. For instance, in *Made to Stick*, the authors talk about scientists who had computed some mathematical formula to such a level of accuracy, it was as accurate as throwing a rock from the Sun to the Earth and getting within one-third mile of the target every time.

Does this statistic stick? Can you realistically visualize throwing a rock from the Sun to the Earth? Can you visualize how close one-third mile is? Are you able to get impressed by this level of accuracy?

But how about something more concrete: *It's as accurate as hitting a golf ball the length of a football field and getting a hole-in-one every time.*

Both of these statistics state the same level of accuracy. But you can visualize one while you cannot visualize the other. It's the same thing with your statistics. If you say "25% of our customers are dissatisfied" that's just a statistic. It's hard to visualize all of your customers and then divide them into four faceless groups. But it's more compelling to explain your graph using language that's easy to visualize, like "The average sales rep has 20 customers. This graph indicates that five of those customers can't wait to do business with another company."

Charts and tables are meaningless unless they are used to tell a story. Don't present dumb charts and unsorted tables. Instead, apply the principles of chunking, Picture and Wallpaper, mumblers and color to clean up charts and tables, then tell a clear story to maximize your chances of winning agreement.

Back to Julia's slide

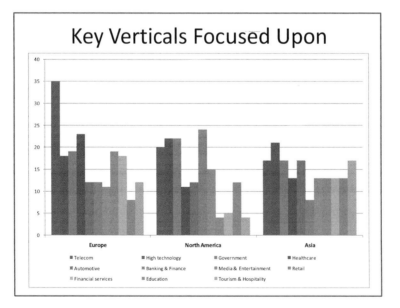

The first thing you notice, that raises a red flag for you, is all the mumblers on the chart: the vertical lines, the busy y-axis and the highly saturated colors in each of the bars. The border around the chart also seems excessively wide. You show Julia how to remove these mumblers.

You next ask *what is the Picture?* This is the main message on the slide and Julia's recommendation and it needs to be specified in the slide title. Once you know the main message, you can determine what on the slide is Picture and what is Wallpaper. After rewriting the slide title you convert all the bars to gray then use a solid color to highlight the three verticals Julia recommends you focus on. You also move the labels to the top of the chart.

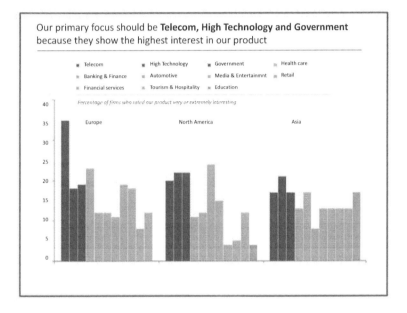

Visually it's becoming clearer where you want the reader to focus his attention. And aesthetically the slide is looking simpler. But you wonder if you have the right chart type. You can no longer match the labels to their corresponding bars without the colors. And the important information is not located in the optical center.

You wonder if a horizontal bar chart might be the answer. You could label each bar and move the relevant text into the optical center. You could even use small multiples to present all this complex information side by side for easy comparison.

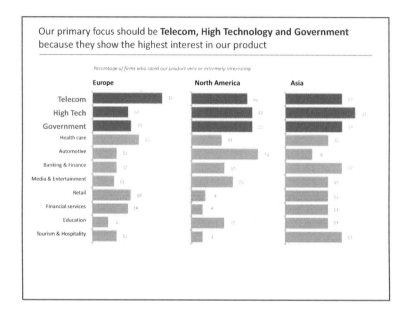

The story in the data is clearer. The recommended industries are clearly the most interested in our product. Your general manager may also want to understand some of the variances, such as high interest in Europe among the Telecom industry and in North America in the Automotive industry. This chart is clearer, more professional-looking and will lead to a more interesting discussion with your general manager.

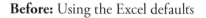

Before: Using the Excel defaults

After: Using Mindworks Presentation Method

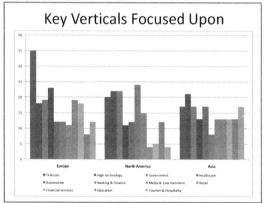

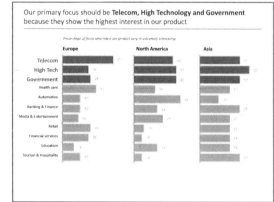

Above-water argument

1. Use the principles of chunking, color, Picture and Wallpaper and mumblers to tell the story in your charts. Start by reducing the chart to Wallpaper and then use color and location to direct the reader's eye to the Picture. Do not depend on Excel's defaults, which create dumb charts and do not know the story.

2. Prefer horizontal bar charts when ranking data items highest to lowest. It puts your data near the optical center, clearly communicates the high-to-low order and allows you to place long labels next to the data. Deviation bar charts are an excellent way to show multiple data series, but Excel does not create them automatically so you need to make a lot of manual corrections.

3. Line graphs are good for showing changes over time. Integrate the labels close to the lines. Break up complicated line graphs into small multiples, or else chunk them into sensible groups of no more than four lines per graph.

4. Pie charts are usually less clear than bar charts. If you do use them, use the principles of Picture and Wallpaper to highlight the relevant pie slice and subdue the remaining pie slices: order them from lowest to highest value with the largest pie slice in the upper-left corner.

5. For tables, focus on the few pieces of data you want to highlight and turn all other data into Wallpaper. Remove mumblers like excessive lines to clean up noisy tables and use borders or cell fill colors to highlight the Picture.

Recommended reading

Anything by Stephen Few including *Information Dashboard Design* and *Show Me the Numbers*. Few's writing is simple and practical, and he shows terrific before and after examples of graphs and tables to illustrate ways to clarify your message and make it more impactful.

Say it With Charts, Gene Zelazny. This is the bible used by consulting firms for selecting the right chart for the message. The approach is simple and effective and you will never approach chart design in the same way again.

The Wall Street Journal Guide to Information Graphics by Dona M. Wong illustrates many of the principles in this chapter, and in the aforementioned recommended reading. This is a practical and highly readable reference manual that will inspire you to create simpler and clearer charts and infographics.

Epilogue

Mindworks Method manager's checklist

I once met a man in the park with a very cute dog.

"Does your dog know any tricks?" I asked.

"Oh, sure!" the man said proudly, "Lots! He knows how to play dead, roll over, speak…"

"Wow, that's great! Can you show me one?"

The man shrugged sheepishly, "I said he *knows* lots of tricks. He doesn't *do* any of them."

You've just learned the Mindworks Presentation Method, which will help you compete in the idea marketplace by communicating your ideas more clearly, more persuasively and more professionally through PowerPoint.

But you need to translate knowing into doing. To help you, I've prepared a handy checklist you can use on your next PowerPoint deck.

To get started, go to the next page and rip it out. Then hang it near your desk. If you manage teams of people, use this checklist when you review their decks.

To your success!

Bruce Gabrielle
Kirkland, Washington
September 2010

Mindworks Presentation Method Manager's Checklist

Download this handout at www.speakingppt.com

	Problem	Manager's question
1. Story	If the deck has an unclear or uninteresting message	1. Who is the reader? What is their question? 2. What is the answer? 3. What is the Inciting Incident?
	If the deck seems to ramble and the structure is unclear	1. How are you breaking this deck into 3–4 sections? 2. *What about* each of these sections?
	If the logic is confused, incomplete or unpersuasive	1. How are you ordering your evidence? Can we start with a cause-effect chain? 2. Where is your emotional evidence? Are you leading with your strongest evidence?
	If the person is working too many hours on the same deck	1. Please show me your planning grid or storyboard.
2. Slide	If a slide is incoherent	1. What is the main message on this slide? 2. Can you write it as a full sentence in the title?
	If a slide seems too busy or overwhelmingly complex	1. How many chunks of information do you have? Do they all need to be on the same slide? 2. Can you chunk them better using proximity, similarity, connections or enclosure? 3. Where are the labels?
	If a slide is full of text or lacks emotional impact	1. What are the trigger words in the slide title? What picture does that suggest? 2. Is there a concrete picture we can use in place of an abstract picture?
	If a slide is full of bullet points and sub-bullet points	1. Is this a briefing deck, discussion deck or reading deck? 2. Does the text follow that style's principles?
3. Design	If a slide has more than 4 colors	1. Do the colors interfere with chunking? Draw attention to the wrong things? Convey unintended meaning?
	If a slide seems to have no focus and the eye has no starting point	1. What is the Picture? What is the Wallpaper? 2. How do you want the eye to move through this slide?
	If a slide is not visually pleasing	1. Can we fix the alignment or remove some of the mumblers?
	If the first reaction is *cool design!*	1. Can we remove some of the mumblers?
	If graphs do not tell a clear story	1. What's the story? Do we have the right graph? 2. Have we removed the mumblers? 3. Have we subdued the Wallpaper and highlighted the Picture?

Does your team want to learn how to *speak PowerPoint?*

Bring the research-based principles found in Speaking PowerPoint to your own company with a full-day onsite workshop. Help your staff use PowerPoint more effectively to influence and persuade in the boardroom.

After this full-day workshop, participants will be able to

1. Eliminate time wasters and complete PowerPoint decks 2-3 times faster.
2. Develop a presentation with a clear message, structure and slide order.
3. Develop a clear and persuasive slide using slide title, text, pictures and animation.
4. Enhance their credibility by creating professional-looking slides and charts using color, alignment and layout.

For details and pricing, please visit **www.speakingppt.com**

"Most PowerPoint trainings focus on product features. This may be the first I have seen on how to use PowerPoint to communicate *effectively*."
- Steve H, Microsoft

"The ideas covered in this workshop can easily save someone days or even weeks the next time you build a presentation."
- Sarah D, Prime 8 Consulting

"Great material and easy to understand. This has definitely improved my PowerPoint skillset."
- Pinak P, The Home Depot

"The session makes you think 'Why *aren't* we doing presentations this way?'"
- Steven B, Microsoft

Bibliography

Bibliography, along with links to the original documents where available, can be found online at www.speakingppt.com

Chapter 1

Arizona State University study as quoted in The New Yorker, Annals of Business Section, May 28, 2001, Pg. 76.

Kaplan, S. (2010). Strategy and PowerPoint: An Inquiry into the Epistemic Culture and Machinery of Strategy Making. Rotman School of Management Working Paper No. 1569762.

Mengis, J., Eppler, M.J. Seeing versus Arguing The Moderating Role of Collaborative Visualization in Team Knowledge Integration, in: Journal of Universal Knowledge Management, 2006, 3 (13), pp. 151–162.

Keller, Julia. "Is PowerPoint the Devil?" Chicago Tribune Wed. Jan. 22, 2003.

Sadoski, M. (1983). An Exploratory Study of the Relationships Between Reported Imagery and the Comprehension and Recall of a Story. Reading Research Quarterly, 19, 110–123.

Sadoski, M. (1985). The Natural Use of Imagery in Story Comprehension and Recall: Replication and Extension. Reading Research Quarterly, 20, 658–667.

Vogel, D., Dickson, G., & Lehman, J. (1986). Persuasion and the Role of Visual Presentation Support: The UM/3M Study (MISRC-WP-86-11), Minneapolis, MN: University of Minnesota, Management Information Systems Research Center.

Childers T.L. & Houston M.J. (1984). Conditions for a Picture Superiority Effect on Consumer Memory. Journal of Consumer Research, 11, 643–654.

Long, S.A., Winograd, P.A. & Bridge, C.A. (1989). The Effects of Reader and Text Characteristics on Reports of Imagery During and After Reading. Reading Research Quarterly, 24, 353–372.

University of Pennsylvania. "Visual Learners Convert Words To Pictures In The Brain And Vice Versa, Says Psychology Study." Science Daily 28 March 2009.

Kreger Silverman, L. (2005). Upside-Down Brilliance: The Visual-Spatial Learner.

Chapter 2

Petty, R.E. & Cacioppo, J.T. (1986). The Elaboration Likelihood Model of persuasion. New York: Academic Press.

Tracey, J.R., Rugh, D.E. & Starkey, W.S. (1965). Sequential Topical Organization of Publications.

Chapter 3

Lagerwerf, L. (2008). Selective Reading of Business Reports: Effects of Graphic and Verbal Advance Organizers. Paper presented at the annual meeting of the International Communication Association, Montreal, Quebec, Canada, May 22, 2008.

Minto, Barbara. The Pyramid Principle. Minto International. 1987.

Chapter 4

Mayer, Robert. How to Win Any Argument. Career Press. 2005.

Stone, V.A. (1969). A Primacy Effect in Decision-Making by Jurors. Journal of Communication, 19: 239–247. doi: 10.1111/j.1460-2466.1969.tb00846.x

Bryant, Adam. "Meetings, Version 2.0, at Microsoft". New York Times, May 16, 2009 p. BU2.

Bransford, J.D., & Johnson, M.K. (1972). Contextual Prerequisites for Understanding: Some Investigations of Comprehension and Recall. Journal of Verbal Learning and Verbal Behavior, 11, 717–726.

Kosslyn, Stephen M. Clear and to the Point. Oxford University Press. 2007.

Chapter 5

Boettinger, Henry M. Moving Mountains. Macmillan Publishing. 1969.

Cialdini, Robert B. Influence. Allyn & Bacon. 2001.

Lagerwerf, L., Bossers, E.(2002). Assessing Business Proposals: Genre Conventions and Audience Response in Document Design. Journal of Business Communication, 39 (4). pp. 437–460. ISSN 0021-9436

Denning, Stephen. The Leader's Guide to Storytelling. John Wiley & Sons. 2005.

Chapter 6

Reynolds, Garr. Presentation Zen. New Riders. 2008.

Chapter 7

Garner, J., Alley, M., Gaudelli, A. & Zappe, S. (2009). The Common Use of PowerPoint versus the Assertion–Evidence Structure: A Cognitive Psychology Perspective. Technical Communication, 56 (4).

Rezaie, A. & Hosseini, M. (2005). The Impact of Interrogative and Declarative Advance Organizers on Iranian EFL Learners' Comprehension of ESP Reading Tasks. Working paper presented at International Conference on Task-Based Language Teaching, Sept 21–23, 2005.

Chapter 8

Blankenship J., Dansereau, D.F. (2000). The Effect of Animated Node-Link Displays on Information Recall. Journal of Experimental Education 68:293–308.

Mahar, S., Yaylacicegi, U. & Janicki, T.N. (2009) The Dark Side of Custom Animations. International Journal of Innovation and Learning.

Chapter 9

Kassin, S. M. & Dunn M.A. (1997). Computer-Animated Displays and the Jury: Facilitative and Prejudicial Effects. Law & Human Behavior, 21, 269–281.

Bright, D.A. & Goodman-Delahunty (2004). The Influence of Gruesome Verbal Evidence on Mock Juror Verdicts, Psychiatry, Psychology, and Law, 11, 154–166.

Bornstein, B.H. & Nemeth, R.J., Jurors' Perception of Violence: A Framework for Inquiry. Aggression & Violent Behav. 77.

Colorado State University. "Brain Images Make Cognitive Research More Believable." Science Daily October 2007.

Mayer, Richard E, Multi-Media Learning. Cambridge University Press. 2001.

Levie, W.H. & Lentz, R. (1982). Effects of Text Illustrations: A Review of Research. Educ. Comm. Technol. J. 30: 195–232.

Sadoski, Mark & Paivio, Allan. Imagery and Text: A Dual Coding Theory of Reading and Writing. Lawrence Erlbaum Associates. 2001.

Carney, R.N. & Levin, J.R. Pictorial Illustrations Still Improve Students' Learning from Text. Educ Psychol Rev 2002;14:5–26.

Lagerwerf, L., & Meijers, A. (2005). Inferred Metaphors or Inappropriateness? Effects of Trope and Openness. Conference Papers—International Communication Association.

Hasher, L., Goldstein, D. & Toppino, T. (1977). Frequency and the Conference of Referential Validity. Journal of Verbal Learning and Verbal Behavior, 16 (February), 107–112.

Bresciani S., Eppler M.J. & Subramanian S.V. (2009). Enhancing Group Information Sharing Through Interactive Visualization: Experimental Evidence.

Tversky, B. & Heiser, J. (2008). Mental Models of Complex Systems: Structure and Function.

Kalyuga, S., Ayres, P. Chandler, P. & Sweller, J. (2003). The Expertise Reversal Effect. Educational Psychologist 38 (1): 23–31.

Horn, Robert E., Visual Language: Global Communication for the 21st Century. MacroVU. 1998.

Chapter 10

Paradi, D. (2009). Annoying PowerPoint Survey. Retrieved August 24, 2010 from http://www.thinkoutsidetheslide.com/articles/annoying_powerpoint_survey_2009.htm

Blokzijl, W. & Andeweg, B. (2005). The effects of text slide format and presentational quality on learning in college lectures. Proceedings of the IEEE international professional communication conference (IPCC): 288–99.

Vogel, D., Dickson, G. & Lehman, J. (1986). Persuasion and the Role of Visual Presentation Support: The UM/3M study (MISRC-WP-86-11), Minneapolis, MN: University of Minnesota, Management Information Systems Research Center.

Johnson, K. (2008). Literature Review: Perceptions and Cognitive Impact of Using PowerPoint.

Mayer, R. & Johnson, C. (2008). Revising the Redundancy Principle in Multimedia Learning. American Psychological Association, May 2008.

Jamet, E. & Le Bohec, O. (2007). The Effect of Redundant Text in Multimedia Instruction.

Mayer, R., Dow, G. & Mayer, S. (2003). Multimedia learning in an interactive self-explaining environment: What works in the design of agent-based microworlds? Journal of Educational Psychology, 95, 806–813.

Le Bohec, O. & Jamet, E. (2008). Levels of Verbal Redundancy, Note-Taking and Multimedia Learning. As cited in Understanding Multimedia Documents, pp. 87–90.

Blokzijl, W. & Andeweg, B. (2007). The effect of text slides compared to visualizations on learning and appreciation in lectures. Proceedings of the IEEE international professional communication conference (IPCC).

Farkas, D. (2005). Understanding and Using PowerPoint. STC Annual Conference Proceedings, May 8–11, 2005, pp. 313–320.

Marsh, E.J. & Sink, H.E. (2009). Access to Handouts of Presentation Slides During Lecture: Consequences for Learning. Applied Cognitive Psychology, 24: 691–706.

Moreno, R. & Mayer, R. (2001, April). Getting the Message Across: The Role of Verbal Redundancy in Multimedia Explanations. Paper presented at the annual meeting of the American Educational Research Association, Seattle, WA.

Atherton, C. (2009). Visual Attention: a Psychologist's Perspective. Presentation to Technical Communication UK Conference.

Mousavi, S., Low, R. & Sweller, J. (1995). Reducing Cognitive Load by Mixing Auditory and Visual Presentation Modes. Journal of Educational Psychology, 87, 319–334.

Mayer, Robert E. Multi-Media Learning. Cambridge University Press. 2001.

Tabbers, H. (2002). The Modality of Text in Multimedia Instructions: Refining the Design Guidelines. ISBN: 90-9016056-0.

Lagerwerf, L. & Bossers, E. (2002) Assessing Business Proposals: Genre Conventions and Audience Response in Document Design. Journal of Business Communication, 39 (4). pp. 437–460. ISSN 0021-9436

Poynter News University. (2010). Beyond the Inverted Pyramid: Creating Alternate Story Forms

Horn, Robert E. (1992) How High Can It Fly-Examining the Evidence on Information Mapping's Method of High-Performance Communication, Lexington Institute.

Eyetrack III. 2004.

Beymer, D., Russell, D.M. & Orton, P.Z. An Eye Tracking Study of How Pictures Influence Online Reading, INTERACT Conference, Rio de Janerio, Brazil (September, 2007).

Chapter 11

Meyers-Levy, J. & Peracchio, L.A. (1995). Understanding the Effects of Colors: How the Correspondence between Available and Required Resources Affects Attitudes. Journal of Consumer Research (September), 121–138.

The Color Marketing Group. The Profit of Color.

3M Corporation. "The Power of Color in Presentations" in monthly newsletter "Meeting Guides".

Woodman, G.F., Vogel, E.K., & Luck, S.J. (2001). Visual Search Remains Efficient when Visual Working Memory is Full. Psychological Science, 12, 219–224.

Kaya, N. & Epps, H. (2004). Relationship between Color and Emotion: A Study of College Students. College Student Journal, 38, 396–405.

Williams, Robin. The Non-Designer's Design Book. Peachpit Press. 2008.

Chapter 12

Sweller, J. (2002). Visualisation and instructional Design. Paper presented at the International Workshop on Dynamic Visualisations and Learning. Knowledge Media Research Center, Tubingen, Germany.

Chapter 13

Song, H. & Schwarz, N. (2008). If it's Hard to Read, It's Hard to Do: Processing Fluency Affects Effort Prediction and Motivation. Psychological Science, 19, 986–988.

Reber, R., Schwarz, N. & Winkielman, P. (2004). Processing Fluency and Aesthetic Pleasure: Is Beauty in the Perceiver's Processing Experience? Personality & Social Psychology Review, 8, 364–382.

Winkielman, P. & Cacioppo, J.T. (2001). Mind at Ease Puts a Smile on the Face: Psychophysiological Evidence that Processing Facilitation Leads to Positive Affect. Journal of Personality and Social Psychology, 81, 989-1000.

Novemsky, N., Dhar, R., Schwarz, N. & Simonson, I. (2007). Preference Fluency in Choice. Journal of Marketing Research, 44 (August), 347–356.

Alter, A. & Oppenheimer, D. (2006). Predicting Short-Term Stock Fluctuations by Using Processing Fluency.

Chapter 14

Heath, Chip & Heath, Dan. Made to Stick. Random House. 2007.

20987021R00167

Made in the USA
Charleston, SC
01 August 2013